Pockets ～

～ *of* Hope

Recent Titles in
Series in Language and Ideology

Pockets ~ ~ *of* Hope

How Students and Teachers Change the World

Eileen de los Reyes
and Patricia A. Gozemba

Series in Language and Ideology
Edited by Donaldo Macedo

Bergin and Garvey
Westport, Connecticut • London

Library of Congress Cataloging-in-Publication Data

De los Reyes, Eileen, 1954–
    Pockets of hope: how students and teachers change the world / Eileen de los Reyes and
Patricia A. Gozemba.
        p.   cm. (Series in language and ideology, ISSN 1069–6806)
    Includes bibliographical references.
    ISBN 0–89789–523–1 (alk. paper)—ISBN 0–89789–524–X (pbk. : alk. paper)
        1. Critical pedagogy—United States—Case studies.   2. Alternative education—United
States—Case studies.   3. Alternative schools—United States—Case studies.   I. Gozemba,
Patricia A., 1940–   II. Title.   III. Series.
    LC196.5.U6 D42   2002
    370.11′5—dc21   00–051925

British Library Cataloguing in Publication Data is available.

Library of Congress Catalog Card Number: 00–051925
ISBN: 0–89789–523–1
        0–89789–524–X (pbk.)
ISSN: 1069–6806

First published in 2002

Bergin & Garvey, 88 Post Road West, Westport, CT 06881
An imprint of Greenwood Publishing Group, Inc.
www.greenwood.com

Printed in the United States of America

The paper used in this book complies with the
Permanent Paper Standard issued by the National
Information Standards Organization (Z39.48–1984).

10 9 8 7 6 5 4 3 2 1

Copyright Acknowledgments

The authors and publisher gratefully acknowledge permission for use of the following material:

Quotations from *It Comes from the People: Community Development and Local Theology* by Mary
Ann Hinsdale, Helen M. Lewis, and S. Maxine Waller, have been included here by permission of
Temple University Press. © 1995 by Temple University. All Rights Reserved.

for students and teachers who are changing the world

Contents

Hope as Situated Pedagogy

Against a landscape of corporate "democracy" that "sanctions misery, chronic hunger, ignorance, or in general, sub humanity,"[1] Eileen de los Reyes and Patricia A. Gozemba's book *Pockets of Hope: How Students and Teachers Change the World*, brilliantly reminds us that in our so-called democracy, the democratic imperatives of voice, equity, and social justice are often relegated to "pockets of hope" characterized by "[t]heir isolation and vulnerability within larger institutions or within dominant economic, political, and social arrangements in communities" that, according to Jean Paul Sartre, "will change nothing and will serve no one, but will succeed in finding moral comfort in malaise."[2] Unfortunately, many educators and media pundits have found "moral comfort in malaise" in their facile call for educational reform that not only trivializes reform itself in the form of cosmetic changes, but also refuses to challenge educators to unveil the hidden ideology of racism, sexism, and other forms of social injustices that serves to devalue and disconfirm the lived experiences, culture, history, and language of subordinate students who are now, more and more, populating our public schools, particularly in urban centers. *Pockets of Hope* also reminds us that the unwillingness of many educators to unpack the schools' hidden ideology serves, at least, two fundamental functions: On the one hand, it muffles the voices of "students, teachers, parents, and citizens who are reinvigorating our democracy by protesting the conservative takeover of public schools" and, on the other, it hides the savage inequalities so powerfully described by Jonathan Kozol's work "with

---

1 Jean Paul Sartre, Introduction in Albert Memmi: *The Colonizer and The Colonized* (Boston: Beacon Press, 1965), pp. xxiv-xxv.
2 Ibid.

its vignettes of East St. Louis, Chicago, Camden, San Antonio, New York, and Washington, D.C. [which] demonstrates that the impoverishment and neglect of urban public schools nationwide persists and is exacerbated by white flight to the suburbs."

Central to the present educational reform that deforms is the language of the market that calls for more competition, accountability, and choice. What these education reformists fail to reveal is that, for example, "choice" represents a positive shock word that creates the illusion that all parents can equally exercise their "democratic" right to choose the best schools for their children. The illusion of choice also reinforces the myth[3] that "every American also has the right to choose where to work, sleep, and to live." However, for Bill Simpson and several other African Americans who attempted to implement the court ordered integration of a public housing complex in Vidor, Texas, the myth became soon a nightmare: Despite his efforts to assimilate quietly, Simpson was subjected for months to Ku Klux Klan threats and racial epithets shouted from passing cars. Unable to endure the unremittingly hostile atmosphere any longer, Simpson decided to leave, as all of his fellow blacks already had.[4]

The illusion also creates a pedagogy of entrapment that makes it undemocratic to argue against school choice. Thus, school choice becomes part of a discourse that brooks no dissension or debate, for to argue against it is to deny one's democratic right to choose. The illusion also hides the conditionality of one's democratic right to exercise choice in other domains. For example, the same conservative ideology that elevates school choice to the level of theology, unabashedly prevents women from exercising their right to choose what to do with their bodies.

It is this lack of ability to make linkages with other bodies of knowledge that has helped conservative educators to prevail in anesthetizing the public's historical memory file concerning the role of the dominant ideology in denying choice to the vast majority of subordinated groups in our society. What conservative educators such as William Bennett, Chester Finn, and John Silber fail to acknowledge is that school choice is part and parcel of a language of management that celebrates testing, privatization, and competition. Because "in the United States, all ideas about renovation of our infrastructure, and even about education and health care, are evaluated mainly for their utility in helping us compete in world economy,"[5] our thinking and

---

3 Henry A. Giroux, *Living Dangerously: Multiculturalism and the Politics of Difference* (New York: Peter Lang, 1993), p. 134.

4 "Weary of the Hostility, a City's Blacks Will Go," *New York Times,* August 29, 1993, p. 24.

5 Jeffrey F. Osbser, "Even in The U.S., Ideology Infects Language," Letter to the Editor, *New York Times,* July 15, 1992, p. A20.

imagination are often straitjacketed in a utilitarian capitalist competition that prevents us from learning about experiments and experiences so convincingly described by Eileen de los Reyes and Patricia A. Gozemba in *Pockets of Hope*. The straightjacketing of our thinking and imagination also prevents us from learning from inspiring democratic experiments in other parts of the world. A case in point is the educational transformation in Sao Paulo, Brazil, under the leadership of Paulo Freire who is considered the most significant educator in the last fifty years of the twentieth century. I say transformation and not reform because undemocratic education should be transformed into sites of hope and not left to the compromised benevolence of educators who relegated democratic aspirations and social justice to isolated "pockets of hope" to spearhead cosmetic reform in an attempt to solve the structural inequalities so all educators will "demonstrate a resolute commitment to education as the practice of freedom."

Instead of isolating education "as practice of freedom" to contained "pockets of hope," educational reformers should deal head-on with the structures of poverty that characterize the lives of a very large segment of students who go to our public schools. To offer school choice to these students and their families without the material conditions that will enable them to access it represents the ultimate pedagogy of entrapment. Put simply, by shifting more public resources away from already decrepit pubic schools to private and middle- and upper-class public schools, reformers are sentencing lower-class students to a de facto boot-camp minimum security detention center parading under the veil of urban public education.

These six pockets of hope described by Eileen de los Reyes and Patricia A. Gozemba represent a desirable alternative to a notion of school reform that has "virtually replaced citizens or even persons as the principal mode of reference to human beings."[6] These six pockets of hope willfully embrace Paulo Freire's imperatives of educational transformation which involve the democratization of the pedagogical and educational power so that students, staff, teachers, educational specialists, and parents come together to develop a plan that is grassroots generated, accepting the tensions and contradictions that are always present in all participatory efforts, thereby searching for a democratic substantivity.

In embracing and prioritizing the democratization of schooling, the participants of these six pockets of hope had to adhere to Freire's call for the decentralization of power. At the same time, they had to create structures

---

6 Ibid.

where teachers, students, parents, and the community could empower themselves so that they could participate in a process where they could think otherwise in order to act otherwise. The participants in these six pockets of hope
understood the substantivity of Freire's notion of progressive and liberatory
education: "In a really progressive, democratic and non-authoritarian way,
one does not change the 'face' of schools through the central office. One cannot decree that, from today on, the schools will be competent, serious, and
joyful. One cannot democratize school authoritarily."[7]

Compare the democratic goals and aspirations evident in these six pockets of hope with the present school reform proposals put forth by our educational leaders. For example, take Chester Finn's argument "against local
control, and giving power to professional educators and lay governing
boards."[8] Or Chubb and Moe's contention that "public schools have been
pulled in too many directions by the 'excess' of democratic demands."[9] That
translates, according to them, as the development of feel good spaces where
students are taught about "multiculturalism, environmentalism, and a thousand other world-saving crusades issues for which neither [students] nor
teachers have even the rudiments of competence."[10] The devaluation of
democratic practice in pockets of hope in our society in our schools exem-
plifies how the substantive practice of democracy always represent a threat to
the dominant ideology. While the dominant ideology often espouses the
virtues of democracy, it simultaneously engages in the creation of anti-democratic structures that prevent the true practice of democracy. This paradox is
succinctly understood by Noam Chomsky when he argues that "because they
don't teach the truth about the world, schools have to rely on beating students over the head with propaganda about democracy. If schools were, in
reality democratic, there would be no need to bombard students with plati-
tudes about democracy. They would simply act and behave democratically."[11]

Acting and behaving democratically is evidently clear in the everyday
practices and aspirations of the participants in the democratic experiments
described in *Pockets of Hope*. The courageous and committed participants in
these six pockets of hope keenly understood Chomsky's notion that "[t]he

---

7 Paulo Freire, *Pedagogy of the City* (New York: Continuum Publishing Company, 1993),
p. 19.
8 Henry A. Giroux, *Living Dangerously: Multiculturalism and the Politics of Difference* (New
York: Peter Lang, 1993), p. 131.
9 Ibid.
10 Ibid.
11 Donaldo Macedo (ed.), *Chomsky on Miseducation* (Lanham, Md.: Rowman & Littlefield
Publishers, Inc., 2000), pp. 16-17.

more there is a need to talk about the ideals of democracy, the less democratic the system usually is."[12] The participants in these pockets of hope also understood the essence of Freire's pedagogy of hope that "teaches us the significance of dreaming, of imagining what could be as opposed to remaining paralyzed in what is. Dreaming keeps these pockets of hope energized and focused. Hope keeps them from despair." Borrowing from Henry Giroux's eloquent articulation of what it means to embrace a pedagogy of hope, Eileen de los Reyes and Patricia A. Gozemba's book, *Pockets of Hope*

> makes a [great] contribution to resurrecting a language of resistance and possibility, a language that embraces a militant utopianism while constantly being attentive to those forces that seek to turn such hope into a new slogan or punish and dismiss those who dare look beyond the horizon of the given. Hope, in this instance is the precondition for individual and social struggle, the ongoing practice of critical education in a wide variety of sites, the mark of courage on the part of intellectuals in and out of the academy who use the resources of theory to address pressing social problems. But hope is also a referent for civic courage and its ability to mediate the memory of loss and the experience of injustice as part of a broader attempt to open new locations of struggle, contest the working of oppressive power, and undermine various forms of domination. At its best, civic courage as a political practice begins when one's life can no longer be taken for granted. In doing so, it makes concrete the possibility for transforming hope and politics into an ethical space and public act that confronts the flow of everyday experience and the weight of social suffering with the form of individual and collective resistance and the unending project of democratic social transformation.[13]

Donaldo Macedo
Series Editor
UMass Boston

---

12 Ibid.
13 Henry A. Giroux, *Public Spaces/Private Lives: Beyond The Culture of Cynicism* (Lanham, Md.: Rowman & Littlefield Publishers, Inc.) In press.

Acknowledgments

We wish to thank the teachers who worked patiently with us for four years: Helen Lewis, Donna San Antonio and Holly Manoogian, Jeff Martel, Al Ferreira, Pi'ikea Miyamoto, Amy Akamine, Janie King, Patricia Buchanan, Elizabeth Hart, and Wayne J. Dudley. Their work is the source of knowledge and inspiration for this book. During the four years that we worked on this book, we had the privilege of working with students of all ages who reassured us that there is great hope in the next generation of citizens and in those who are struggling to reclaim their place in our democracy. We hope that this book stands as testimony of their leadership and courage.

We met Donaldo Macedo in 1993, when we were looking for guidance with the Language Intensive Interdisciplinary Program (LIIP) at Salem State. From that day on he has been a loyal, caring, and inspiring ally. It was through his constant support and patience that we reached the end of this journey. We are eternally grateful for his powerful presence in our lives.

Karen Kahn understood deeply every thought, sentence, comma, and period in this book. She read our chapters returning them with copious comments and working with us from the beginning of this project to the last moment. We wish to recognize her wise advice and her soulful work.

We wish to thank Kathleen George who transcribed countless tapes and asked us probing questions about our work. Sandy Martin, Priscilla Forance, Barbara Taylor, Alexa Gutheil, and Gastón de los Reyes Jr., read various chapters and commented on them deepening our understanding. Pat Ould, who was a colleague and ally of ours in women's studies and the LIIP, theorized many of the ideas about pedagogy with us over the past seven years and read much of the book adding many crucial insights.

The Spencer Foundation helped us complete this work transforming what began as a labor of love into a viable project.

—E.M.d.l.R. and P.A.G.

I learned how to teach from Patricia Gozemba. She insisted that faculty in the Women's Studies program which she directed had to teach with her and learn how to become feminist teachers. This experience, coupled with our collaboration in the LIIP, motivated me to challenge her to write about teaching and learning. Ask and you shall receive. What began as a modest request ended up being a pocket of hope, a much larger project than I ever envisioned. I was blessed with having in Gozemba a mentor teacher and scholar who made taking the first steps in the academy a joyful process full of possibilities and hope. For this I thank you.

I wish to thank my family, Gastón, Gastón, Jr., René, and Alexa, for their love, support, and patience.

—E.M.d.l.R.

I am grateful to Larry Smith of the East-West Center in Honolulu for offering me a fellowship and providing me with a welcoming space to begin the work that became this book. I thank my union the MSCA/MTA/NEA for struggling to assure that faculty receive funds to support research. Salem State College President Nancy D. Harrington understood the potential of the Language Intensive Interdisciplinary Program from the outset and supported it as well as my efforts in working on this book.

My students have been a constant source of inspiration and energy and I have faith that they all will change this world for the better. My friends, the best friends in the world, have been very patient as I worked on this project. To Margaret Nielsen and Karen Rudolph, I send special thanks for their hospitality during the time that I needed it most. To Karen Kahn, my partner, you understand it all and as always you are the best.

As I begin my thirty-eighth year of teaching, I thank Eileen de los Reyes for having convinced me that I, finally, ought to write about pedagogy. The intellectual process of working on this book offered many rewards and I look to Eileen and the next generation of scholars to assure that Freirean and feminist scholarship survives in the academy.

—P.A.G.

CHAPTER I

Introduction:
Education as the Practice
of Freedom

> The academy is not paradise. But learning is a place where paradise can be created. The classroom, with all its limitations, remains a location of possibility. In that field of possibility we have the opportunity to labor for freedom, to demand of ourselves and our comrades, an openness of mind and heart that allow us to face reality even as we collectively imagine ways to move beyond boundaries to transgress. This is education as the practice of freedom.
> —bell hooks, *Teaching to Transgress: Education as the Practice of Freedom* (1994)

Despite the unrelenting attacks on public education ranging from scathing assessments of students to withering condemnations of teachers, there are pockets of hope—physical, intellectual, emotional, spiritual, and political communities—where students and teachers are engaging possibility and challenging despair. Collaboratively, they are creating a "paradise" in their classrooms. The six pockets of hope that we present here are widely diverse, but they all demonstrate a resolute commitment to "education as the practice of freedom." The "classrooms" of these projects range from secondary schools to a college campus, from community centers to mountain lakes, from Hawai'i to Massachusetts to Appalachia. The very existence and success of these projects and of others like them offer hope for the future of democratic education and, perhaps more significantly, for democracy.

When we first began using the term "pockets of hope" to describe democratic educational projects, we were surprised that it resonated so readily with so many people. If we asked teachers, professors, parents, students, college administrators, or principals if there was a pocket of hope in their school, they often named a project they found inspiring. Inevitably, they identified a teacher who was the motivating force behind the project. When we spoke with community activists and concerned citizens about pockets of hope in their communities, they, too, could name the people and projects that gave them hope. Consistently, these pockets of hope share similar characteristics: a democratic teacher, a community that serves as an empowerment zone, a democratic pedagogy, and participants actively engaged in changing the world.

In *Pockets of Hope: How Students and Teachers Change the World,* we celebrate liberatory teachers and their emancipatory pedagogies that engage students in what Paulo Freire and Donaldo Macedo (1987) call "reading the word and the world." These six democratic projects offer hope about the ways in which all students can acquire academic, social, and political knowledge and skills that will serve them well as citizens in our democracy. In all of the educational settings in which they work, these highly competent, creative, and courageous teachers whose work we follow challenge their students in what Freire (1993) describes as "problem-posing" education. Provocative academic questions; intellectual, spiritual, and psychological challenges; political dilemmas; and social issues engage these students and teachers in classrooms where ideas are freely explored and rigorously examined. These teachers purposefully connect the world in which they and their students live with the work of their democratic classrooms, making education relevant and exciting.

In naming these projects "pockets of hope," we wanted to draw attention to two characteristics: first, their isolation and vulnerability within larger institutions or within dominant economic, political, and social arrangements in communities, and second, their capacity to enliven hopes and dreams. Inspired by Freire's *Pedagogy of Hope* (1994), we began to see these projects as enclaves of hope. Freire explains that he does not "understand human existence and the struggle needed to improve it, apart from hope and dream" (8). He sees hope as an ontological need, part of who we are as human beings and what keeps us alive—as opposed to existing in a living death. But he suggests to us that having hope is not enough, for "hope needs practice in order to become historical concreteness" (9). He reminds us "One of the tasks of the progressive educator...is to unveil opportunities for hope, no matter what the obstacles may be" (9). It is this task that teachers in pockets of hope take up seriously yet joyfully in creating vital spaces where students love to be.

In *Pedagogy of Hope,* Freire also teaches us the significance of dreaming, of imagining what could be, as opposed to remaining paralyzed in what is. Dreaming keeps these pockets of hope energized and focused. Hope keeps them from despair. The inspired engagement of life and living, the caring nature of the relationships between students and teachers, and the contagious laughter and fun we experienced make these pockets of hope the spaces where we want to live and work.

In these pockets of hope, teachers and students share what hooks (1994) calls an "openness of mind and heart," which makes it possible for them to dream of and move toward a truly democratic society in their daily work. The six pockets of hope that we focus on are highly productive learning environments of the sort that are rarely featured in the media. Why are they and so many others like them ignored? Why are the failures relentlessly trotted out by the media? Who gains and who loses when public schools are identified as failing institutions? In countering the bleak portrayal of education that saturates the media with examples of teachers and students working for positive change in their lives and in the world, we invite readers to begin interrogating more critically popular discourse about public education.

THE POLITICAL CONTEXT OF EDUCATION AT THE TURN OF THE CENTURY

The hard-fought and highly effective legal, legislative, and grass-roots progressive political struggles around education in the 1950s, 1960s, and 1970s advanced democracy in this country. *Brown vs. the Board of Education* (1954) promised equal opportunity for African Americans. Title IX (1972) furthered opportunity for people of color and opened up educational opportunities for females in programs from grade school through graduate school. The civil rights movement and the black studies movement, the women's movement and the women's studies movement, the farm workers movement and the ethnic studies movement challenged our society and our schools to live up to the promise of democracy. The grass-roots democratic movements in communities inspired educational movements in schools that challenged obstacles to educational equality and access; interrogated curriculum around race, gender, and class at all educational levels; and introduced liberatory pedagogical strategies. Social activism also legitimated as topics for discussion in classrooms: power, oppression, transformation, and engaged political struggle.

Renewed interest in liberatory pedagogies such as that of John Dewey and especially that of the Brazilian educator Paulo Freire generated a deep concern about how teachers were teaching and students were learning. Freire's *Pedagogy of the Oppressed* (1970, 1993) spurred on the development of critical pedagogy, which questioned both what was taught and how it was taught. Feminists deepened and broadened the analysis of critical pedagogy by focusing on gender and the inequities inherent in the entire educational landscape

(Weiler, 1991). *Schooling in Capitalist America* (1976), by Samuel Bowles and Herbert Gintis, laid bare the lie of the American dream in detailing how public schools continued to reproduce the inequities of the larger society. Progressive educators made important intellectual, political, and social links between schools and the world and underscored the importance of educational projects in renewing and expanding democratic ideals for all people. A growing consciousness of the pervasive inequalities in our society and in our educational systems sparked the dreams of teachers, students, and community activists to agitate for equal opportunity and to make significant advances.

By the early 1980s, however, the backlash to this hopeful era was firmly established nationally. The Reagan-Bush administration's *A Nation at Risk* (1983) signaled a renewed conservative focus on education, which would become a highly contested terrain over the next two decades. With the sustained help of the media, this carefully crafted diatribe shocked the country into believing that our schools, which were finally moving in the direction of democratic promise, paying attention to race, class, and gender, were failing to prepare students to compete in the global economy. Dire predictions of the United States falling behind economically, and thus politically, served the conservative goal of attacking the liberatory gains made in public schools and colleges in the three previous decades. Equity, diversity, and multiculturalism, key concerns of democracy, were pitted against technological advances and global dominance, key concerns of capitalism. Capitalism held sway. Ironically, the very slackers and incompetents to whom *A Nation at Risk* pointed are the young people who have led the United States at the turn of the century into its unchallenged position in the global economy. Nonetheless, in 1998 the conservative Center for Education Reform published *A Nation Still at Risk: An Education Manifesto,* renewing the relentless attack on progressive reform and the promise of equality for all.

Determined to ignore gender, race, and class as issues of equity, which affect outcomes in schools, conservatives blame poor results on standardized tests (which often are racist and sexist) on teachers, on curricula, and on students unwilling to learn. Rather than seeking real solutions to the enormous problem of providing high-quality education to poor and working-class students, particularly in urban areas, the conservative strategy of dealing with the challenge is humiliation through broadly publicized reports of failure— shaming and blaming—the authoritarians' punitive strategy. Since the early 1980s, conservatives have carefully constructed media images of burned-out teachers and failing students to convince the public that we are wasting resources on dysfunctional schools. Their goal—to dismantle the public school system—is only thinly veiled in their rhetoric of high-quality education for all.

The deeply conservative political context within which educators struggle is driven by a strategic alliance of corporate elites and religious fundamentalists. Their goal—an authoritarian and highly undemocratic educational system that trains submissive workers—is hardly a system to which we would want to entrust the generations on whom we will count to preserve democracy. We hope that understanding both the strategies being used to dismantle public education and the strategies that courageous teachers use to resist conservative and corporate control will inspire more people to join in the struggle to reinvigorate our schools and our democracy.

Dismantling Public Education

Public schools face relentless attacks from four ideological sectors: capitalist entrepreneurs who want skilled yet compliant workers for the new global economy; conservatives longing for a return to authoritarian pedagogy and a white male Eurocentric curriculum; religious fundamentalists agitating for school prayer, polarized gender roles, "abstinence only" sex education curricula, and creationism; and big business staking out claims on what they see as upward of a $370 billion "school industry." The possibility of racial, social, and economic justice inherent in *Brown vs. the Board of Education* and Title IX in particular is no longer a "dream deferred"; it is a dream derailed.

As we enter the new millennium, public schools and liberatory education struggle for survival across the United States. Among the strategies that conservatives are using in repressing high-quality democratic education are school choice (private school vouchers), charter schools, and high-stakes testing. These three strategies have a high profile in public discourse critiquing schools.

School Choice. Rather than being summarily dismissed as unconstitutional, the debate about school choice is part of the national discourse, with pilot voucher programs in several states, including Wisconsin, Florida, and Ohio (Crowley, 2000, A24). In Massachusetts, where the vote on vouchers comes up annually, Governor Paul Cellucci declared himself in favor of vouchers, contending, "Choice and competition are very powerful tools for public schools" (Crowley, 2000, A24). His rhetoric carefully masks the reality that vouchers are tools for dismantling public education by draining off necessary funds and supporting, instead, religious, private, and corporate school ventures.

All too often, urban families of color are caught in a bind cleverly devised by proponents of privatization. As high-stakes tests reveal poor scores for urban youth of color, their parents begin looking for alternative schools. Instead of improving the public schools by providing them with books, computers, attractive and well-kept physical plants, and small classes, conservative politicians encourage turning toward private schools. As students take their public school, per-pupil appropriation to for-profit schools, urban schools become more impoverished and pockets of despair are multiplied. What begins as a family's strategy for survival results in collective actions that further embattle our public school system, an already fragile institution in our democracy.

Charter Schools. As legislative debates about increasing the numbers of charter schools (private schools supported by public funds) continue, corporations are positioning themselves for the windfall. Writing in the *Boston Globe* (April 30, 2000), Barbara Hall reports that nationwide there are over 1600 charter schools (J 9). Edison, Advantage, and Sabis International operate chains of schools in the United States, some of them charter schools, where public funds are turned into private profit. Like most other corporate ventures, they are anti-union.

Paul Dunphy points out that the "Microsoft co-founder, Paul Allen, has channeled $30 million into Edison. Wall Street raider and trader Theodore Forstmann, elevated to sainthood by the media for raising millions in voucher money for poor children, is capitalizing on his largesse through several ventures, including a network of charters called Victory Schools" (2000, 4). One can only wonder whether corporations, even educational corporations, are as interested in educating citizens to participate in our democracy as they are in producing competent yet docile workers for the global economy.

High-Stakes Testing. In a master stroke of control and surveillance, those who want to limit democratic practice in the schools have instituted high-stakes testing, which is used to justify failing students and denying them high school diplomas. Rather than considering teacher recommendations, grades, and student portfolios for promotion or graduation, high-stakes tests are slated to become the single standard in many states. In April 2000, the *New York Times* reported that 26 states have high-stakes tests, which by the year 2003 students must pass to receive a high school diploma (Steinberg, 2000, A22). The unfortunate response of numbers of beleaguered teachers is to teach to the test so that they and their students will not be humiliated when the scores are publicly unveiled. In this climate of fear, less creative and demanding pedagogy focusing on memorization becomes the norm and school becomes less challenging for all students.

In Massachusetts, where the Massachusetts Comprehensive Assessment System (MCAS) administers tests to fourth, eighth, and tenth graders each year, the pitfalls of high-stakes testing are being revealed. Vito Perrone, the former director of Teacher Education Programs at Harvard Graduate School of Education, worked with Massachusetts teachers in reviewing MCAS tests. They concluded that the tests are "poorly written, filled with trivia and ambiguities, excessively long and lack a recognizable educational purpose" (www.Fairtest.org). Deborah Meier, the founder of the highly successful Central Park East schools in New York City as well as the new Mission Hill Elementary School in Boston and the first public school teacher to win a MacArthur Foundation "genius" award, cautions against the use of MCAS. "Success for all kids—rich and poor—requires high standards linked to rigorous, performance-based assessment. The path the MCAS leads us on will not reach this vital goal. Instead it will weaken the quality of many schools and do little to cause real improvements where they are needed" (www.Fairtest.org).

A strong grass-roots movement of teachers, parents, students, and citizens is intent on exposing the anti-democratic ploy of high-stakes testing. Sandra Alvarado, executive director of the Latino Parents Association, in Boston, understands how the MCAS represents corporate ideology. "We know there's a problem with this test because we know our children are definitely not dumb. MCAS [is] not a valid instrument, unless the purpose is to create a ready-made army of people who will clean the hotels of Boston, Springfield and Worcester" (Alvarado, Spring 2000). An editorial in the same newsletter indicated the resolve of parents to fight: "Politicians tell us the MCAS is here to stay. This is a democracy. The MCAS is not the only choice. It is not our choice."

Perhaps the most heartening reaction to high-stakes testing has been the response of high school students. On April 13, 2000, the *New York Times* reported in a front-page story that "in recent months, parents, teachers and students have rallied and railed against new standardized tests" in Illinois, Massachusetts, Wisconsin, Ohio, Louisiana, and Florida, among other states (Steinberg, 1). The Student Coalition Against MCAS with its appropriate acronym (SCAM) used the Internet to organize rallies across Massachusetts and to encourage boycotts of MCAS. Their web page (www. scam-mcas.org) provides a critical analysis of the high-stakes test and strategies to organize against it. In Wisconsin, politicians actually rolled back the requirement.

The students, teachers, parents, and citizens who are reinvigorating our democracy by protesting the conservative takeover of public schools deserve high praise. In the finest American tradition of Frederick Douglass, Susan B. Anthony, Thurgood Marshall, Rosa Parks, Martin Luther King, Jr., and Cesar Chavez, they are calling attention to injustice and raising the consciousness of the public. These students, teachers, parents, and citizens are organizing public protests; deconstructing the biases, errors, and foolhardiness of the tests; lobbying legislators; gaining attention for their issue; and raising consciousness. Their focus on schools is especially important because it is there that youth should be preparing for an active role in our democracy.

The Challenges in Public Education

Our nation's schools, particularly in urban areas, do face enormous challenges. Two of Jonathan Kozol's books published a quarter of a century apart, *Death at an Early Age: The Destruction of the Hearts and Minds of Negro Children in the Boston Public Schools* (1967) and *Savage Inequalities: Children in America's Schools* (1991), illustrate the persistence of the problems. Kozol's first book signaled the awareness of idealistic progressive teachers who saw the intensity of racism and classism in northern urban schools that mirrored the long decried and publicly exposed inequities of the South. *Savage Inequalities*, with its vignettes of East St. Louis, Chicago, Camden, San Antonio, New York, and Washington, D.C., demonstrates that the impoverishment and neglect of urban public schools nationwide persist and are exacerbated by white flight to the suburbs. Both books point to appalling public policy that has clearly abandoned children of color, setting back progressive gains imagined in *Brown vs. the Board of Education.* Allowing students to languish in environments where they cannot learn is shameful, but students and teachers are not the perpetrators of this national embarrassment—they are the victims.

Yet there are pockets of hope, democratic classrooms, in even the most educationally desperate cities, like New York and Chicago, that deserve support and emulation. Deborah Meier demonstrates in *The Power of Their Ideas* (1995) some of the day-to-day democratic practice in the Central Park East public schools in Harlem, where predominantly black and Latino students in K–12 soar to success. Stephen Wolk, in *A Democratic Classroom* (1998), describes how in his elementary school classrooms in Chicago, students discover democracy by living it. Both Meier and Wolk are teachers, researchers, community builders, and activists for democratic education. They celebrate intellectually rich classrooms where students are challenged to become critical thinkers and independent learners by teachers who understand and use democratic pedagogy. Their success in public schools points to viable alternatives to private school vouchers, charter schools, and high-stakes testing.

FINDING ALLIES AND SHARING OUR STORIES

Committed to progressive education that leads to increased participation in our democracy, we offer in this book case studies of struggle and accomplishment in six pockets of hope where students and teachers are changing the world. Although ostensibly very different, these projects—the Language Intensive Interdisciplinary Program at Salem State College in Salem, Massachusetts, for students who are not native speakers of English; Project 10 East, a gay-straight alliance at Cambridge Rindge and Latin High School in Cambridge, Massachusetts; the Appalachian Mountain Teen Project, a community-based, early-intervention project for rural youth in Wolfeboro, New Hampshire; the Highlander Research and Education Center in New Market, Tennessee, a community-based education center for southern and Appalachian leaders from working-class and poor communities; the Peer Education Program at Roosevelt High School in Honolulu, Hawai'i; and Aloha 'Aina, a special education science program at Castle High School in Kane'ohe, Hawai'i, dedicated to reclaiming Hawaiian culture—share a core commitment to democratic pedagogy. By creating participatory learning environments, the teachers engage students in what Freire calls education as a practice of freedom, not education as a practice for freedom at some future time.

Four of the pockets of hope are in public schools and two are in the community. All of them are largely unheralded learning and teaching communities in which Freirean and feminist pedagogies engage students in rigorous academic work and projects of social change that contribute to assuring the future of democracy. Although only half of the teachers would identify themselves as having been influenced by Freirean or feminist theory, all of them are engaged in practice emblematic of those theoretical positions.

As these teachers and their students study science, history, composition, mathematics, health, mediation, economics, environmental studies, community development, they also learn how to use the knowledge that they collaboratively construct to understand and transform their lives. Significantly, the democratic pedagogy of each of these projects connects students to larger democratic projects in their communities and the world. Democracy is a passionate and lived experience for teachers and students in pockets of hope.

In these pockets of hope, we found a disciplined and serious commitment to having students of all ages gain the skills necessary to make decisions about their own lives, education, and future. The test for these students was in "real" time and in "real" life. For students in Project 10 East, creating "safe schools" required a concerted effort to change state law, which meant understanding the structure of government and being capable of articulating their vision of a just society before state legislators. For adults in the Ivanhoe Civic League, working to set up general equivalency diploma (GED) classes for themselves and negotiating the political structure to fund their work became dual strategies to move themselves out of economic distress.

The success in these pockets of hope with a wide range of students in terms of age, race, ethnicity, sexual orientation, regional differences, class, and traditional academic ability points to the possibilities of education linked to culture and the life of the spirit as well as to the political and social purposes of a visionary democracy. None of these pockets of hope narrowly focuses the educational process to training workers who accept hierarchies of class, race, and gender seemingly fundamental to sustaining the inequities of our capitalist economy. Rather, each focuses on developing critical thinkers who are willing to challenge injustice. They become thinking subjects who pose real questions about the world in which they live, reflect on them, develop theory, and take action to test their theories. In such an education, students are fully cognizant of the education that they are receiving and conceiving, and they enjoy the results of the changes that they initiate and implement. Students in these projects are willing and able to dream with intense passion of new possibilities for themselves and their communities. Keeping alive hope in democracy by living it in their classrooms, these students become democracy's best hope.

The teachers in these projects are typically regarded by their students as the toughest, holding the highest standards and always pushing to make students think critically, become highly competent in their subject area, act democratically, and engage as participants in their classroom and school and then in their broader communities outside school. Each of the classrooms in these pockets of hope is what hooks (1994) calls "a location of possibility," and in those spaces the teachers and students are engaged in "education as a practice of freedom."

Our Project. The impetus for developing these case studies began with our own experience at Salem State College in creating the Language Intensive Interdisciplinary Program (LIIP) for first year English as a Second Language (ESL) college students (see Chapter 2) and in teaching women's studies. Our research is thus generated from our own experience as feminist and Freirean teachers who believe that democratic practice must be taught, learned, and lived in the classroom. Both the LIIP and women's studies were viewed by students and by numbers of other faculty as pockets of hope at our otherwise traditional college, where what Freire (1993) dubbed the "banking method" of education largely prevailed.

We realized that the LIIP, which our administration funded as a commitment to ESL students, provided a space for us to construct a community of students and faculty who were committed to democratic pedagogy, academic excellence, and civic engagement. Though our community was vibrant, it clearly stood outside the mainstream and suffered the isolation of other marginalized programs like African American studies and women's studies. Our experience prompted us to wonder about teachers in school and community settings who shared our Freirean and feminist philosophy and practice of education. We wanted to have a dialogue with teachers to understand their work and ours. We wondered, How do teachers who believe in education as preparation for active participation in a democracy create and sustain their classrooms? How do they build their communities? How do they teach? How do they keep their strength and nourish their hope? How do they link their classrooms to projects of change in the world? We decided to enter into a dialogue with teachers and students engaged in democratic educational projects.

As teachers, concerned with the politics of education, we also saw this project as a way to introduce the voices of more teachers and students into the debate about public education. We understood the ignominy of having spent decades in the classroom and being ignored in the shaping of education policy. We agreed with Henry Giroux (1988), who, in describing the function of teachers as transformative intellectuals, noted that "many of the recommendations that have emerged in the current debate either ignore the role teachers play in preparing learners to be active and critical citizens or they suggest reforms that ignore the intelligence, judgment and experience that teachers might offer in such a debate" (121). Like Giroux, we see teachers as transformative intellectuals, but we believe another sector in the educational community is also being ignored—students. In our view, teachers' voices are of central significance, but the critical voices of students must also be heard and respected in any discussion of education.

Using the insights of teachers and students in writing these case studies, we hope to offer credible and viable possibilities for transformation in schools and communities. The creation of more pockets of hope is central to our political project. Our dream is that in learning about these educational projects, teachers, students, parents, and community members will be inspired to sustain their own pockets of hope, forge new alliances, engage in dialogue, and demand more of their educational systems.

Who We Are. As a political scientist and a junior faculty member, de los Reyes, who was raised in a middle-class family in Puerto Rico, brought to our work a grounding in critical, colonial, and post-colonial theory, as well as a lifetime commitment to the independence of Puerto Rico and to other colonized countries still fighting for their sovereignty and their freedom. As a lesbian feminist and a senior faculty member in English and women's studies, Gozemba, who was raised in a working-class Irish family in the Boston area, brought a grounding in feminist and liberatory pedagogical theory and practice, as well as a lifetime commitment to activism around issues of teacher unionism, gender, race, class, and sexual orientation. The common ground that initially allowed us to develop a shared language and vision was the work of Paulo Freire, particularly *Pedagogy of the Oppressed* (1993) and *Pedagogy of Hope* (1994).

Gozemba's experience in women's studies and de los Reyes's in political science naturally led us to think about the centrality of power in our own project, the Language Intensive Interdisciplinary Program, and in other educational projects that intrigued us. We came to realize that the clarity of teachers and students about how power operates not just in school but in the world was a key characteristic of a pocket of hope. *Teaching to Transgress: Education as the Practice of Freedom* (1994) by bell hooks and *Truth or Dare: Encounters with Power, Authority, and Mystery* (1987) by Starhawk would become key feminist texts for us in opening up a vision of the way power operated in pedagogical settings. Starhawk's typology of power, which she based on her own pedagogical and activist experience, resonated with us. She elaborates on the concepts of "power-over," "power-from-within," and "power-with" throughout *Truth or Dare,* and describes them succinctly in the first few pages:

> *Power-over* shapes every institution of our society. This power is wielded in the workplace, in the schools, in the courts, in the doctor's office. It may rule with weapons that are physical or by controlling the resources we need to live: money, food, medical care; or by controlling more subtle resources: information, approval, love. We are so accustomed to power-over, so steeped in its language and its implicit threats that we often become aware of its functioning only when we see its extreme manifestations (9).
>
> *Power-from-within* is akin to the sense of mastery we develop as young children with each new unfolding ability: the exhilaration of standing erect, of walking, of speaking the magic words that convey our needs and thoughts.
>
> But power-from-within is also akin to something deeper. It arises from our sense of connection, our bonding with other human beings, and with the environment.
>
> Although power-over rules the systems we live in, power-from-within sustains our lives. We can feel that power in acts of creation and connection, in planting, building, writing, cleaning, healing, soothing, playing, singing, making love. We can feel it in acting together with others to oppose control (10).
>
> *Power-with,* or influence: the power of a strong individual in a

group of equals, the power not to command, but to suggest and be listened to, to begin something and see it happen. The source of power-with is the willingness of others to listen to our ideas. We could call that willingness respect, not for a role, but for each unique person (10).

Starhawk's typology of power became a critical tool in helping us understand how teachers in pockets of hope achieved noteworthy results in their work with students of all ages and from many different backgrounds. Across all of the pockets of hope, we observed teachers and students naming and challenging power-over; developing and nurturing power-from-within; and generating and modeling power-with. Some of the teachers and students talked about racism, sexism, homophobia, and classism. Others used the language of fairness, justice, and equality. All of them understood power deeply and knew how it must be shared in a democratic classroom and in a democratic society. They all spoke a language of democracy and all of them were committed to making democracy more of a reality.

While only some of the teachers consciously constructed feminist and Freirean classrooms, they all arrived at that practice through an attention to creating conditions in which students came to understand how power operates in our society. We saw these teachers inspiring their students to become engaged citizens by becoming active participants in their classroom, their school, their communities—people who could, as one of the students said, "rise to ask questions."

After initially interviewing these teachers, we realized that in talking about their practice in the classroom, we were constantly moving to something larger—citizenship and ultimately the vitality of our democracy. This prompted us to read more broadly and think more deeply about the roots of American democracy and the lack of political participation evident today. We considered how in the eyes of many U.S. citizens, democracy has been downsized to the simple act of voting, what Sheldon Wolin (1996) sees as "an illusion of perpetual political motion" (34). Yet, over the past 20 years, fewer than 50% of eligible voters ever took part in even that most minimal of democratic activities. Far, far fewer actually participate in trying to make our democracy a just place for all of its people.

We began to see the pockets of hope as effective learning communities capable of empowering students and of restoring our weakened democracy. Mansbridge asserts that "because no democracy ever reaches the point at which justice is simply done, democracies need to recognize and foster enclaves of resistance" (1996, 58). We realized that each of the pockets of hope, including our own, was indeed the kind of enclave for which

Mansbridge was advocating and in which she saw the hope for democracy.

CONNECTING POCKETS OF HOPE: METHODOLOGY

By the time we conceived of the idea of writing this book, de los Reyes was on the faculty of Harvard Graduate School of Education and Gozemba had spent a semester researching and reflecting on pedagogy at the East-West Center in Honolulu. We had also written "A Dialogue of Hope: Faculty in the 1990s" (Gozemba and de los Reyes, 1996), which defined some of our views about how democratic teachers could survive by building political alliances and creating community. Finding five other projects to study, along with our own, flowed naturally from connections that each of us had with other democratic teachers.

At Harvard, de los Reyes learned about the work of her graduate student Donna San Antonio, with the Appalachian Mountain Teen Project (AMTP) and was impressed with its outreach to working-class and poor white youth. Our initial two-day site visit to AMTP in Wolfeboro, New Hampshire, and our interviews with a number of people connected with the project convinced us of its value.

Gozemba, while a fellow at the East-West Center in Honolulu, had begun interviewing Pi'ikea Miyamoto and her students in the Aloha 'Aina project regarding their cultural and political work in reclaiming the island of Kaho'olawe from the U.S. Navy. Gozemba's interest in mediation had also led her to interview Janie King with the Hawai'i Department of Education's Conflict Resolution Program and, at King's suggestion, Hunter Halliniak, a peer education student at Roosevelt High School. While the central purpose of these initial interviews was not an exploration of democratic education, that focus clearly emerged in the interviews. After de los Reyes and Gozemba jointly studied the transcripts and interviewed Miyamoto and King, we decided to include those projects in the book.

The work of Highlander Research and Education Center of New Market, Tennessee, founded in 1932, appealed to both of us because of its long-standing commitment to expanding the practice of democracy through adult community education. Its central role in the labor, civil rights, and environmental movements as well as in grass-roots community economic education had earned Highlander a notable history in democratic education. In *The Long Haul* (1990), the autobiography of one of the founders, Myles Horton, and in *We Make the Road by Walking* (1991) by Horton and Paulo Freire, their visions of democratic education emerge. Research about Highlander prompted us to go there to investigate the possibility of doing a chapter on one of their teachers or projects. On our initial trip to Appalachia, Candie

Carawan of Highlander suggested that we attend a conference on service learning in Virginia. There we heard Franki Patton Rutherford of Big Creek People in Action talk about Helen Lewis of Highlander. Our preliminary work with Lewis began three days later at Highlander. Ironically, while there has been extensive research in writing and film about the work of Horton and other males who were part of Highlander, scant attention has been paid to the women of Highlander. Women like Zillah Hawes, Zilphia Horton, Septima Clark, Bernice Robinson, Candie Carawan, and Helen Lewis have made enormous contributions to the success of Highlander's democratic agenda. In focusing on Lewis, a strong feminist, we could tell an important part of the story of Highlander.

Gozemba had worked with Al Ferreira, founder of Project 10 East, in offering a workshop on lesbian and gay teachers for their union, the Massachusetts Teachers Association/National Education Association, and knew of Ferreira's work with the gay/straight alliance at Cambridge Rindge and Latin High School. After we conducted two in-depth interviews with Ferreira about his philosophy of education and pedagogy, viewed Ferreira's appearance debating on *Larry King Live,* and studied articles written about Ferreira's work, we decided that Project 10 East was a dynamic example of the work we wanted to document.

The process of deciding on all of the projects involved visits and interviews. In two cases, listening to students led us to their inspirational teachers, Amy Akamine of Roosevelt High and Helen Lewis of Highlander. After analyzing our initial interviews, we realized that all of the teachers (1) had long-term commitments to democratic pedagogy; (2) viewed education as preparation for a life of active involvement in their communities in school and in the larger world; (3) saw the importance of linking what, how, and why they teach with a larger social project; (4) viewed pedagogy as a transformative process for themselves and their students as they jointly engaged challenges; (5) understood how power operated in their classrooms, in their school, and in the society; (6) were risk takers.

To allow us to engage fully in each of the projects and come to an understanding of their day-to-day work, we each focused on three and ultimately wrote about them. De los Reyes continued work on the LIIP and began following AMTP and Project 10. Gozemba, who taught at the University of Hawai'i in 1997-1998 and spent time there in the following years, continued her work with the Aloha 'Aina Project and the Peer Education Program at Roosevelt High School and took on exploring the work of Lewis in Appalachia. Over a four-year period, both of us visited all of the projects, participated in their activities, and reviewed all of the transcripts of interviews with teachers and students as well as field notes that we each had written. From our collaboration in analyzing the data we had collected emerged our vision of the ways in which democratic pedagogy functioned at its best.

Individually, we interviewed each of the teachers at least six times over a two- to four-year period, and in addition we spoke jointly with them at least twice; that allowed us to assist each other in building on knowledge of their work. We interviewed groups of two to five students who had participated in these projects at least three times and, in most cases, up to six times. Interspersed with these group interviews were interviews with individual students, allies, principals, or other administrators or workers in the school or community projects. In every case, those interviewed reviewed the transcripts and had an opportunity to edit them or expand on them. Most significantly, the transcripts became the basis of reflection, analysis, and theory building for the teachers, students, and us. The students gained agency in the process. At Project 10 East, one of them cautioned de los Reyes about how to describe a student revolt against too much adult participation in the group: "Make sure that you get this right." Another student in Roosevelt's Peer Education Project shifted Gozemba's focus from looking at students only in the role of peer mediators to looking at their work as peer educators, peer partners, and peer supporters. "It's all connected," he said. "You've got to look at the total picture. Mediation is an important part of sharing and listening but being a peer partner and supporter is part of what makes it work. Then all of it is what makes these students effective peer educators."

A great deal of the fun and deep emotional and spiritual learning for us occurred as we engaged in each of these projects as participant observers. We attended board meetings, camped out on the bomb-scarred island of Kahoʻolawe, paddled canoes in a New Hampshire lake, witnessed student presentations and celebrations, and attended community meetings. Our engagement in the remarkable and ordinary events of each project gave us a deep sense of its Freirean and feminist pedagogy. A rich portrait of each project emerged from our interviews and our participation in and observation of the projects. As our book neared completion, students and teachers reflected with us on the accuracy of our analysis.

We organized our research as six case studies, which allowed us to preserve the uniqueness of the projects in our descriptions and give a sense of the communities in which they exist. This also gave us the opportunity to develop a broader analysis that can explain how teachers and students are able to create and sustain democratic communities in a wide variety of contexts. Each of the case studies contributed to a larger theoretical framework (Stake 1994) of how democratic pedagogy functions in a variety of educational settings. The case studies become eloquent narratives of the lives of teachers and students, and, in a sense, they are teaching and learning biographies, capturing the drama of the pedagogy in everyday life in "classrooms." We became better listeners ourselves as we developed relationships with the teachers and students.

Given the nature of our study, we focused on understanding how teachers create a democratic community with their students, how academic learning takes place, how power is distributed in the classrooms, how the pedagogy employed by teachers supports the practice of democracy, and how they create the conditions for democratic citizens to emerge. Finally, we looked at the kinds of alliances that support these pockets of hope, allowing them to survive.

Patti Lather's feminist approach to critical research and liberatory pedagogy in *Getting Smart: Feminist Research and Pedagogy With/in the Postmodern* (1991) guided us in thinking about the methods and purposes of our research. With empowerment for both teachers and students, researchers and the researched as a central concern of ours, Lather's "focus on three interwoven issues: the need for reciprocity, the stance of dialectical theory-building versus theoretical imposition, and the question of validity in praxis-oriented research" grounded our approach (56). Recognizing the need for reciprocity, which, Lather says, "implies give and take, a mutual negotiation of meaning and power," we shared our own work in the Language Intensive Interdisciplinary Program with teachers and students and we eagerly engaged in dialogue with them about the LIIP (57). We explained the other projects that we were investigating and arranged for these world class teachers and some of their students to meet with each other and some of our own students for dialogue and reflection, particularly about the concepts of pockets of hope, power, and democratic pedagogy. Two of these meetings took place in Hawai'i, involving teachers and students from four of the projects. We also presented with some of the teachers and students at conferences of the National Women's Studies Association, the New England Educational Research Association, the Far Western Philosophy of Education Society, and the Conference on Pedagogy and Theatre of the Oppressed. The reciprocity that evolved made possible provocative dialogues between the researchers and researched and assured that theory and analysis of practice emerged mutually and were discounted if they did not seem plausible to teachers and students.

Across the projects, our discussions of power, using Starhawk's theory of power-over, power-from-within, and power-with, generated deep analyses of teachers and students about their own pockets of hope. Lather argues that when this "dialectical theory-building" or "collaborative theorizing" is used, it "both advances emancipatory theory and empowers the researched" (64).

In following these strategies, we indicated to the researched that we, too, as teachers were, as Lather points out, "rooted in a commitment to the long-term, broad-based ideological struggle necessary to transform structural inequalities" both in schools and in society (65). As students became more involved in the research with us, they became further convinced of their growing capacity to bring about change in their schools and communities. Moving from the position of interviewees who gave answers to the questions, the teachers and the students began to see themselves in a larger context where they were sharing important stories with those in other institutions and communities who, like them, are engaged in unique projects. These new understandings expanded their vision of their own project and the possibilities of creating change. As a result of the book new friendships and alliances have developed that further strengthen each of the individual projects.

Finally, Lather's emphasis on the little-known theory of catalytic validity resonated with us. She explains that "catalytic validity represents the degree to which the research process re-orients, focuses and energizes participants toward knowing reality in order to transform it, a process Freire (1993) terms conscientization" (68). Lather's bold acknowledgment of the political purposes of research as serving as a catalyst for action strikes us as refreshing in an academic world where pseudo-neutral objectivity is glorified even as it guides and often undergirds conservative and reactionary political agendas.

In approaching this research as teachers and researchers with a series of questions generated through our own experiences, we had the objectives of deepening our understanding of teachers committed to democratic pedagogy and of inspiring others to create similar educational projects. We call the results of our research "teacher and student knowledge," which is akin to what Peter Park (1993) calls "people's knowledge" and stands in opposition to elite modes of inquiry. We make no claim for being separate from the researched, objective, or apolitical. We are teachers and intellectuals with a passion for democracy.

In working with these teachers and students and in drawing those of them who were not part of the larger national discourse about education into that debate, we hope to contribute to expanding the base of concerned citizens committed to transformative education. We particularly want to pay tribute to the teachers in these projects: our colleagues in the Language Intensive Interdisciplinary Program (LIIP), Patricia Buchanan, Wayne Dudley, and Betsy Hart (Chapter 2); Amy Akamine of the Peer Education Program and Janie King of the Hawai'i Department of Education (Chapter 3); Al Ferreira of Project 10 (Chapter 4); Pi'ikea Miyamoto of Aloha 'Aina (Chapter 5); Donna San Antonio, Holly Manoogian, and Jeff Martel of the Appalachian Mountain Teen Project (Chapter 6); and Helen Lewis of Highlander

(Chapter 7). We end this work reassured by their skills, their grace, their compassion, and their vision.

DEMOCRATIC EDUCATION: THE PRACTICE OF FREEDOM

In each of these projects the teachers and students spoke eloquently about the ways in which they shared power, interacted with each other building community, learned new knowledge and skills and engaged in projects of changing the world. They spoke the language of democracy—a language of freedom, responsibility, and justice; in fact, this language infused their conversations with each other and with us. In this section, we use their voices to highlight key characteristics of pockets of hope.

The Central Role of the Democratic Teacher

Teachers with a passion for democracy play the central role in pockets of hope. Their commitment to sharing power and engaging themselves and their students in the "practice of freedom" transforms their educational projects from the all too common power-over paradigm to a power-with experience. By intentionally building community, democratic teachers establish the conditions in which students access their power-from-within as they engage in the process of co-constructing knowledge. In structuring experiences that call for students to work in alliance among themselves and with others outside their educational project, teachers assure that students learn the process of building power-with, which will sustain them as they become active participants in their communities working for fairness and justice.

All of the teachers in these pockets of hope are fully present intellectually, spiritually, and emotionally for their students. Their presence in the midst of their students in a writing class or on a mountain trail is a welcome change from the power-over posture that is so often thought of as natural to a teacher. They begin every course or project intent on sharing power with their students. These teachers understand that in whatever they and their students do, the ultimate goals are to build skills and knowledge that will help the students become autonomous individuals and full participants in our society.

The teachers are diverse in terms of age, race, ethnicity, gender, class, and sexual orientation, but they share crucial characteristics: courage, openness, coherence, and vision. Lewis of Highlander exhibited enormous courage in her convictions and found herself "fired from some of the best colleges and universities for nurturing radical students." Ferreira, a gay man, courageously came out of the closet in order to support gay students he perceived as isolated and alone.

All of these teachers were open about their lives with their students, revealing their innumerable strengths while recognizing as well their mistakes and vulnerabilities. Many welcomed students into their homes on special occasions. Miyamoto, San Antonio, and Manoogian as part of their work camped out with their students for days or even weeks at a time. Ferreira, after speaking to a Latino group at the high school about Project 10 East, shared with his students his uneasiness about the venture because he had "a lot of stereotypes about that group." Later, recognizing that his stereotype was unfounded, he modeled for students the honesty it takes to admit to buying into oppressive stereotypes. In all of the pockets of hope, students encountered teachers who were whole people, at ease with their lives and totally engaged in the process of working with students.

Students saw a coherency in the lives of these teachers who "walk the talk." Wayne Dudley, a history professor in the Language Intensive Interdisciplinary Program, feels fiercely committed to literacy in Africa and involves his LIIP students in book drives for African schools and colleges. Working in alliance with other students in local schools and community groups, they have sent 3 million books to schools and colleges in many parts of Africa. Some of those same students in the LIIP rose to challenge the faculty for unilaterally choosing to focus much of a semester's work on one topic, human rights, without consulting them. Having read hooks and Freire, they understood that we were not being true to our educational philosophy—we were not walking the talk.

Faculty like Dudley who have a vision for change inspire students. Miyamoto, who has worked for over 20 years on reclaiming the island of Kaho'olawe for the Hawaiian people, models for her students the necessity of sustaining a vision over a long period. Her vision inspired one of her students, Keawe, to articulate his vision of establishing a high school study program on the uninhabited island, which would allow indigenous Hawaiians an opportunity to learn all of their academic subjects in a way that he felt would be culturally appropriate.

These teachers also share love, respect, and trust with their students, and their bold act in doing so elicits the same response from their students. Students look at these teachers with a sense of awe. Maxine Waller, a community leader who worked with Helen Lewis, describes her as a "soul educator," someone who "always gives you stuff to feed your soul." Maurice, a student of Akamine's in the Peer Education Program (PEP), marveled that in her class students do 90 percent of the work during a class, whereas in other classes they sit back as passive spectators and barely do 10 percent. He laughs, thinking about how he gave her the ironic name "Boss," which has stuck with her. In Akamine's classes, students learn to be responsible; they become the "bosses" of their own lives, because she gives them the chance to do so in a caring environment. In pushing students to share with each other the love, respect, and trust that she shares with them, Akamine transforms her classes. Maurice explains that she cares about having them learn, but the critical difference in this class is that, in addition, the students know that she cares deeply about them as whole human beings and this inspires them to achieve more.

Confident, competent, and caring, these teachers are powerful even when silent. Their protective presence in the classroom is always felt. Dan, a student of San Antonio and Manoogian in the Appalachian Mountain Teen Project (AMTP), poetically captures the safety all of these democratic teachers create in their projects. "It's like a spider web; they're at the center of it and we are around." In this protective web, he went on to explain, participants get to experience the "magic" of the project. Time and time again, students told us that the source of the magic in their projects was the teachers. Diane in PEP spoke of how Akamine could take one of the most diverse groups of students in Roosevelt High School and get them all to collaborate on extraordinary peer education projects that demanded the highest academic skills and enormous poise. She called it "Boss' magic." In truth what seems so compelling for all of these students is teachers who care deeply about them, have enormously high standards, and believe in the potential of every student.

Creating Community

In each of these pockets of hope, the teachers initiate and then with their students consciously create community—that magical web. Essentially, the community becomes an empowerment zone, in which students build the intellectual, emotional, and political skills necessary to allow them to become self-actualized participants in their communities at school, at home, and in our democracy.

Sofia, a college student in the LIIP, described how it worked. "This is what the program is all about—building a community where everybody can feel comfortable to work and to succeed." She added, "We feel free to learn...because it comes from the heart. It's a sense of family." Rebekah Luke, a community ally in Aloha 'Aina, recalls how Miyamoto told her that "she wanted the students to realize that this is an 'ohana (family). That we are all one 'ohana." The sense of comfort and confidence that students develop in consciously constructed empowerment zones that feel like "family" directly contribute to their building power-from-within. Without this kind of support, which the teacher initiates but eventually they and the teacher sustain, many students would languish, never fulfilling their potential.

The initial step toward building community is simply transforming the physical space where people gather into a welcoming place. In all of the classrooms, either in the community or in schools, circles of chairs replace the hierarchy of rows. With this arrangement, the teachers indicate their commitment to face-to-face dialogue, the foundation of a democratic community. Akamine explains how PEP participants are affected. "Our classroom setup encourages equality. We sit in a circle. We sit on chairs of equal height." Hunter, one of her students, speaks to the effect of this arrangement: "I think…students don't talk in most classes, because other students aren't listening to them. They feel oppressed. They feel as if they shouldn't say anything because it's useless. But when you're forced to look at people, you're forced to show expression to them." At Highlander Research and Education Center when poor and working class adults congregate to envision change in their communities, rocking chairs arranged in a circle await them. For students of all ages this simple humane gesture transforms classroom dynamics of power-over to a configuration that allows people to recognize fully each other's humanity and to acknowledge the potential that each person brings to the circle.

While sitting in a circle seems to be such a small act, the norm in most classrooms and most community meetings is still rows. The teachers in pockets of hope go further. Welcoming art work on the walls greets all who enter the space to learn. A refrigerator, some old comfortable chairs, pictures of the students at work, and signs of their accomplishments typify the classroom landscape. What begins as the teacher's classroom quickly becomes a mutual space—our space. The teachers and the space that they share with students communicate that this is a place that welcomes the whole student. In every instance such a space empowers students to become part of the welcoming ritual, putting their mark on the space—truly making it a place for all of them.

The teachers in each of these projects consciously engage the participants in activities such as team-building exercises, theatre and music, and the simple act of sharing food and "talking story" to create community. By engaging in these activities, participants build their power-from-within and bond in ways that make it possible to enjoy each other and take their place comfortably in their project and outside it in larger communities. In Ivanhoe, Virginia, community members decided to use a renewed Fourth of July celebration to have fun and educate the community. Lewis recruited a puppeteer with expertise in building larger than life-size puppets. She worked with youth and adult community volunteers to develop a morality play of sorts recalling the closing of industries in the community and the people's efforts to revive the community. This event energized people and built enormous solidarity for the struggle that would continue with powerful forces outside their community.

Learning the democratic skills of participation comes easiest to those who learn them in a caring community where the art of collaboration—as opposed to competition—is fostered. The sense of solidarity that students build with each other is eminently important. Janie King, an ally of Akamine, speaks of the importance of building community in schools so that there will not be any "forgotten kids," isolated and alienated teenagers who, because they lack community, take power and use it in ways that put their health and safety at risk—as well as that of their peers and teachers. Forgotten adults, who have struggled to survive in the hollows of Appalachia, have been revitalized as Lewis has worked with them in efforts to rebuild their communities. Maxine Waller described the people's transformation poetically, "We have been on a train for the last hundred years and we've rode as passengers. And now we're not passengers; we're engineers" (Hinsdale, Lewis, & Waller, 1995, 48). Lewis's experiences in projects throughout Appalachia demonstrates that building community creates the democratic power-from-within that can change people's lives.

Pedagogy

"Reading the Word and the World." Michaela, a student in Project 10 East, repeated a critique of traditional schooling that we heard from many of the participants in pockets of hope: "I don't know if people can ever learn from a school situation how to function in society. I know that I can't. That's not what taught me how to function in society." She goes on to point out that finding Project 10 in her high school made all the difference in teaching her how to "function in society" for there she found a teacher and other students who engaged in dialogues of critical importance to them intellectually, emotionally, and politically. In Project 10 East, in researching and speaking out before their peers and the state legislature about issues like homophobia and racism, they "read the word and the world."

But students can find traditional academic courses where they also engage in reading the word and the world. In the Language Intensive Interdisciplinary Program, first-year ESL college students in a composition course read Jonathan Kozol's *Savage Inequalities* (1991) and bell hooks's *Teaching to Transgress* (1994). The books provided the students with a lens through which they could reflect on their own experiences in some of the Boston area's most neglected public schools. Out of their class discussions and their writing about their own experiences, they developed sophisticated critiques of bilingual education and they decided to take action. They came up with a suggested plan for improving the bilingual programs at each of their high schools and they organized a conference for Latino high school students that focused on coaching them through the process of preparing for and applying to college.

Dialogue. Key elements in both the LIIP and Project 10 East examples were the emphases on relevance and dialogue. In all of the pockets of hope, rich, serious, and purposeful dialogue characterized the interactions among participants and their teacher. Speaking and listening—the foundation of democratic pedagogy—were at the core of the teaching and learning process.

Sofia, a student in the LIIP, related a conversation she was having with other students in the program about what they called the "perfect" classroom. "We were talking yesterday about how for [many] people, a perfect classroom is one where all the students are silent and the professor is always talking. [laughs] I couldn't understand, how that could be true." She then asks the critical question, "How does the professor know that students are learning, if they don't express themselves?" Unfortunately, Sofia came to learn how common those "perfect" classrooms were. Countless students pass through authoritarian classrooms in which the "banking method" of education prevails: teachers make deposits in students' heads. Every so often the teachers give tests in which the students repeat, usually in writing, what the teacher said. In the event of a national or state test, the students repeat what someone outside the classroom determined they needed to know. To succeed in such classrooms, the students must learn to be docile, passive, and capable of enduring endless boredom.

Lewis, influenced by Freire's work, described the role of the teacher in the dialogical classroom as that of an animator who "poses problems and gives students the confidence to analyze their problems and plan ways of overcoming them" (Lewis & Gaventa, 1988, 4). She cautions that "teachers should be more facilitating, advising and the learners more active and responsible" (5). She sees the teacher playing the active role of animator, the person critical to the learning process, continually moving the discussion to deeper levels, steering participants away from "gossiping" or "sharing their ignorance" (5). And significantly, Lewis reminds teachers that "people remember the best what they have said, not what they are told" (5). Finding one's voice in a supportive community is a transformative experience.

San Antonio reminds us of the other critical function in a dialogue, listening. "Something we forget is how radicalizing it is to just be taken seriously...to be given an opportunity to speak your own experience and to have it be listened to." Ferreira agreed with San Antonio and explained that teens are "acutely aware of the fact that their voices are not heard by the adult community." Dan, a student of San Antonio, shared with us his insight about why most schools don't work for teenagers. There the students have come to know, he argues, that "kids should be seen, not heard." Educated to be silent and compliant, these students grow up to be silent and compliant citizens. By contrast, democratic teachers believe that students who have found their voice and eagerly listen to their peers become the next best hope of democracy.

Ferreira of Project 10 East identified four elements that he saw as essential if students and teachers were going to have what he calls "dangerous" dialogues about challenging subjects like homophobia, sexism, and racism. According to Ferreira, participants must (1) accept that they can disagree, (2) not be afraid to say anything, (3) get away from "political correctness," and (4) be willing to take risks in order to create change.

Collaborative Construction of Knowledge. In the six very different learning environments in the pockets of hope highlighted in this book, we observed students and teachers sharing the roles of teachers and learners. These teachers recognized that students of all ages came to learning experiences with a great deal of knowledge. Richard, a Hawaiian student in Miyamoto's Aloha 'Aina project, entered her class with a great deal of expertise in cultivating taro. Miyamoto, herself a native Hawaiian, prized this knowledge and eagerly learned from him. This experience of having his expertise recognized in school bonded Richard to the project and kept him connected to it even after he had completed his science requirements.

In Ivanhoe, Virginia, adult students told Lewis that they wanted to do a history of their community. She decided to offer a course for this purpose. Kay Early, one of the students, comments on how that class's collaborative process initially shocked her but eventually helped her to recognize her skills.

> When I heard that there would be a history class about Ivanhoe, at Ivanhoe Tech, I said to myself, "Now that sounds like fun. I'll just go down there and learn about Ivanhoe." Boy, was I in for a big surprise! I thought that this would be a regular class, with textbooks and a teacher who lectured and gave tests. There were no books and a teacher who said, "You the class, will do research for the history of Ivanhoe."
>
> I spent many hours, usually on Sunday afternoons, touring every graveyard in and around Ivanhoe. Church records were vague and hard to come by. I took a week's vacation to go through my husband's grandaddy's trunk which contains old letters, ledgers, bills, tax tickets and pictures dating back to the mid-1800s. (Hinsdale, Lewis, & Waller, 1995, 97–98)

For students such as Early, being a part of this collaborative construction of knowledge gave her a new view of the possibilities inherent in democratic pedagogy.

We discovered that students in pockets of hope work more diligently than most other students we have observed. The pedagogy of democratic teachers is demanding. Their students—adults in Appalachia, ESL students in a college in Massachusetts, or native Hawaiians in special education science—testified to the rigor of their courses. Special education students whose opinions are usually ignored because they are perceived as having few insights speak poignantly about how teachers affect them. Kaleo said with pride, "You come to Miya and you do more." Richard contrasted this with what happened in another teacher's class. "He doesn't push us. He just says, 'You don't want to do it. Take an F.'" Kaleo acknowledged, "If we just act dumb, then that's what makes her mad." In all of these projects in courses from special education science to college world civilization, the intellect of the students is recognized and challenged through problem-posing education.

While democratic teachers clearly take responsibility for planning in their classes, they understand completely the ways in which learning is an organic experience and not predictable. The knowledge that everyone in the classroom brings to the circle transforms everyone's understandings and keeps the classroom alive. Lusted defined pedagogy as "the transformation of consciousness that takes place in the intersection of three agencies—the teacher, the learner and the knowledge they together produce" (quoted in Lather, 1991, 15). In pockets of hope, where students and teachers work together collaboratively, one finds neither a teacher-centered class nor a student-centered class; instead we find what Palmer (1998) calls a subject-centered class, where the focus is on ideas. Students such as Michaela in Project 10 East, Richard in the Aloha 'Aina project, Kay Early in Ivanhoe, Virginia, and all of the others with whom we spoke see the ways in which what they are learning connects to their lives and broadens and deepens their understanding of the world. What is inside them counts, just as the new ideas to which the teacher is introducing them count. Therein lies the crucial vitality.

CHANGING THE WORLD

In pockets of hope, nurturing learning communities, where human beings are recognized for the unique talents and insights that each of them has, possibility is engaged as an ongoing process. Hunter saw it happening for students in Akamine's classroom. "Most students don't believe in what they can do. But in PEP everybody comes in to do what they need to do. I look at how well this class is run just by us students and how students can do so much for themselves and not need, well need minimal, supervision from adults. If we really want to do something, we can do it." In sharing power with her students by experimenting with different approaches to teaching and learning, Akamine creates opportunities for students to discover that they are capable of taking charge of their own education and taking action.

It is significant that teachers in pockets of hope don't shy away from opening the doors of their classrooms to the larger world. Instead, they see the school and the larger community as spaces where their students can test their knowledge and their skills. Students begin their education for democracy by taking small steps in their class or school. Eventually, they spread their wings and test their power in the larger society.

Having noticed that some of the profoundly disabled special education students at Roosevelt High School had become the butt of jokes in the cafeteria, PEP students brought up the issue in class and decided to take action. They began sitting at lunch tables with the special education students. Because many of the PEP students were "stars" at the school, their action turned heads, and, eventually, other students gravitated to the tables, creating a supportive environment that persists as a PEP tradition. In allying themselves with many student groups at their high school, PEP demonstrates the importance of sharing power-with a broad range of students.

Hunter's belief that students in PEP can accomplish whatever they set out to do is a belief that resonates throughout all of the pockets of hope. In every project, students became engaged in projects of change in their communities. In Wolfeboro, New Hampshire, members of the Appalachian Mountain Teen Project joined with the AFL-CIO and the American Friends Service Committee to organize a conference for teenagers addressing the conditions of their part-time employment. They discovered that they have rights as workers and did not have to accept unsafe working conditions. In West Virginia, the Big Creek People in Action joined forces with Highlander Research and Education Center in Tennessee to create Democracy Schools where citizens in McDowell County could learn how to become involved in the practice of democracy, especially in holding elected leaders accountable. In Massachusetts, students in Project 10 East testified before the legislature to get a safe schools bill passed that would assure counseling and support for gay and lesbian students in the state's public schools. On the day that they went to the governor's office for the signing of the bill, one student said in amazement to her teacher, Ferreira, "Do you realize that we are making history?" Ferreira later reflected with us on "how powerful it is for these young people who have been involved in changing a state law...who will be able to look back and say, 'I helped change the direction.'" In pockets of hope, students and teachers move easily from making discoveries in the classroom to connecting their learning to larger communities of which they are a part. Confidence, gained through the process of research, dialogue, and reflection, creates new insights that lead them to desire freedom, justice, and equality.

In every pocket of hope, teachers understood and then taught their students the importance of building alliances both within their schools and community projects and then with the world outside. Miyamoto, Akamine, Ferreira, as well as we understood that all change agents need allies among the administrations at our schools. Lewis emphasized that isolated Appalachian communities had to build alliances around and over mountains. San Antonio and Manoogian recruited a powerful alliance of feminists and other progressive community members in New Hampshire to support their efforts with teens. In modeling the ways in which they shared power-with others, the teachers taught their students important lessons about collaboration and ways to succeed in achieving change by working in alliance.

Experiencing the energy, vision, and capacity for dreaming that we found in these pockets of hope expanded our own vision of democracy. We learned how these teachers and students generated an understanding of the world that allowed them to engage it actively and positively. And we relearned with them that a participatory democracy is possible. In each one of these pockets of hope we found the seeds of democracy carefully planted and nurtured.

THE TASK BEFORE US: A CALL TO ACTION

All of us have a stake in the vitality of our public schools and in democratic community organizations. They are the life blood of our democracy. Robert Putnam in *Bowling Alone: The Collapse and Revival of American Community* (2000) describes the increasing sense of alienation that people are feeling in our democracy and notes the ways in which it undermines the social capacity of our society. We believe that our nation is at risk of forgetting the importance of citizen participation in preserving our democracy and is at risk of engaging in historical amnesia about powerful memories of struggle.

In *Pockets of Hope: How Students and Teachers Change the World,* we capture the truly extraordinary work of very committed groups of teachers and students in participatory democratic projects. These students and teachers are reinvigorating democracy by sharing power in the classroom, analyzing the way power operates in their communities and the world, and challenging inequities that stifle the voices of the disempowered and dispossessed.

Our observation of these six educational projects over a four-year period has given us an opportunity to see both their resiliency and fragility. In the case studies that follow, the stories of teachers and students who forged ahead and would not allow their efforts to be thwarted by fear, funding threats, conservative attacks on public education, or corporate and political attempts to undermine their efforts to democratize their communities are inspirational.

Threats to their funding were constant. For example, the Peer Education Program lost its funding for four years in a row in the Hawai'i legislature, and it was only through the lobbying of students, parents, concerned community allies, school administrators, and teachers that the legislature restored the funds. The Appalachian Mountain Teen Project went each year to the selectmen in the town of Ossipee asking for funding for their work with teenagers in the community. For years, the selectmen have refused to put AMTP's request for funds into the town budget. But because parents and community allies in Ossipee understand how much of a difference the program makes in teenagers' lives, at the annual town meeting citizens always reject the recommendation of the selectmen, revise the budget, and appropriate the funds for AMTP.

Each pocket of hope survives because the skilled democratic teacher at its center understands the importance of having allies. Miyamoto's Aloha 'Aina project found important community allies in Rebekah Luke and Tet-Choi Fung, who brought special skills to tasks the group wanted to complete. Big Creek People in Action in McDowell County is establishing Democracy Schools because of their support from Helen Lewis and the staff at Highlander Research and Education Center—and Highlander has survived because of the contributions of its community allies. Ferreira's role in Project 10 East's gay/straight alliance grew because of the support of Cambridge Public Schools superintendent Mary Lou McGrath and high school principal Edward Sarasin. Released from his teaching load, Ferreira became the full-time director of Project 10 East and was able to devote himself fully to creating a safe-school environment for students who were gay, bisexual, and transgendered.

The remarkable achievements of each of these projects breathe life into our democracy. Five years ago, we heard Jonathan Kozol speak at the Cambridge Public Library, just steps away from Project 10 East's space, on the occasion of the publication of his book *Amazing Grace: The Lives of Children and the Conscience of a Nation* (1995). Kozol, worried about who is carrying on a tradition of struggling for equality for children and poor people, challenged his audience of typical liberals and progressives with the question "Who's developing the farm team?" The question resonated with us and is responsible in part for our writing this book. Over the past four years, we have discovered that teachers and students in pockets of hope are creating the "farm team." Young and adult learners in pockets of hope are being groomed for the major leagues—leadership positions in their communities. Their teachers' legacy to our society are generations of students who can take on the responsibility of sustaining our democracy.

For our readers who feel committed to participatory democracy—to the practice of freedom, justice, and equality—we offer a challenge similar to Kozol's. Thousand of pockets of hope across this country need the support of community activists committed to democracy and justice. Find the pockets of hope in your schools and in your communities and figure out the ways in which you can become their allies: lend a hand in a classroom; help buy additional supplies or send students on field trips that expand their horizons; or talk with school administrators, school committee members, and local politicians and civic leaders about the success of these projects. Community educational projects also need allies who will volunteer time, help them raise money, and defend them when they challenge established authority. To fend off the conservative agenda of high-stakes testing, charter schools, and vouchers, committed citizens need to get involved in the debate over educational policy at local and state levels and present an alternative vision of "educational reform."

The teachers in pockets of hope need support so that other teachers will step forward and expand the circle of democratic educational projects. In the current conservative atmosphere pervading schools, teachers find it difficult to take risks. We need community allies, politicians, superintendents, principals, and college presidents who will support the creation of more pockets of hope. As Deborah Meier (1995) has shown in her work in the Central Park East Schools in Harlem and in the New Mission Hill School in Boston, it is possible to create entire schools that are pockets of hope. In the midst of such acrimonious debate about the future of our schools, we hope that those of you who care about educating students to take an active role in our democracy will listen to the voices of students and teachers. In doing this, we can all learn about the ways in which their work both nurtures academic accomplishment and furthers the goals of our democracy. Too often the voices of students and teachers, the very people who understand best what works in educational settings, are ignored in favor of listening to corporate and political leaders, who have not set foot in a classroom in years. The inspirational voices of the teachers and students in this book should convince us that we cannot rest until all schools are pockets of hope.

CHAPTER 2

Breaking the Cycle, Rising to Question: The Language Intensive Interdisciplinary Program

Eileen de los Reyes

> Freedom is acquired by conquest, not by gift. It must be pursued constantly and responsibly.
> —Paulo Freire (1998)

A NEW VISION

The education of students of color and students for whom English is a second language (ESL) is contested political terrain. Caught up in the language of deficiencies and low standards, these students find themselves relegated to the periphery of schools and colleges. During my tenure as project director of Student Support Services at the Salem State College Learning Center, a federally funded program for students of color conditionally accepted by the college, I became intensely aware of how this process of marginalization works.

Often spoken about as ill-prepared, intellectually deficient, and in need of remediation, ESL students were the objects of countless meetings. These meetings seemed always to revolve around building hurdles to ensure that these "ill-prepared" students were meeting appropriate "standards" for admissions and graduation. Yet, for every faculty member and administrator who believed these students were academically deficient, another believed in their potential. The tension between these groups defined the parameters of the always heated and often acrimonious discussions.

In response to the prevailing notion that ESL students were a "problem" for the college that needed to be resolved, Patricia Gozemba and I created the Language Intensive Interdisciplinary Program. Our alliance began when, in desperation, I put almost all incoming ESL students from the Learning

Center in Gozemba's English Composition course. Gozemba already taught freshman composition in Avenues for Successful Communication (ASC), an innovative, interdisciplinary program that also included courses in history, speech, and communications. The students' experiences in ASC, as well as Gozemba's insistence that something had to be done to improve the quality of education for Salem State's most marginalized students, gave me confidence in her work.

I was also Gozemba's best hope for coming up with a plan to educate the growing population of ESL students on our campus. She figured that since I had an accent, I had a solution. As our conversations became more frequent, we realized that we shared a deeper political understanding of education. When I became a faculty member in the Interdisciplinary Studies Department, my assignment was to create what we called the Language Intensive Interdisciplinary Program (LIIP).

Building an Alliance

In some ways, our shared political vision surprised us. We came from such different backgrounds in terms of class, age and experience, ethnicity, and culture. Although we both described ourselves as being from the Left of the political spectrum, we understood that this was a necessary but not sufficient condition for working together. We needed to find common ground that would allow us to develop a shared language and vision. The work of Paulo Freire, particularly *Pedagogy of the Oppressed* (1993) and *Pedagogy of Hope* (1994), became the bridge that linked our ideologies. The critical analysis of relations of power, the understanding of teachers and students as makers of history, and our belief in possibility and hope provided us with a foundation for deeper discussion and reflection.

Our discussions began with a shared concern for our students, who we could see were struggling to survive in an academic institution that failed to meet their needs. While some faculty and administrators bemoaned the flood of ESL students, whom they perceived as "lowering standards," we asked critical questions about their lives: Why were they hungry? Why were they working 40 hours a week? Why were they responsible for supporting their families? Why were they sick and unable to access medical care? Who was benefiting from their oppression? We saw these questions as relevant to our educational theory and practice. We could not resolve each student's individual problems, but we could use the classroom as a place to explore how our lives and those of our students were linked to the larger structures of power and powerlessness that define the social order. In this manner, our classrooms would become microcosms of the larger society, as opposed to isolated and disembodied spaces where, with benign neglect, the reality of oppression is never acknowledged. With this approach to theory and practice we did not intend to avoid the urgent and time-consuming challenge of finding solutions for students in crisis; yet, we hoped our students would come to understand that individual solutions are seldom permanent or satisfactory.

As our analysis of relations of power in society deepened, our vision of education expanded. We explored the realm of possibility and hope and reaffirmed our belief that all students have a right to a democratic education. We concluded that the idea of democracy had to take concrete form in our classrooms. For us, this meant that we expected our students to be fully conscious of the education they were conceiving and receiving and to use their education to imagine and implement social and political change that would improve their lives. Students educated in democratic practice, we believed, would have the will and the capacity to dream with intense passion of new possibilities for themselves and for those around them. By building a program based on democratic practice, we were convinced that our students would not only learn English more easily, but also become fully engaged in the teaching and learning process, build community, and develop democratic leadership skills that would make them effective leaders in their communities.

This chapter documents the development of the Language Intensive Interdisciplinary Program, from 1993 to 1997, and how we struggled to transform our ideas into practice. During these years, the program continued under our leadership. I was the program coordinator for the first three years, at which time I left Salem State to become a faculty member at the Harvard Graduate School of Education. Gozemba took over as the acting coordinator for the 1996–1997 school year. In 1997–1998, a new coordinator began directing the program, and, as a result, it has taken a different direction.

Initial Questions

We began the formal process of designing the LIIP by identifying three key questions: (1) Which student population would be admitted to the program: immigrants or internationals? (2) What would be the benefits and drawbacks of keeping non-native speakers of English together in first-year classes? (3) How could we send the message to the students that we believed in their ability to lead and engage with us in the process of teaching and learning?

International Students vs. Recent Immigrants. After much discussion, we decided to include both international students and recent immigrants in the LIIP. This proved to be a highly controversial decision. Although many faculty argued that the program could not bridge the cultural, socioeconomic, and educational differences between these two groups of students, we wanted to challenge the misconceptions and biases that led to the assumption that

33

international students were wealthy and, therefore, "successful" in school, while immigrant students were poor and, therefore, "unsuccessful." We argued that this assumption ultimately tracked both groups: international students became the college's money-making venture; recent immigrants became an area of neglect. By enrolling both groups in a single program, we made the statement that all students had a right to a democratic education in which they would be encouraged to engage as thinking subjects capable of transforming themselves and their communities.

Separation vs. Integration. Another key question was whether to keep the ESL students together in all of their courses. While we had seen this work in the ASC program, we shared the concern that language acquisition might be inhibited by limiting the exposure of ESL students to native English speakers. However, we had both observed that ESL students seldom spoke in class-rooms where they were the only ones who had accents and did not speak English fluently. ESL students adrift in the mainstream often seemed confused and lonely. Their isolation appeared to hinder learning and lead to alienation. Donaldo Macedo, whom we consulted on this question, agreed that keeping a group of ESL students together during their first year would be a good strat-egy for developing confidence and creating a solid academic base.

Leadership. We believed that preparing students to be competent and compassionate leaders was an essential part of their education. To convey this belief to our students best we decided to integrate student mentoring into the program's structure. We envisioned student mentors working as translators on two levels: first, mentors would function as translators between the lan-guage of the teacher and the students' languages. This meant we would need to choose mentors who, whenever possible, spoke the languages present in our classrooms. Second, mentors would engage in a more complicated process of translating the academic discourse used by faculty members to a language that could be readily understood by the students. This process would not involve translating from English to different languages; instead, it would respond to differences between the faculty and students in terms of their class background, ethnicity, and culture, helping to mediate differences in power and authority between teachers and students. In addition, student mentors, we realized, would understand the difficulties faced by non-native speakers of English in an academic environment and, consequently, would be able to provide a bridge of understanding between students and faculty.

Implementing Our Vision

After making these three key decisions, we organized the LIIP within the Department of Interdisciplinary Studies (IDS). In 1993–94, the LIIP consisted of a small community of 6 faculty members (1 African American, 1 Latina, and 4 English-speaking whites), 6 student mentors, and 21 ESL students who had been admitted to the college and invited to participate in the LIIP. This structure remained essentially the same for the duration of our tenure with the program.

The process of identifying the six faculty members was relatively simple. Every institution has teachers who are passionate about their teaching practice. These teachers are often struggling alone, a condition that limits their impact to their own classrooms. Gathering them in one program and creating the conditions for them to do their work in a supportive and challenging environment magnify their impact at the institution. We identified faculty who exhibited a set of characteristics: a willingness to take risks, a commitment to innovative programs, and passion and caring demonstrated through their love for their students. We knew that many of these faculty were already "overcommitted," particularly because, in addition to teaching, they often participated in political activities outside the institution. We hoped that offering them the opportunity to be a part of a community that appreciated and celebrated their work would draw them to the LIIP. Here, we argued, was a chance for them to be at the center, rather than the margin, of a teaching and learning community. Much to our delight, each and every faculty member invited to participate in the program agreed immediately.

We designed the LIIP initially to include two semesters of core courses: English Composition, Speech Communication, World Civilization, Microcomputers, Mathematics, and the First-Year Seminar, a course which introduces students to academic life and the college community by focusing on the social, psychological, and intellectual issues facing all first-year students. Students would earn 16.5 college credits each semester, allowing them to advance at the normal pace of first-year students. In the 1997 academic year, as a result of the recommendations from LIIP students, the program added the sophomore-year World Literature sequence.

The college supported the LIIP by approving a budget that included stipends for at least two mentors in each course as well as a one-week summer program for faculty and mentors. The summer program included workshops on ESL teaching and learning and intensive discussions on issues of race, language, culture, and discrimination. During the week, the LIIP faculty and mentors debated, revised, and affirmed a series of program principles and objectives, which we agreed to reaffirm in our curriculum, activities, and actions during the school year (*see page 36*).

PROGRAM PRINCIPLES	PROGRAM OBJECTIVES
• *We believe that education is political and that our mission is to prepare students to be active participants and agents of change in a democratic society.*	• *To create programs that promote leadership and foster mentoring relations. To give all participants real opportunities to make decisions, to make choices, and to define their own voices.*
• *We believe in equal opportunity for students to receive an education in which critical thinking is at the center of the teaching and learning process.*	• *To create programs of the highest academic standards that challenge students to find new answers, as opposed to reciting old ones.*
• *We believe that for us to succeed we must create a confidence zone— a community where students, faculty, and student mentors feel safe and comfortable taking risks and engaging in new and innovative projects.*	• *To create programs in which students participate actively and collaboratively in the learning process.*
	• *To create programs in which all members feel they are part of a community where their opinions are valued and their beliefs and values respected.*
• *We believe in having fun while teaching and learning.*	• *To create an environment that allows the teaching teams to succeed and to accomplish their shared as well as their individual goals.*
	• *To create programs and activities where we have the opportunity to have fun.*

Every other week at our faculty-mentor meetings, we continued to urge ourselves and our students to stay focused on the principles and objectives. The main strategy consisted of reflecting on our day-to-day practice and examining the ways in which it remained consonant with the principles and objectives. Through these discussions, the LIIP faculty and mentors became a cohesive unit, sharing a vision, a curriculum, and a pedagogy.

IMAGINING, CREATING, AND LIVING IN COMMUNITY

Our first priority, as the 1993 fall semester began, was to create the conditions for a community to develop. This process began with our own collaboration. Students and faculty realized that the LIIP was the result of Gozemba's and my forming a community of two. Betsy Hart, the LIIP speech professor, observes, referring to Gozemba and me, "I think the two of you formed a community among yourselves...whether you realize it or not, just that sense of community exudes from you as a group." The passion we put into imagining the program generated the sense that this was exciting work; we invited others to expand the community by joining in our intense discussions. But we did not stop there. These discussions were intended to guide us in taking actions that would encompass our shared ideas, hopes, and dreams.

Creating a Home Space and a Community of Hope

Our collaboration found support in the physical space in which we worked. Since our offices were both on the third floor in the library, everyone around us knew that we were in each other's offices talking about the program, writing proposals, calling people at the college, and discussing our courses. Everyone who came to talk with us became involved in the conversation taking place at that moment. Our tiny "offices" (library carrels) were quickly overrun. Consequently, the conversations moved outside our offices. We transformed the third floor of the library, where the Interdisciplinary Studies Department was located, into the LIIP space: the physical space that indicated to both students and teachers that we had a community, or a home space, at the college.

Understandably, students who used the third floor to study found the space too noisy. Slowly but surely they started moving elsewhere. We avoided becoming isolated by encouraging interaction between the LIIP students and women's studies students who often came to the library to talk with Gozemba or me about other courses we were teaching. This expanding community was further strengthened when students from the LIIP started taking women's studies courses. Since we co-taught the introductory women's studies course with the director of the Honors Program, Patricia Ould, who also had an office in the same floor, these students, too, became engaged in conversations with LIIP students. Eventually, students in the Honors Program for whom English is a second language became members of the LIIP community.

As a significant number of students began to see the library as their "home space," it became a place where students knew they would always be able to engage in discussions of their courses or current events, where they could find personal and academic support, and where they could just meet up with friends to plan social activities. For us, the space became one where education was taking place the whole day—teaching and learning was no longer confined to the time slots in which our classes met. In essence, the library became an extension of our classrooms.

The location of the LIIP community facilitated collaboration among faculty members as well, generating ongoing innovation and cohesiveness across the program. Patricia Buchanan, who taught English 101–102, explains that we would confer a lot simply because our offices were across the library from each other and we could just run across the hall. We could, on the spur of the moment, plan something where our classes would interact." In comparing her other courses to those she taught in the LIIP, she notes, "When you are teaching a class and you are just teaching that class, that is all you do. Even though we share the students, we are not sharing the experience, either their intellectual experience or their emotional experience." The LIIP collaboration, which was strengthened through the creation of a "home space," provided the opportunity to share that experience in a deep and rewarding way.

For the faculty, this experience of community was rejuvenating. Betsy Hart explains:

> I felt always an extraordinary sense of renewal.... When we actually get the time to get together and plan something or work with students, there is something that happens that is unlike anything else you can plan on. It's just the renewal, a reinforcement and excitement that says that it's okay to do this. I get something really extraordinary from that.

Unlike other teachers who are equally committed to their work, but who have succumbed to the prevailing pessimism in public institutions, faculty in the LIIP were part of a community that helped to renew our hope and our love of teaching.

To keep our optimism alive and transform our space into a community of hope, each faculty member made a commitment not only to being an excellent teacher but also to participating in the LIIP community. This added time to our already busy schedules but was ultimately rewarding. In our meetings, we were careful not to spend all our time discussing the problems typical of any program. A significant part of every meeting included celebrating what worked, the moments when, as Wayne Dudley, who teaches the World Civilization sequence, explains, we could see "a glimmer of light flickering" in our students or when they transformed an idea into "a practical everyday movement to enhance the quality of lives of others." By celebrating our accomplishments and those of the students, we kept ourselves energized and creative. Our home space became a joyful community of hope.

The third floor of the library both facilitated the emergence of our community and became the tangible expression of its existence. Committed to the success of our students, we found that they responded to our optimism, challenging themselves and each other to participate fully in the teaching and learning community. The community of hope that emerged as a result sustained every member as we, individually and collectively, struggled through difficult times and celebrated remarkable achievements.

Creating a "Confidence Zone" for Students

In constructing the LIIP, we imagined it as a "confidence zone" that would address the isolation ESL students felt in "mainstream" classrooms. The confidence zone, we believed, would create the conditions for students to speak without the fear of being ridiculed; as a result, they would quickly become more comfortable using English. The students responded immediately to the space we created. Sofia, a Puerto Rican student, explains her fears and how the program created a community of support for her:

> I was so lost, because not being an American student, I [was afraid that] I'd go to a class where everybody would speak English fluently and [no one would have] an accent. So I was kind of worried. But when I got to the class on the first day, I saw that everybody in this class had something in common— we all came from a different country, we had different backgrounds. And I felt comfortable, I said, "Whoa, I am going to be around people that instead of criticizing my work, they are going to encourage me to do my work and even help me." This is what the program is all about—building a community where everybody can feel comfortable to work and to succeed.

With time and care, the confidence zone became an empowerment zone—a nurturing and supportive community in which students found their power-from-within. In this community, students and faculty felt protected and secure from devastating racist and ethnocentric comments to which they were always vulnerable.

Repeatedly, students spoke about the LIIP as a community of support that felt very much like a family. Nancy, a student from the Dominican Republic, explains her experiences in this community:

> Another thing that helps us with the pressure is that we are all
> united and everybody is concerned about the students. For
> example, I missed a class, and Eileen asked me why I missed
> that class. So everybody is concerned; it is a big whole family.

Though it should be commonplace, our students were surprised that we
expressed concern when they missed our classes. They didn't see the question
as intrusive; rather, it communicated that they were an important part of the
community and that their presence or absence mattered. Sofia, too, uses the
metaphor of family to describe the community. She notes that everyone is
honest and open, and that atmosphere allows learning to take place: "You
[faculty] feel free to give constructive criticism and we [students] feel free to
learn from that, because it comes from the heart. It's a sense of a family that
we have created." It is in the context of a caring and nurturing "family" that
students gained the confidence to reclaim their voices, learn the language,
and prepare for their college experiences outside of the program.

A New Understanding of Education

Having seen students of color at the college become isolated and removed
from the larger community, Gozemba and I were conscious of our desire to
make the LIIP a space of empowerment and freedom. We insisted that the
students learn to engage the college in an assertive, responsible, and effective
manner. Within one year, we expected our students to be fully prepared to
move into the college community and take the full range of courses offered.

The LIIP provided students with both a political analysis that gave them a
deeper understanding of their place at the college and in the classroom and
practical criteria for choosing courses with positive learning environments.
Osvaldo, a Cape Verdian student, notes that the program taught him the
importance of speaking up in his classes:

> I got into my mainstream process, I was the only student of
> color in my class.... I didn't open my mouth.... It doesn't even
> faze me anymore, but it used to. At one point I used to get so
> uptight about it, I would be afraid to walk into the classroom.
> And you can't be afraid to walk into the classroom, because
> when you get out of the classroom and you graduate and you
> go into society, are you going to be afraid to walk into the work-
> place? How are you going to live? How are you going to partic-
> ipate, in the widest sense, in the community? And you need to
> make people know that you are an individual, you are not just

somebody that you group together and push to the side. And that's part of what you learn in the program.

By creating an empowerment zone within a nurturing community, the LIIP gave students the opportunity to sharpen their language skills. We encouraged students to take risks in developing arguments and expressing their opinions. When they entered the larger college community, they were prepared to claim their space. Moreover, students understood that they could return to the LIIP community for support and feedback, and many continued to look to the third floor of the library for intellectual and emotional sustenance. Here they could renew themselves among supportive friends and mentors as they struggled to remain visible and vocal in the larger community.

Tricia, a Jamaican student who mentored in courses that Gozemba and I taught outside the LIIP and participated as a senior mentor and trainer in the yearly LIIP mentoring workshops, reflected a pattern we saw developing among LIIP students. She looked for environments throughout the college that were similar to the LIIP. Tricia's intentionality in seeking out certain kinds of classes demonstrates that students who experience a confidence zone develop criteria for identifying these spaces throughout their college experience. She explains:

> I notice in a lot of my classes we write and the teacher speaks. But I found that a lot of the classes that I take we get in a circle, like my psychology or women's studies classes. I try to stay within those classes, because I don't feel so intimidated.... Every semester I try to take classes that are like that, [rather than] going to class and listening to the teacher go on and on when she/he doesn't even know your name.

Instead of choosing courses in which the teacher always occupied the center of the classroom, lecturing while the students listened, Tricia valued what she called a "community classroom," where students were encouraged to engage in discussions. As a result of being in these community classrooms, Tricia found that she could continue her education outside the classroom by "stopping someone from a class and just talking about politics."

Like Tricia, the LIIP students became used to the idea of having conversations outside the classroom about political issues such as immigration, bilingual education, human rights, or religion. They too sought out "community classrooms" that encouraged this kind of serious discussion among peers, welcoming the opportunity to speak, debate, and learn from each other and from the faculty.

Once LIIP students experienced the "community classrooms" Tricia describes, they began to view their education differently. No longer did they see themselves as passive recipients of knowledge; nor did they expect to slide through school, just "getting by." Having developed their confidence in their ability to engage in serious dialogues with other students and teachers, they became more demanding of the institution. They began to make decisions that ensured that the education they wanted and deserved was the one they received. Students who are used to going to classes, sitting silently, and leaving for the next class forfeit this critical part of their education. Unfortunately, if students do not experience a different kind of classroom, they cannot imagine a different kind of education.

Together the LIIP faculty, mentors, and students created a learning community grounded in clear political and pedagogical principles. These founding principles—(1) that education is political and our mission is to prepare students to be active participants and agents of change in a democratic society and (2) that students must have equal opportunity to receive an education in which critical thinking is at the center of the teaching and learning process— found concrete expression in the everyday practice of the LIIP.

These principles, which provided a foundation on which to build a home space and a community of hope, sustained our students as they developed their language and critical-thinking skills. As our students became more confident, they were able to move successfully to college courses outside the program. Students like Osvaldo viewed the process of leaving and engaging with the rest of the college as an example of what they would need to do the rest of their lives. They also understood, however, that the LIIP community would always welcome them back; this pocket of hope would always be a place where they could feel the camaraderie of being with others who shared their struggles.

Our greatest hope for the LIIP was that it would become a community in which faculty, mentors, and students together would find their power-from-within and develop their power-with others to transform the conditions of their lives. We expected our students to become engaged in creating a college community that would meet their needs and those of other marginalized students. Ultimately, we hoped the students would transfer what they learned in the LIIP and at the college to their participation in the society at large. To do so, however, we recognized, they would first need to reclaim their power and their voice and be educated in the practice of democracy.

DEMOCRACY, POWER, AND VOICE

In this country, democracy is more often discussed than practiced. LIIP faculty and students, just like students and faculty everywhere else, knew intimately how education worked in authoritarian classrooms. We all had experience in classrooms where teachers held all the power and students were expected to absorb information passively, where docile behavior and an ability to memorize were rewarded with good grades. This kind of classroom, however, does not prepare anyone to participate in an assertive, active, and critical manner in a democracy—the ultimate goal of the LIIP.

Gozemba and I, over many years of teaching, had come to believe that democratic practice must be taught, learned, and lived in the classroom. LIIP provided an opportunity for us to share what we had learned. Fundamental to that practice was the reconsideration of relations of power. We envisioned the LIIP community as one in which teachers and students would challenge the prevailing notion that power rests solely with the teacher. We encouraged LIIP faculty and students to create classrooms where everyone could speak and be heard, where every member could dissent and have his or her grievances addressed, and where students and teachers would share in the decision-making process in an equitable and responsible manner. An education in democracy, we all agreed, would require that we do more than theorize: democratic practice had to become a part of our everyday lives, inside and outside the classroom.

Faculty Rethinking Power

Faculty who joined the program came prepared to engage in the process of creating a democratic community. They understood the challenges and struggles of rethinking relations of power in the classroom. Wayne Dudley defines his "ultimate goal" in education as "engendering a sense of power among the students to take charge of their own lives." This sense of power gives students the ability "to think for themselves and to cultivate qualities of leadership." By cultivating these qualities, he says, students are able to "become agents of change not only for a generation of this time but in the future and [under] a different set of circumstances."

The LIIP faculty viewed education as a way for students to take charge of their own lives—that is, to access their power-from-within. Buchanan reflects on this process:

> How do I get the students to take charge of their own learning,
> to be aware that they can do it on their own, and that, no mat-

ter what I do, no matter how many [assignments] I check off, this is irrelevant? What I am trying to get them to see [is that] they are in charge of their own learning, and by extension, their own lives. My power is what I can do with these students to get them conscious of their own power in their own lives.

Dudley identified strategies for sharing power with his students. During the first weeks in the LIIP, he asked students to stand in front of the class and introduce themselves in their own language. This simple exercise transformed the classroom as students, strengthened by the power of their own language, told others who they were. Students in the course collaborated with the speaker, translating for those who didn't speak the same language. By inviting students to bring who they were into the classroom, Dudley created the space to develop what he calls "student power."

Being aware of power in the classroom did not mean that the faculty relinquished all power to the students. LIIP faculty recognized the difference between educating students in the practice of democracy and simply giving over the classroom to every student whim. A democratic classroom is not a "permissive" classroom or one without high standards for learning. At times students made the mistake of confusing democracy and cooperative learning with previous experiences when "group" work had meant "no" work. LIIP students, however, soon discovered that LIIP was not an easy ride. The faculty sent a clear message that the LIIP academic standard was high and that students would need to decide how to approach the challenge. The power to succeed was in their hands, as was the power to fail. Buchanan, speaking about students who at times took longer to rise to the challenge, notes:

> So part of giving students power is also giving them a little power to fail for a while. And one of the nice things about having the students for the entire year is that we can assess them, we can see that they have the ability.... There are students who recognize [this] and grab hold of what is possible for them.

The LIIP students quickly recognized that unlike other courses whose faculty sometimes felt sorry for them because of their poor language skills and let them pass, in the LIIP faculty would not do so. The professors respected them as intellectuals and, consequently, expected them to do their work. They also knew that even if they chose not to work, we would always love and respect them. For us, the power to fail always entailed the power to succeed. It was quite common that a student who got a D first semester in a course would demonstrate his or her full potential during the second semester and, eventually, become a mentor for that class.

By respecting the possibility that all students could become powerful intellectuals and contribute to the community in a significant manner, LIIP faculty created the conditions for participatory democracy to develop. Students recognized in this process the hard, disciplined work required to participate in society in a responsible and informed manner. We seldom found students who, when given an authentic invitation to participate and develop to their full potential, would refuse to do so. Instead, students often returned to their own high schools and asked that students be treated fairly. "Fairness" meant that they be required to do meaningful intellectual work that would prepare them for full participation in their communities. A student in the program, angry at her own miseducation in high school, went back and told her high school teachers that "whether they are good students or bad, whether you like them or not, you should be demanding that they work."

Extending an Invitation to Co-Construct Knowledge. Many teachers believe that democratic practice means giving students some decision-making power, for example, deciding when they are going to have a test or what kind of notebook they want to use. But these teachers still reserve the power to define knowledge and decide how it is delivered. In other words, they still reserve for themselves the most important form of power in education, the power to think and construct knowledge. Democratic practice in the classroom means that students and teachers engage in the project of constructing knowledge together.

We began this process of co-constructing knowledge by analyzing structures of power and powerlessness and how they functioned within the LIIP community, the college, and society in general. Instead of focusing solely on grammar and language remediation, we created spaces to analyze, discuss, and define issues that affected our lives. The classrooms in the LIIP were places where students brought their lives front and center as context and text to be engaged and discussed.

For example, in the First-Year Seminar, during an exercise to identify the issues that were causing stress in the students' lives, they explained that they were working 40 hours per week as well as attending school full time. Three young women talked about working until 10:00 P.M. every day and then going home to study until 3:00 A.M., only to begin the same cycle again the next day. We heard stories about serious financial problems in their homes, about how exhausted they were, about carrying on while physically sick. Others felt homesick, with their parents away in Japan, Cambodia, and

Vietnam. One student told the class that he had lost all his family in the war in Cambodia and he was alone in this country. Most were not eating because they had no time. We suspected that money was also an issue. One woman brought home the seriousness of the situation when she explained that when passing cemeteries she would long to be there so she could rest. This student was working long hours both at the college and at her job.

Through this exercise the students became aware that their individual problems were, in fact, shared by every student in the program. They were all overwhelmed by their responsibilities and were all seeking individual solutions. In the discussion, it became clear that their shared experience called out for a collective solution. Otherwise many of the students would fail to succeed—they simply could not keep up these grueling schedules for long. To help provide more support for the students, the program offered some immediate solutions: the counselor who co-taught First-Year Seminar added stress-reduction exercises to the beginning of each class. We also added more counseling support that students could readily access. Yet, all of us were painfully aware that even when we deployed all kinds of supports for our students, a number of them would not be able to cope with the financial and/or emotional demands and would likely drop out. Staying at the college required a heroic effort of all of our students.

Our response to this constant crisis was moving with our students from an analysis of their individual experiences to a larger social analysis. Paulo Freire's *Pedagogy of the Oppressed* (1993), Jonathan Kozol's *Savage Inequalities* (1991), and bell hooks's *Teaching to Transgress* (1994), which students were reading in Gozemba's and Buchanan's courses and mentors were discussing in the summer workshops, provided a language and a lens through which to examine their education and their position in society. As students began to explore their everyday experience through these texts, they found these authors offered new insights and explanations for the stress, disappointments, and confusion that often made their lives unmanageable. The insights the students gained from reading these texts motivated them to begin analyzing other aspects of their lives. For example, Buchanan cites the work of a group of students in her course who decided to research bilingual education programs. According to her, "They were so mad because, they said, 'No, they didn't teach us enough, the classes weren't hard enough, they didn't give us enough information, we were far behind.' There was a real strong sense of I deserve more."

For students to believe that there is an authentic invitation to share their experience and co-construct knowledge, they need to experience their teachers as learners. Faculty in the LIIP were authentically surprised by how much their students taught them. This created the space for students to educate the faculty as well as others in the classroom, disrupting the usual balance of power. Dudley, who believes that education is a "continuous process" in which teachers and students search for answers and not the "absolute truth," critiques the role of the teacher in the classroom:

> Am I the ultimate source of knowledge? No. I may have done a tad bit more reading, I may have some opinions, which I will express in a more vehement tone, but I want to hear your side, because in the process, I can learn a great deal more than if I close my eyes to your opinion.

Hart sees her mission as a speech teacher as giving students the power of their own voice, which is critical to their participation in democracy. In the process of teaching, however, she learns from her students' experiences and knowledge:

> My power is to motivate them to find a voice, to give the speech. I say to them, "In this forum, you have a unique opportunity. You are in charge. You have ten minutes of time, three times a semester, to change the way we think. You educate me." And I mean that totally and sincerely, every single semester I learn more than I teach.

At the end of the teaching and learning journey, LIIP faculty and students celebrated having co-created something new: new knowledge that emerged from the dialogue among a group of individuals who brought to the classroom different experiences, cultures, languages, hopes, and dreams.

Engaging in Difficult Dialogue and Dissension. The democratic journey on which students and teachers collaborate in the construction of knowledge is not always pleasant. Often, it involves struggles, arguments, dissension, and hurt feelings as teachers and students negotiate across differences and constantly re-evaluate relations of power.

While we were talking about the condition of women around the world in one of my First-Year Seminar classes, the discussion between Japanese women and men in the course became so heated that they began speaking in Japanese, continuing for quite some time. Both the students and I understood that the discussion was of such importance to the Japanese students that it was necessary to switch to their native tongue. Speaking in their own language allowed them to get more out of the discussion, because they could explore the issue more deeply. When they finished, one of the Japanese women gave the rest of the class the bottom line: Japanese women are not as liberated as Japanese men in the class would like us to believe; as a matter of fact, they are quite oppressed. The tension in the room was high and the mood serious. Clearly, the Japanese students in the course understood that they could generate as much tension as they needed in order to have an honest and meaningful discussion about the subject. The fact that they switched to Japanese signaled that they understood that learning in this case did not have to do with the correct use of English, but with the nature and intensity of the dialogue.

Teachers and students soon discovered that a democratic project in which everyone was able to speak and be heard often generates intense discomfort. This feeling of discomfort had to be accepted as an essential component of a larger project. Living with discomfort, learning to question what causes it, and doing something about it were among the most powerful lessons we learned in our teaching and learning about power, powerlessness, and democracy. Faculty were forced to a new level of awareness, in which we could not retreat to our comfort zone, reclaiming the power vested in us by the institution whenever dissension erupted. We had, after all, committed to sharing power and had encouraged the students to disagree, argue, and organize for change when they felt it necessary to do so.

The faculty learned this lesson most clearly when LIIP students brought to our attention their dissatisfaction with an integrated human rights module that had formed the core of the LIIP curriculum during the spring of 1994. The faculty were pleased with the success of the module. Marjorie Agosin, a Chilean human rights activist and poet, made a presentation on human rights, read her poetry, and screened films on human rights in Greece and Argentina in an all-day forum. Later in the semester, Herb Spirer, a statistician, presented his work documenting violations of human rights around the world. His presentation connected with the methodologies in the students' statistics course, the study of colonialism in World Civilization, and topics they had selected for their speech course. We also ran a film series in which we showed *Night and Fog; Killing Fields; Hiroshima, Mon Amour;* and *Missing.* These late afternoon screenings were well attended, and after each screening, students related personal stories that connected to the topics in the films.

To conclude the module, the students were asked to write a research paper on a topic of their choice dealing with human rights issues. The results of the students research, which covered diverse topics such as Japan's use of biological weapons in China during World War II, Trujillo's massacre of Haitians in the Dominican Republic, the United States' decision to drop the atom bomb on Japan, the purge of the Jewish intelligentsia under Stalin, and the rights of mental patients in experimentation protocols, were impressive. We celebrated the successful completion of the projects and the module. Yet, much to our surprise, when we met with students who had participated in the module and had now become mentors, the feedback on the interdisciplinary module was tentative, and in some instances, negative. They even had a chant: "Human rights left and right, we are tired of it." The mentors pointed out that the module was too long, and if given the opportunity, they would have chosen another interdisciplinary topic that would have been more relevant to their interests.

The faculty were upset and stunned by the students' feedback, but as a democratic community, we realized that we could not let our hurt feelings get in the way of hearing what the students had to say. We quickly realized that they were right. We had not involved them in choosing the topic or deciding how long the module would be. At no point during the entire semester did we ask for their feedback about the content or process.

As a result of the mentors' feedback, we asked the mentors to poll the new group of students for suggestions on the subject matter for the spring interdisciplinary module. They chose to study popular culture and its impact on the economic, political, and social fabric of the United States. This time, the students worked on the design of the module along with the faculty. The shorter module, which focused on a topic of their choosing, worked much better than our "great" module. The lesson in sharing power and democratic practice was loud and clear.

Students' Understanding of Power

The LIIP students became increasingly aware of how power was distributed in the classroom. They looked for ways to share power with the professor and became more assertive as they tapped into their own power-from-within. They argued that if a professor didn't willingly share power, students had to assert their own. In a training for new mentors, senior mentors facilitated a discussion about sharing power. Georgia, a student from Greece and a new mentor, still expected the teacher to direct the class:

> In the classes I am taking now…students are trying to do work
> in groups, but it is really up to the teacher's power. If the teacher
> doesn't really motivate the students and set the direction…
> nothing is going to happen.

Tricia, a "veteran" mentor, pushed the point further by explaining that the teacher needs to make it clear that he or she is interested in sharing power by giving students room to participate:

> I think that when power is distributed it comes from the
> teacher. When you go into a classroom, it is up to the teacher
> to show, "Well, I am not going to stand here and teach you
> something and drill it into your head and that's how it is."

Having said this, Tricia realized that even in this kind of classroom, students
can take power. In her view, the students must rise to question and challenge.

> I believe that power comes from within. How you have power
> is by saying what you have to say and someone listening to you,
> not just you listening to them. A lot of teachers just expect you
> to listen. And our parents tell us that we have to listen to them
> always. You need to break the whole cycle of just listening, and
> just rise to question. Like one of my favorite movies, *Higher
> Learning*, says, you need to raise the question. That's what we
> have to do, and that's how we have power—you have to ques-
> tion everything. Sometimes people will not agree—your beliefs
> might be totally different—but they must be willing to hear
> and not just shush you up.

A student who has gained this level of understanding and explains to others
why they need to rise to question and challenge the teacher to listen to them
is enormously powerful. When Tricia argued that students could raise the
question and demand the education they deserved, other students began to
believe in their own power to make change.

These discussions on power in the classroom moved students to think
more deeply about the process of education. In doing so, they reclaimed their
voices and defined their own vision of education. Sofia relates a conversation
she had with other students as part of her presentation at the Pedagogy of the
Oppressed Conference in Omaha, Nebraska (1997):

> We were talking yesterday about how for [many] people, a per-
> fect classroom is where all the students are silent and the pro-
> fessor is always talking. [Laughs] I couldn't understand, how
> that could be true. How does the professor know that students
> are learning, if they don't express themselves? If they don't see.

The question Sofia poses is intriguing: "How does the professor know
that students are learning, if they don't express themselves? If they don't see."
The answer, of course, is that they give tests every so often to see what the

students have learned. But Sofia was puzzled about something more immediate. If a teacher is lecturing, how does she or he know that the students understand what is being taught? Without dialogue, in which students and teachers ask questions and propose answers, the teacher postpones finding out whether anyone is learning until the time of the exam—possibly weeks or even months later.

Does postponing knowing whether your students are learning matter? It matters to students, who understand that the outcome can be more serious than flunking a test. Tricia connects this kind of learning to the structure of power and powerlessness in society. She says, "We are still going to have people who want the system in power and people walking around like little robots...just listening to what they have to, not having a mind of their own, not saying anything, not getting involved." This kind of teaching treats students like robots: they are expected to learn what the teacher tells them. The teacher maintains power by refusing to allow dialogue to take place. But Tricia doesn't want to learn to be a robot. She wants to know how she can be educated to become an active participant in society. Tricia challenges teachers to revise their practice, so that they do not continue to reproduce hierarchical social relations in which a small group holds power over the majority. The LIIP students came to understand that in reproducing power-over, the educational system attempts to silence and pacify them. This realization provided a powerful lesson in understanding why it was important for each of them to develop their ability to speak and be heard.

The Power of the Mentors

Our belief in re-visioning relations of power was reflected in the structure of the LIIP. Mentors were expected to collaborate with the faculty in creating democratic classrooms and envisioning the process of education. From actually teaching a course, to helping students with the crisis of finals, to helping faculty grade papers, the mentors became powerful leaders who guided the faculty and students with their advice and their insights.

The experience of having been in the program allowed mentors to understand at a personal level what it meant to be a LIIP student. Their compassion for the students was heartfelt, but this did not mean that they were "easy" on them. In fact, quite often the mentors were harder on the students than the faculty were. Having experienced the obstacles that students of color and students for whom English is a second language face, the mentors wanted to ensure that all students were as prepared as possible when they transitioned into the mainstream. In some cases, a mentor's stance was unyielding and undemocratic. The faculty saw this as an opportunity to educate. When a mentor, armed with a red pen, was overly critical of a student's work, Dudley pointed out that "you may very well have one standard for yourself...and a more rigorous standard for others. Where is the inconsistency? Do you want to be judged by the standards that you apply to others?"

The faculty modeled democratic teaching practice for the mentors, guiding them as they developed their own skills. But the mentors faced a different set of challenges than those faced by the faculty. For example, the mentors could not presume that new students would respect them as teachers because they did not hold the institutional power invested in the role of "professor." As a result, they argued that the faculty needed to convey, through their actions in the classroom, that the mentors had the power to teach. As Joselito, who is Puerto Rican, explains, "[If faculty treat the mentors as students], the students are not going to listen [to us]." The mentors realized, and made clear to faculty, that, particularly in the beginning of the school year, their power was contingent upon the messages conveyed by the faculty in the classroom.

Mentors also realized that though students wanted to know the "right" answer—and hoped that the mentors would deliver them from the painstaking and laborious process of learning—mentoring was a complex relationship that was not facilitated by giving someone "the answer." The mentors learned to be patient, teaching students that their mission as mentors was the same as that of the faculty: educating them in the process of learning by considering different alternatives and making their own decisions.

Given this reality, the best educators of new mentors were the mentors themselves. The experience of thinking about their practice and sharing what they learned with other mentors generated a vast source of knowledge about teaching and learning. This knowledge was passed from one generation of mentors to the next, ensuring that they shared fundamental principles and benefited from knowing about the successes and failures of other mentors. For example, Georgia, a new mentor, and Tricia, a senior mentor, share some of their understanding of teaching and learning in the following exchange:

> *Georgia:* I usually went for help for speech when we had a presentation.... We had two mentors, so I went to see one at one time and she helped me out. I had to go to the other one and I heard completely different ideas. You have to decide which one is better. That's good, because you meet that in real life. You have different choices and you really have to decide which one is the best.
> *Tricia:* When students come in they expect you to tell them what the right answer is and you give them choices and this is new to them. And they come back with something else and

then you have to drill it into their head, "This is your paper...
and you need to decide what you want to put in your paper."

This conversation shows how the mentors had fully incorporated the LIIP's
principles into their own teaching. In working with students, they focused on
getting them to think about their choices and to explore new ways of thinking. Tricia furthered this idea by explaining to new mentors that the process
of thinking and learning is reciprocal. For her, mentoring "is not something
that you study, it is the feeling of thinking." This powerful "feeling of thinking" is something mentors had learned and were able to share. By asking
mentors to think with them, students engaged in the process of co-constructing knowledge.

Importantly, when students realized their own power to teach and learn
from each other, the faculty were no longer at the center of the teaching and
learning process. In these democratic classrooms, the shared power of students, mentors, and teachers generated the collective strength and knowledge
necessary to tackle critical issues that affected our lives. We used our power
as teachers to empower our students, so that they developed the skill and
confidence necessary to pose questions and find answers to their own puzzles
and dilemmas.

Fundamental to the LIIP was the understanding that education is a joint
process in which faculty and students engage in the co-construction of
knowledge. Faculty didn't see themselves as all-knowing sources of information, but rather entered the classroom ready to learn with their students. To
engage in this kind of educational project, however, it was essential to examine relations of power and powerlessness and how they are reproduced in the
classroom setting. Not surprisingly, as the learning community began to
examine relations of power, the conversations often became uncomfortable
and tense. When issues of class, race, gender, culture, power, and authority
were at the center of the dialogue, we moved into territory that had caused
everyone personal pain at one time or another. Yet to remain silent about
these issues, in order to keep the conversation "safe" and comfortable, would
have imposed artificial limits on necessary discussions. Without examination
of these issues, democracy could not have flourished.

In addition to opening a space for uncomfortable dialogue, democratic
practice demanded that the faculty accept and take seriously dissent among
the students. Faculty overcame their personal feelings of disappointment and
frustration that accompanied criticism by reaffirming their commitment to
the larger political project. By remaining committed to the LIIP's mission of
educating active participants in a democratic society, faculty embraced

intense and uncomfortable dialogue as well as serious critiques of their practice offered by students who were taking responsibility for their own education.

By giving students the opportunity to define their own education, the LIIP trained educated democratic leaders. The mentoring program was critical to fostering leadership skills. As mentors taught students to think critically and make their own decisions, they instilled in themselves and others "the feeling of thinking." By evolving into capable teachers who could work without the faculty, mentors further de-centered power in the classroom, giving students in the LIIP clear evidence that leadership was possible and expected of all students. LIIP students quickly demonstrated their abilities to access their power-from-within, share power-with others through the co-construction of knowledge, engage in critical analysis, and teach and learn from one another, making it clear that they were prepared to engage in democratic action on campus and in society.

THE POWER TO ACT AND TRANSFORM THE COLLEGE AND SOCIETY

The LIIP faculty believed that by engaging in projects of change, students would gain essential knowledge, skills, and experience that would help prepare them to participate effectively in society. Logically, the college community offered the perfect place to gain this understanding and experience. Methodically, faculty moved with students from an analysis of language and its social and political uses to organizing for change at the college and, finally, to engaging in projects that have an impact in their communities. We found that taking action and analyzing the outcome with our students made for an ideal education in democratic practice.

Taking the First Steps

Students in the LIIP learned to analyze texts carefully so as to understand the social and political use of language. By reading texts that connected with their lives, students began to view language differently. Instead of a tool used against them to their exclusion, language they found in the difficult texts resonated with their experiences. Above and beyond the correct use of grammar, students began to view language as a tool of oppression or possibility. Janet, the only native English-speaking mentor in the program, relates a conversation with other mentors:

> We were at lunch today discussing regular classes and the language-intensive classes, and Tricia and I stopped and went, Well, if those are "regular" classes, is everything else "irregular"

or "bad"? [laughs] Wait a minute, no, it's not. So it's kind of fun that we can sit down and sort of pull language apart and change it so that it fits our purpose a little better. Or rather doesn't oppress people.

Deconstructing language was just the first step in taking on the more complicated challenge of having a positive and transformative impact at the college and in the community. The need to tackle the financial aid problems of our students provided an opportunity to learn how to organize and mobilize. While working in the financial aid office, Janet found that there were "a disproportionate number of non-native speakers getting completely dumped by financial aid." As she explains, the discrepancies in the treatment of the non-native speakers' awards "really offended my sense of justice, because at Salem State, to describe us as working class is absolutely accurate. We don't have a lot of money at all." She began working with Gozemba to educate LIIP students about their rights. She started taking students in small groups through the whole financial aid process, showing them what to do and letting them know that they had "a voice and they were worthy and they deserved that money as much as anybody else."

After Janet's first year working with the LIIP students, she began training Sofia, a mentor in the program, to do financial aid advocacy. These two mentors then expanded their field of action, becoming captains in the local walk for abused women and children. Janet and Sofia viewed the financial aid work and the fundraising walk as their projects of social change. For them, the LIIP community had become the learning ground for organizing and becoming active participants in society. They organized and interacted with the college from a position of strength. As Janet describes it, her involvement "illustrated in a real sense how much power and potential each student has to make a difference, instead of sitting around and being a victim and poor me." The LIIP community built self-confidence so that students felt capable of expanding their field of action to include the towns and cities where they lived. They knew that individually and collectively they had the power to make a difference.

Moving from the College to the Community

One of the clearest examples of our approach to reconfiguring power, transferring leadership from the faculty to the students, and connecting the college to the community was the spring 1995 Latino Conference, *Breaking Boundaries: Setting Goals*. Throughout the first year and a half of the LIIP, faculty and students became aware of the serendipitous and sometimes very painful routes Latina/o students took to college. In our biweekly team meetings of faculty and mentors, the idea emerged to return to the mentors' high schools to smooth the way for other Latino students to come to college. Eventually, we decided that we could have the greatest impact by holding a conference. Fueled by their dream of easing the college application process for their peers, the mentors became the catalytic force in shaping the conference.

From the beginning, the planning group of mentors (including five Latinos, three African Americans, and two Anglo American students from the LIIP and other IDS programs) and I envisioned the conference as one defined, organized, and implemented by student leaders. This didn't mean that the faculty intended to abandon the students, who had never planned an event for 200 students. Faculty would take on the initial leadership and training, so that leadership and responsibility could be transferred to the students as they became ready. Ultimately, the students simply seized power when they felt ready.

Producing the invitation to send to area high schools provides an example of how the students quickly took on leadership roles. I produced the first draft, which the students organizing the conference revised no fewer than 10 times. They were very concerned about the precise language that would be used. Specifically, they wanted the conference to be inclusive and to ensure this was reflected in the invitation. The final paragraph dealing with this issue read:

> The Latino students and our allies at the College represent those young men and women who have been able to break boundaries by identifying goals and defining a path of success. We have organized with other students at our college to insure that our work represents the vision and aspirations of all races, ethnic backgrounds, and languages. We envision ourselves as pro-active members of our communities and wish to engage with the students in the high schools in a dialogue about possibilities for success.

The discussion surrounding the final wording took place in front of the chair of IDS and the dean of Arts and Sciences, who argued that the invitation should not be on behalf of Latina/o students only. The dean felt that if the conference were dedicated to Latina/o youth it would not be as inclusive as it could be. He also objected to the use of the word "allies," which he believed sounded too political, but the students stood their ground. Arguing forcefully for the wording they had carefully chosen to convey their message, they sent the invitation out to area high schools.

The organizers decided to divide the 160 high school students who registered for the conference into groups of 8 to 10; each group would be facilitated by a Salem State student. Student leaders were recruited from throughout the college to participate as group facilitators. In addition, each group was assigned a faculty member or an administrator whose mission was to assist the student leaders throughout the day.

The day opened with the keynote speaker, the Puerto Rican poet Tato Laviera, who presented an inspirational challenge on going to college and succeeding. Five workshops followed, focusing on the application process, financial aid, choosing majors and minors, choosing a career, and deciding whether to commute or to live on campus. These workshops reflected the experiences of the college students, who found these issues difficult to sort through when they were graduating high school and considering college.

The students organizing the conference stayed true to two principles: excellence and inclusion. Having been neglected in their own high schools, where Latina/o students were very often regarded as mediocre and unreliable, the mentors were determined that this conference run flawlessly, making the political statement that they were indeed capable of producing excellent work. For example, the organizers felt that if the logistics were designed correctly, they could welcome and process 160 students in a half-hour, leaving more time for the workshops. To the administration's and faculty's amazement, they finished right on time, setting the tone for the day.

The process of recruiting student leaders to facilitate the small groups resulted in perhaps the most diverse working committee that ever operated at our college. Student leaders included African Americans, Asian Americans, Anglo Americans, Japanese, and Latinos from the Dominican Republic, Puerto Rico, and Mexico. The campus community seemed astonished that this diverse coalition of allies chose to take time from their summer break—and most probably from work—to engage with the Latina/o high school students. Having seen the campus divided by race, gender, and ethnicity, many faculty expressed surprise when they saw non-Latina/o students addressing issues not immediately relevant to them. We were not surprised, however, because we knew that the foundation for this coalition of allies had been built by the LIIP students' ongoing work with women's studies and honors students and with other associations at the college.

LIIP faculty contended that the political climate of the LIIP created the conditions that inspired the college students to lead a younger generation. Having become engaged in defining their own political vision, the students reflected on the obstacles to their success and were determined to make it easier for those coming up behind them. Deciding that all students at the college should take on the responsibility of opening the doors to Latina/o students, they made sure the student leaders represented the diversity of the college community. In taking action, the LIIP mentors taught a larger lesson to our campus community about excellence, inclusion, and alliances leading to social and political transformation. Hart (1997, 58) expresses the pride we all felt in seeing our students succeed: "I really don't have words to describe how I felt as I listened to my student in that public forum.... I had to restrain myself from dancing around the room when he finished."

The students from the LIIP undertook more personal and painful actions as well, taking advantage of their own inner strength and the support of their community. One of our students took action against a faculty member who warned her and a friend that they could not speak Spanish in the hallways. The student went to the IDS chair for advice and insisted that the situation be dealt with. The college supported the student and reprimanded the faculty member.

LIIP students also found new ways to challenge racism on campus more broadly. Some became involved in the antiracist Human Action Theatre and others created an anti-racism umbrella group, which they hoped would function as the place where all student organizations would gather to plan a coherent strategy for dealing with institutional racism on campus. Students from the LIIP also became involved in student government by either campaigning for their favorite candidates or running themselves.

The success of the LIIP program in building alliances across campus and transforming the campus community was recognized by the student council in 1997. The program was given a $500 award that was matched by another $500 from the college administration for its leadership in promoting the multicultural goals of the college. Specifically, the award recognized the LIIP for building alliances among the Honors, Women's Studies, and the Language Intensive programs. In a very real way, the program had moved from the margin to the center, with LIIP students receiving recognition for their contribution to the college community.

CONCLUSION

As Gozemba and I first set out to develop an ESL program for first-year students at Salem State College, we envisioned creating a program that would educate students to become active participants in a democratic society.

Gathering a group of faculty who believed in their mission as agents of change, we presented an invitation to students to reconsider language and rethink their lives. Our students accepted the invitation and instead of focusing solely on the mechanical aspects of language, found power in seeing language as a means to read and revision their world. Language, we argued, is used as a tool to oppress, separate, and diminish. Language, we believed, had to be transformed into a tool for liberation.

Gozemba and I conceived the project as an act of resistance. We never believed that ESL students were "deficient," in need of "remediation," "substandard," or any other of the derogatory terms used to separate ESL students from the so-called mainstream. We wanted something radically different for ourselves and for them. We thought of the LIIP as an opportunity to put together a program that incorporated all that we had learned and dreamed of throughout our lives as educators. We loved our work and had fun creating the program. The love and joy in taking on this challenge proved to be contagious. Anyone who visited our "home space" could share in the intense work and also in the laughter, the regular visits to the local coffee shop, and the parties at Gozemba's house, where Japanese students learned to dance "salsa" and Latina/o students learned to prepare sushi. As a result, we created a community in which humor and love for teaching and learning were expected and encouraged.

We believed that a political education had to take place within an environment of hope, where a community of committed students and teachers could emerge. This community of hope provided shelter for students and teachers from a larger institution that was, all too often, unsupportive. In this pocket of hope, students experienced a moment of silence and freedom to recover their power-from-within. The texts they read, which reflected their own lives, confirmed what they always knew: that they had been intentionally and systematically relegated to the margins of society. Moreover, through dialogue with their teachers and other students they began to see the pattern of marginalization of other ESL students. They began to ask questions such as, Why is this happening? Who is doing this? What will I do? The "feeling of thinking" and their own power as intellectuals gave them the confidence and the skills necessary to find the answers to these questions. Once they found the answers, they understood that they had the responsibility to act. They remembered that there were students in high schools, who, as they had, needed to know.

Students found in their individual and collective power the strength they needed to break the cycle of oppression and rise to question. They began to believe that they had the right to demand an education that did not treat them as "robots." They tested their individual and collective power in the LIIP, at the college, and in their communities. When life did not go as anticipated, they returned to their pocket of hope, which always welcomed them when they needed to recover their strength and refocus their energy. Everyone understood that it was important that after recovering their power and strength, they go back out and reengage in the struggle.

CHAPTER 3

Crossing the Bridge:
Peer Education and Mediation

Patricia A. Gozemba

During the spring of 1995, I took a leave from teaching at Salem State College to work on a problem that I saw as both political and pedagogical: how to make the promise of a high-quality democratic education available to some of the most vulnerable students at Salem State College, immigrants still struggling with the English language. I spent a semester as a fellow at the East-West Center in Honolulu reflecting on pedagogical strategies and imagining how to apply innovative teaching strategies within the context of Salem State's linguistically and culturally diverse student body. Teaching in the Language Intensive Interdisciplinary Program (LIIP, see Chapter 2), I, like a number of my colleagues, worried that there might be specific skills that I did not have that would work better for our students. Months of reading, reflection, discussion, and writing about English as a Second Language constantly led me back to my own Freirean and feminist pedagogy and its inherently democratic practice. The catalytic moment in the semester occurred when I entered into dialogue with a Hawai'i Department of Education administrator, Janie King, and an articulate and reflective student, Hunter. King, the State Resource Teacher on Conflict Resolution, and Hunter, a native Hawaiian and a sophomore in the Peer Education Program (PEP) at Roosevelt High School, inspired me with their deep commitment to democratic pedagogy. Their views of pedagogy resonated with the philosophy and practice of the LIIP and challenged me to begin thinking more deeply about the commonalities in such apparently different programs.

King's work as an English teacher had been known to me for almost 10 years. I had visited her middle school and high school classes to observe how she had implemented the peer response process in writing courses with students who were not speakers of standard English. A highly competent and challenging teacher, King motivated students to take a more active role in their own learning and to excel. Her work as an administrator promoting conflict resolution arose out of her commitment to fostering democratic school climates in which all students could learn more effectively. In her position as State Resource Teacher on Conflict Resolution, she brought peer mediation, peacemaking, peacekeeping, and peer counseling to schools throughout Hawai'i, training teachers, administrators, students, custodians, secretaries, and security guards in both the philosophy and the practice of conflict resolution. By 1995, her work was making an impact in 66 of the 76 middle and high schools across all the islands of Hawai'i.

In my first interview with King, she told me, "Pat, you've got to go to Roosevelt High and meet Amy Akamine and her students in the Peer Education Program. I send everyone there who wants to know about any form of conflict resolution or peers helping peers." Five days later, in June 1995, King arranged for me to join her for lunch with Hunter, one of Akamine's students. Hunter's description and analysis of peer education, mediation, and Akamine, whom he referred to as "Boss," made me want to go to Roosevelt.

A few days after our interview, as I was working in my office at the East-West Center, King called to tell me the story of what she had just experienced at Roosevelt. An Australian scholar who was studying bullies and their effects on school climate had gone to her office that day to research what was happening in Hawai'i. King spent the morning with him sharing videotapes and books that she had developed for the statewide program and then took him to Roosevelt High. It was one of those hectic days right toward the end of the school year, but Akamine and her students welcomed the guests.

King recounted how as Akamine's class of 25 students started, Kimo, a big and very physically powerful young Hawaiian boy from Papakolea, a native Hawaiian Homestead community, asked to share something with the class and the visitors. Once known as a bully and a poor student, he began by saying that before being in PEP, "I never thought I could talk." He then, King recalled, "told the story about going to an office that day and trying to find out about his grades and encountering some problems." King laughed as she recalled the scene: "In the old days he said that he might have blown up and screamed 'f___ you,' and stomped out and probably gotten himself in big trouble. But because of his experiences in Amy's class and learning how to talk things out, he realized that there are other ways to approach conflict." King added that it made her feel proud when he related that "he just calmly went across the hall to the principal's office and said, 'I really need some help here,' and they immediately solved the problem for him. It is touching to see him so proud of that. Then, when he told us that he was actually going to be a senior next year, I've never seen such a radiant smile." King emphasized that Kimo "has really survived—really 'crossed that bridge' from Papakolea into the wider community."

Coming out of Papakolea, an insular Hawaiian community, to find one's way among the racially and economically diverse population at Roosevelt, represents a big step for many young Hawaiians like Kimo. While there literally is a bridge that connects the community, the metaphor speaks much more of the courage of finding one's power-from-within to negotiate in the world. King believes that "it's symbolic to cross that bridge and take risks and join the world out here." King summed up her analysis of Kimo's coming to voice. "That's why courses like this are so important, because they enable kids to find their inner voice, the one that is really who they are, instead of the one that is distorted by fear and shame." Kimo was a bully partly because he didn't trust his voice.

During the same class period, the RHS principal, Charles Goo, stopped by unexpectedly and the Australian visitor got a chance to ask him about the program. Goo, King recalled, "went on and on about how wonderful Amy's program was and how mediation had really helped to change the school. In fact, he got all choked up, teary-eyed, and this is a stoical guy. I was dumbfounded when I saw that and I was very touched that here was a leader of the school who appreciated the program as much as I did and who saw the impact that mediation and that kind of approach could have on a school."

I reminded King about how Hunter had told us the week before that Goo had dubbed PEP "the pulse of the school" and committed himself to working with PEP students to solve problems in the school. "Yes, he said that again today," King exclaimed. "I know you're busy finishing up work before you leave in a few weeks, Pat, but I wish that I had called you and dragged you over there today. It was another one of those amazing days in Amy's class."

I wished she had, too. King's story of Kimo, once a bully, but nonetheless one of the most vulnerable students in the school, stayed with me, offering hope about what teachers and students are doing. Back in Salem, my experience in transcribing the interview with King and Hunter and reflecting on it with my LIIP colleague Eileen de los Reyes inspired us to begin developing the concept of pockets of hope. We began to see the centrality of democratic practice in nurturing courage, empowerment, and academic and personal success in students' lives.

Seven months later, in January 1996, I returned to Honolulu on semester break and resumed the process of interviewing King and Hunter, and, most exciting of all, I met Amy Akamine and more of her students. The conversa-

tions and experiences, which began in 1995 and continued to 1999, intensi-
fied during the 1997–1998 academic year, when I taught at the University of
Hawai'i at Manoa, just a few miles away from Roosevelt. Over the four years
of observing this pocket of hope in which students and their teacher were
changing the world, I had my faith in democratic pedagogy confirmed.
Hunter, just finishing his sophomore year at RHS in 1995, when I first interviewed him, was in the middle of his sophomore year at the University of
Hawai'i when I last interviewed him in 1999. At that time he participated in
a roundtable discussion on pedagogy along with Akamine and King. As an
undergraduate, he brought to the table a view of democratic education that
now spanned our unit of analysis for this book, high school through adult
education.

REFLECTION: BUILDING A DEMOCRATIC SCHOOL CLIMATE

The alliance of two pockets of hope—one at the Department of Education
(DOE) and the other in the Peer Education Program at RHS—is remarkable
for its uniqueness. Rarely do creative teachers like Akamine find administrators like King and Goo who understand what they are doing and give their
full support. But alliances like theirs are the most effective forces for empowering students. By sharing power-with each other, the adults model the
democratic ideal that they are attempting to instill.

King describes a healthy school as one in which a "democratic climate
prevails—where individuals respect each other and grow, realizing their intellectual, moral, and psychological potential." She has promoted that kind of
environment in schools throughout Hawai'i, but, she says, "It takes leadership within the school to really transform the school climate." When a principal like Goo recognizes the importance of mediation and peer education,
he acknowledges the significance of having students find their power-from-
within. When a student like Kimo, who had previously solved problems with
his fists because he thought that he couldn't talk, actually advocates for himself by negotiating the channels of communication at the school, the school
has succeeded. In overcoming fear and shame and, more significantly, sharing his vulnerability and accomplishments with his peers, teacher, and guests,
Kimo demonstrates that he has "crossed the bridge." But he could do this
only because of the enormous foundation of power-with that the students
and their teacher had developed.

In this community, Kimo felt empowered to bring up his experience,
despite the presence of important visitors. PEP students feel a sense of ownership of their classroom space and a sense of pride about the importance of
their work. Sharing their insight and vision is a natural extension of their

work together. The PEP program at Roosevelt demonstrates on a day-to-day basis that administrators, teachers, and students can work toward creating a democratic school climate that enhances the potential of all students to find their power-from-within; to act collaboratively, sharing power-with their peers; and to change themselves and the world, sustaining hope in all of their activities.

ROOSEVELT HIGH SCHOOL'S PEER EDUCATION PROGRAM

At Roosevelt, a fairly traditional high school of 1,500 students, PEP attracts a broad spectrum of boys and girls who train to be peer supporters, educators, partners, and mediators. Using a health-based curriculum provided by the state, these student educators learn to teach K–12 classes on subjects ranging from nutrition to alcohol abuse to sexuality to teambuilding to mediation; they also mediate conflicts among their peers and provide leadership across culturally and economically diverse school communities. The PEP students are in special education, the mainstream, the ESL program, and honors; they are among the leaders in student government and the once shy and reserved and, in some cases, once alienated; they star on male and female athletic teams and in the drama club; they are straight or gay or questioning their sexuality. In this school, which classifies 49 percent of its students as Asian, 23 percent as Hawaiian or part Hawaiian, and 10 percent as Caucasian, PEP students are all of the above as well as African American, Hispanic, and Samoan. Their class backgrounds vary widely because the school serves both the most affluent and the poorest neighborhoods in Honolulu.

To secure one of the 20–25 slots available in each of the two sections of PEP, students have to be nominated by an employee at the school and interviewed by Akamine, who consciously constructs a diverse group of peer educators representative of the school population. Students gain elective credit for taking the Peer Education Program, which meets for four class periods a week as well as for additional out-of-class projects. Technically, students could apply to be in the program for their four years at Roosevelt, but Akamine recommends that they participate no more than three years so that a maximum number of students can become part of PEP. Returning students in the program establish remarkably high standards of commitment for the newer generation; seniors and juniors forge alliances with freshmen and sophomores, defying stereotypical divides in most high schools.

The Hawaiian philosophy that undergirds this program and a number of others in the school is visible on the walls of the 25- by 30-foot PEP classroom. Posters in Hawaiian and English read: "Be *Akamai* [smart]. Think First. AIDS Is Preventable." "*E kuka kuka kaua* [discuss strife]. Communication Is the

Key." Their big yellow banner with red letters reads, "PEP Posse Roosevelt High School." The homey feel makes the room a welcoming oasis for students. Akamine's desk and computer are off in one corner. A refrigerator is in another corner. A big comfortable couch is along one wall. Stackable chairs are arranged in a circle.

On a large bulletin board along a wall are four human stick figures composed of photos of the current year's PEP students. On the blank face of one stick figure are the words "Peer Supporter," on another "Peer Educator," on another "Peer Partner," and on another "Peer Mediator." PEP students, in learning all of these roles, become leaders in the school community.

In this democratic space, PEP students learn and teach important lessons in how power operates. This room is a place to which many RHS students are naturally drawn. Something is always happening here throughout the day and after school. Here they nurture friendships and alliances. They dream of changing the world. They plan how to do it.

Deeply committed to democratic practice and to a culture of caring about each other and the world, PEP students and their teacher form a loving and supportive community where learning to listen is essential. Maurice, a former PEP student and a 1993 graduate of RHS who was volunteering in 1996–1997 in PEP, while attending the University of Hawai'i, suggests that "most students would love to have a friend or someone their own age to talk their problems over with," and goes on to add, "that's one of the big draws of our program." When one thinks of the rash of school shootings by alienated students, most notably the one at Columbine High School, it is evident that schools need programs in which students can find peers who will listen to them and with whom they can discuss their issues. Four months after the Columbine shootings, Diane (RHS '98), who was in PEP for two years, told me that such an incident would never have happened at Roosevelt because Akamine and PEP would have been aware of the problems and done something about them.

Diane, a white student, who described herself as "quite a hermit" at RHS before discovering PEP, might have become one of what King calls the "forgotten kids"—kids who are not making it and are alienated and in trouble. Diane, a student who struggled with issues of sexual identity and experienced some pretty difficult moments in school and in her family, reflects about PEP, "You know there really weren't any bad experiences in that class." But before PEP there were "bad experiences" in school for Diane.

King is concerned that educational systems are not adapting to meet the needs of vast numbers of students who do not succeed in traditional classrooms. "Rather than changing, they just cast off these kids." In contrast, in peer education and mediation, King sees "a real sense of kids increasing their self-confidence," growing in self-esteem as a result of discovering that they can solve their own problems and they can, as well, help other people solve their problems. Both she and Akamine agree that students who have found their power-from-within become more inclined to engage in other activities at school—they become participants, not just spectators. They have an increased sense of their own empowerment and realize that they can actually get things done. King asserts that through programs like PEP, "students learn how the system works a little bit more at the school. They know that they are not helpless and that if they can use the right approach, they can really get what they want." They become agents of change.

Statewide Alliances

As one of 26 peer education programs statewide and one of the mediation programs that exist in close to 80 percent of the secondary schools, the Roosevelt Peer Education Program is in a unique statewide alliance. Jasmine, a freshman, feels excited connecting herself to the nearly 1,000 peer educators statewide each year. Just knowing that there are other peer educators working in their schools and communities gives her the sense, she says, that "we're making a difference. For every person who we help to change their own lives, we're making a difference."

King fosters the relationships among all of the mediation programs through student-designed and student-run conferences that her office facilitates. The 1995 conflict resolution conference, which I attended, demonstrated to me the remarkable poise, maturity, and creativity of the mediators. Roosevelt mediators have long been the mentors for newly emerging programs. King asserts that many schools have made mediation part of peer education programs because they are a perfect fit: "mediation fits into the idea of emotional health, the health of relationships." Having an ability to "manage conflict in healthy ways," King argues, is essential for all of us and she maintains that students should learn this in school.

Maurice recalls that throughout his high school career at RHS, "We went out to different high schools and different conferences and we were really proud of our program.... We became the model program for peer education in the state." They also, not surprisingly, became the model program in mediation. Maurice, who is Hawaiian and African American, presented at conferences with King, and later, Hunter and other RHS peer educators became guest speakers in a course King taught at the University of Hawai'i. Akamine's students taught educators, school personnel, and students about peer education and mediation throughout the state.

The statewide alliances that these students become a part of serve the important function of connecting them to a critical mass of students who like them are working to change the world.

Peer Supporters: Building the 'Ohana

The kind of community that gets built in Akamine's classes, King believes, is one in which students, "manage conflict in healthy ways; they talk things out. There's trust and fellowship and love. There's a lot of fun. There's a sense of support and caring. People know each other. There's a sense of not leaving people out. There's a sense of belonging and just a tight-knit feeling that this is my school. This is my place. I have a place here." In such an environment, the vast majority of the students perform at their optimal level.

Akamine and her students create the space for everyone to "cross that bridge" over whatever impediments stand in the way of their tapping into their own power-from-within. Maurice explained, "the most important thing that we share in this class we can sum up in one word. That word is 'growth.'" Maurice laughed, thinking about it. "In fact, Boss always likes to say she'd rather have you fail than succeed in everything in life, because if you always succeed you never see yourself growing. It's the time when you fail that you then later see the most growth."

To a large extent, it is Akamine's vision of herself as a person in the process of growing that lends essential vitality to PEP. Over and over again, she insists on how much she learns in the process of collaborating with her students. Her openness and her sense of caring and giving set a strong example. She is the first to note, "This kind of program is not for everybody. You really have to be a person who is willing to look at yourself and be willing to give to others. And people have to take care of themselves first to be able to give to others."

These students are not missionaries, living their emotional lives through "helping" others. They are people in the process of looking critically at their own lives and behavior in their PEP class meetings, as they simultaneously reach out to educate, to mediate for, to support, and to form partnerships with their peers. The support that the students get from each other in the class allows them to develop the self-esteem, power, and leadership skills to participate more broadly in the school community and in the community in which they live.

"The content of the course is important but they have to feel good about each other to be able to work together," Akamine insists. In PEP, students will face fears and challenges that will push them to their limits academically and personally. To be successful in such an environment they need the support of both peers and adults. To achieve this solidarity, Akamine begins early to break down any alienation that might exist and to build an *'ohana*—a supportive family or community.

Because of the wide range of demographic differences among students in the class, students who in most schools would never speak to each other get to know each other quite intimately. Students with a father in prison, students who have been abandoned by their parents, students torn apart by family divorce, students whose mom and dad are supportive, students going on to prestigious colleges, students whose highest hope is to graduate from high school learn to know each other. Akamine observed that when students know each other, they "take care of each other." Hunter notes the importance of this strategy. "In some cases students don't have a supportive family so when they come here then we give them the support that they need. When they do something good, everyone in the class supports them. Good job. Good job." Maurice adds to that, "they know that this is a family that they can have—literally."

From the beginning of the school year, Akamine consciously strives to build relationships among students within each of the two sections that she teaches and then across the two sections. For larger projects out in the community, the two sections will work together and Akamine wants them to be tight. She tells them, "We're one group. We're one *'ohana*."

Fashioning an *'ohana*, a family, in a conscious way, tells the students that there are responsibilities but there are supports. Usually within the first month of the academic year, the PEP students are excused from most of their other classes for two days to work at the team building that will make them an *'ohana* and to learn mediation skills (see "Peer Mediators: Negotiating Power" in this chapter) that will allow them to work strategically in their school, their families, and their various communities. These days are critical to the success of the year. Akamine's skills and charisma are nowhere more evident.

Team Building Exercises. September 24, 1997. It's 8:00 A.M., already 80 degrees, and 40 students are gathered in the shade at the Roosevelt High School athletic field. It is the first day of their two-day training, and Akamine is briefing them on remembering to keep drinking water to prevent dehydration. They'll be in the sun most of the day. All of the students wear tags on which they've written their names and drawn their animal totems. The two classes of peer educators are mixed together in a scrambled eggs exercise. Akamine begins the introductions, gesturing and chirping like a beetle, "I'm Beetle Bug Boss." The kids crack up. The next student says, "Hi, Beetle Bug Boss," and then he imitates her gestures and adds, "I'm Rudy Red Rooster," then struts and does a "cock a doodle do." All 40 of the students will repeat the name, gesture, and animal sound of all PEP students, and Akamine will breeze through them all at the end. In 15 minutes, they will have learned the names of everyone in the *'ohana*, laughed, and put themselves out there taking risks. No one begs off participating. Everyone is engaged in this and the next five exercises that follow. They are bonding.

In the concluding exercise of the day, two rows of 16 students each stand facing each other. Eight of the pairs hold a metal pole, thus shaping a horizontal human ladder. The others in the lines and those not in the ladder will "spot" and be safety checks for the challengers. The daunting and somewhat threatening challenge is to crawl crab-like across the poles, holding on to them with your hands while balancing your feet on them, all the while being supported by your classmates holding the poles. Akamine asks, Who will go first? A student suggests, "Boss, you do it." Akamine strikes an attitude and grimaces at them. They cheer her on. She kicks off her rubber slippers and approaches the ladder, climbs up on it, and begins crawling across it as the students scurry about spotting her and making sure that she will not fall. She is all smiles throughout the process, and upon reaching the last rung, she jumps off to their cheers. "Okay, people. Let's keep it safe and see how many we can get across." The last student to try it is Harry, a very big boy who is reluctant and afraid but clearly wants to do it. Everyone pulls together to hold the poles and brace him. There are a few hairy moments, but he emerges from the other end of the human ladder smiling. His classmates give him a huge round of applause. He clearly has taken on the deepest challenge of the day.

Akamine debriefs them: How did it feel being on the ladder? Why were people willing to try climbing the ladder? Why were people hesitant to participate? How did you feel after you had participated? Again males and females of all ages are willing to share their fears and embarrassment. Their honesty is remarkable. One student says that he was really proud of Harry's courage and that it made him feel good to be a part of the support team. The students nod their heads in agreement. Harry gets another round of applause. Throughout the activities, they have learned important lessons about caring, respect, trust, teamwork, listening to each other, and supporting each other. They have bonded at physical, emotional, and intellectual levels, and they have all had fun. An *'ohana* is emerging.

As students participate in all of these activities, they develop their power-from-within. Akamine's goal of building a powerful *'ohana* is achieved as each student takes physical and psychological risks in a safe yet challenging environment. Risks such as these are decidedly different from what much of school is about, but these risks become the baseline from which Akamine will nurture power-from-within.

The team-building exercises provide a foundation for the kind of ongoing support that students offer one another in PEP. The strength that the students get from each other in PEP allows them to develop the self-esteem, power, and leadership skills to participate more broadly in school and in the community.

Diane sees the attitudes and behavior of PEP students affecting the whole school. "When I was a freshman, I'd never bother to go around and help in any way but when I noticed the PEP students, I started to get other ideas." Peer educators exercise leadership formally and informally. "If there's a fight and there's some of us around, most likely that will be broken up," says Diane. A few years later and out in the working world, Diane sees the skills she learned as useful—to listen, provide support, and look for solutions. "A lot of times at work there are people who are mad at each other. It's hard for me because they are older but I will try to at least get them to talk to each other. I can't necessarily do it in a formal fashion, such as mediation, but I do use things that I learned in Peer Ed."

A major skill that PEP supporters give to their peers is the art of good listening. Akamine relates that in college as well as at work, PEP graduates "feel like magnets" because people come to them when they need to talk. Akamine is the preeminent role model and increasingly the peer supporters become skilled themselves. Diane calls it "Boss's magic. Everyone cares and that, I think, comes from her, ultimately. The caring that we ended up having for each other in the class began with Boss."

King wishes that all teachers were like Akamine: "better communicators who can talk things out and not be so autocratic—people willing to listen to kids more." PEP becomes the perfect vehicle, King contends. "Amy's kids build a strong sense of community among themselves first. There they can find support for each other when they go out in the school and in the community." She adds, "the community that they create in the class transcends the class," and that is a marker of effective education.

Peer Educator: Pedagogy

Initially Akamine's pedagogical practice is seamless to her students. They know that there is something radically different that they feel about this class and how it operates, but it takes them time to understand the pedagogy. After a few weeks in the class, they want to demystify the pedagogy so that they can use it in their own ventures into teaching. For most of the students, this course becomes their first experience in examining pedagogical practice and how it is shaped by the power relationships that manifest themselves in school, particularly in pedagogical practice.

Maurice analyzes how power operates in most classes from the teacher's perspective: "It's my way or the highway." In such classes, students are expected to become followers of the teacher's lead or leave the class. There is no possibility of collaborative construction of knowledge, for, in most of Maurice's classes, both at RHS and later in college, the teacher was the center of the classroom. He sees the teachers sometimes caring, but in a way that does not inspire students truly to achieve their potential. "I don't think that teachers care enough about their students. I really feel that they just truly care about getting that subject taught and making sure that their kids get good grades so that they can move on to college." Clearly, this is not enough for Maurice or for Hunter, who both agree that when it is clear that the teacher cares about them, they put out more effort and become empowered.

In classes where the teacher exercises power-over them, students sit back and expect those teachers to do all of the work. In contrast, Maurice says, "When we are in this classroom, we do 90 per cent of the work and Boss does 10 per cent." They soon learn, as they prepare to teach their own classes, how much work it takes to get the students to do that 90 per cent and how critical it is to create those conditions which will allow students to be so engaged.

Hunter gives testimony to the way that a democratic classroom such as Akamine's changes students' self-concept and develops their power-from-within. "Most students don't believe in what they can do. But in PEP everybody comes in to do what they need to do. I look at how well this class is run just by us students and how students can do so much for themselves and not need, well need minimal, supervision from adults. If we really want to do something, we can do it."

Understanding the dynamic of apathy that pervades most classrooms, students in PEP, who will have to go out and teach their peers in K-12 are forced to think about how they can banish apathy and get their peers engaged and "into" their lessons. PEP students do not go out and lecture to other students. Maurice says that's because "they know that's not the way that they would learn." The PEP class, they quickly realize, is not a teacher-centered classroom, but neither is it a student-centered classroom. Akamine inspires a greater sense of purposefulness. It is very much what Parker Palmer (1998) calls a subject-centered classroom, where the great problems that they are struggling with engage both teacher and students alike.

Akamine's practice thus becomes critical in inspiring generations of peer educators who will have opportunities to enter classrooms and transform their own and other students' ideas about learning and power. Akamine suggests that "a teacher has to be willing to see himself or herself as a partner in education, not the master of the classroom." Her recognition of the power-over dynamic that dominates most classrooms leads her to encourage peer educators to model the best practice they encounter, not the worst. It begins simply with paying attention to the conditions in the classroom. "Our classroom setup encourages equality," Akamine insists. "We sit in a circle. We sit on chairs of equal height. If someone sits out of the circle, other students encourage that person to move in. I think how a teacher sets up their classroom is often indicative of his or her teaching style." The classroom configuration is also often indicative of a teacher's understanding of the politics of education. In their circle, Akamine and the students nurture their democratic space.

Hunter argues how important it is in a class to be sitting facing each other. "When we're not facing each other it's like talking to yourself. You see no one's expression and it's like 'why am I even saying this? Never mind.'" His observation makes perfect sense and he speculates further, "I think that's why students don't talk in most classes, because other students aren't listening to them. They feel oppressed. They feel as if they shouldn't say anything because it's useless. But when you're forced to look at people, you're forced to show expression to them. It helps a lot."

In Hawai'i the practice of "talking story" is clearly one of the major cultural ways that learning takes place. Although the talking is important, it cannot be underscored frequently enough that listening to each other plays an equally significant role. In Akamine's class, talking story involves sharing experiences and knowledge in a purposeful dialogue. Nalei observes, "In our class we have a lot of equality. We're all heard.... If we have an opinion we can say it without getting bashed down because we all respect each other." King observes that getting students to listen to each other is the hallmark of a great democratic teacher like Akamine. In her classroom, students internalize the practice of listening and learning from each other as they develop their power-from-within building alliances among each other.

Hunter recalls how he felt as a freshman walking into the PEP class and noticing juniors and seniors already there sitting in a circle. "I felt intimidated at first because of the older students, but once I got going sharing and working with them, I couldn't stop." Akamine acknowledges the important role that the more experienced PEP students play for students less accustomed to a democratic classroom. "You learn the behavior. You walk into class and you just observe first and then you see how everybody's speaking and you internalize that and then you put yourself forward in the same manner."

The students see themselves as working with Akamine even though they all jokingly refer to her as "Boss" and actually call her "Boss." Maurice gave her that name when he was a junior. He says, "Everyone in the class was bigger than her but she commands so much respect, despite her size. 'Boss' is a small word but it holds big meaning so it just attached to her." Maurice acknowledges that the name is totally ironic because of all of the teachers he has encountered she is the least bossy and the one who most insists that stu-

dents act responsibly on their own. Maurice describes what happens after a
PEP class has decided on its projects. "She says this is your job now and you
have to go out and do it. And that's what we do." Hunter understands that
Akamine is shifting power to them, and he jokes, "By her giving us the
responsibility we truly feel that we have the responsibility to do our job well
so that she looks good." He continues, more seriously, "We feel as if we're in
charge now. By giving us the power, she gives us more confidence."

Maurice describes their process, "We choose our topics for lessons from
the state PEP curriculum and from ideas that the class has come up with and
then we have to write out our lesson plans and describe how we are going to
teach them." He underscores their learning process: "Boss doesn't supply
plans to us. There are a lot of books in our classroom and in the library and
we have to do research on what we are going to do and decide if it suits the
age level that we are teaching."

Far from being aloof and pushing the students off on their own, Akamine
is always there as the caring adult who will aid them in finding their power-
from-within, what Hunter calls "confidence." In PEP there are few quizzes or
tests and the students work collaboratively co-constructing knowledge about
the subject areas in which they will teach. Students do not go out and teach
unless they have demonstrated to Akamine and the class that they are prepared.

Hunter says that it is often difficult to convey to people outside class what
happens in it because its mode of operation is so different from what happens in the rest of school. Maurice remarked that once he heard a teacher
refer to PEP as "a fun class" in a clearly demeaning way. Hunter interjects that
teachers such as that one do not understand that "it's hard work but it's fun."
PEP is no easy course. Even stars like Maurice and Hunter have gotten a B in
some quarters because they did not put out the extra effort to earn the clearly
defined points for community outreach work that would qualify them for an
A.

Maurice points out that a goal of peer educators is to promote "unity,
teamwork and opening up feelings." Once they break down some of the barriers that make achieving that goal difficult, Maurice claims that "learning is
easy." He elaborates, "Often in high school it's the barriers of friendship and
peer pressure and drugs and society and parents that cause the problems that
keep you from learning." Being talked at by adults turns off many teenagers.
The rare adult who wants to share information and experiences with them
and not just tell them everything truly engages them. Maurice contrasts the
PEP pedagogy with the dominant pedagogy of the school. "In math and
English the teacher is telling you what to do. They are telling you what you

should know. In this class we are not telling each other. We are sharing. I think it's easier to learn if you share, rather than if you tell."

Experienced in democratic pedagogy, PEP students go out and teach, modeling new ways of teaching and learning for some students and teachers alike. Maurice addresses the challenge Akamine faces with each group in PEP. "What she is teaching is hard. I really think that she is teaching the toughest subject in the schools. She is teaching you how to leave your fears behind, go in front of a class of your own friends and teach them something they think they know everything in the world about." It is also being committed to your peers and to your vision of a world that you would like to see.

Peer Partners: Building Alliances
Preparing for and Teaching a Special Education Class. In addition to teaching the standardized health-based curriculum, PEP students use their pedagogical skills to support special education students. Part of the mission of PEP is to encourage peer support and collaborative work with disempowered communities and to have the PEP students determine ways of sharing power with them. With this challenge, PEP students have worked with homeless shelters, nursing homes and convalescent hospitals for the aged and for young people who have been permanently injured in automobile or motorcycle accidents. Some of their most sustained work, however, occurs with the severely learning impaired special education community at RHS.

On a Monday morning, Hunter and Diane begin a class discussion of ideas that they have for a lesson that PEP will teach to a RHS special ed class of students who range from moderately impaired to those with Down's syndrome. After some considered discussion about facilities, the students' capabilities, and pedagogical strategies, the idea that the class gets most enthusiastic about is teaching how to measure. In doing this project, their goals will be building support and an alliance with the special ed students, reinforcing teamwork, and teaching the students measuring strategies. Akamine gives her approval and suggests that Hunter and Diane talk over their ideas with the special ed teacher.

A week later Hunter and Diane are the lead teachers and 20 other PEP members are partners with the special ed students. PEP is welcomed with open delight into an area the size of two large classrooms—much hugging and high-fiveing from all of the students. Akamine and the special ed teacher move off to the edges of the classroom and chat, all the while keeping a watchful eye. Hunter and Diane demonstrate how to build a paper airplane and throw it. The special ed students begin following the instructions, and their PEP partners offer assistance as needed, but the emphasis is on coaching and empowering. After 10 minutes, the 20 special ed students have functional airplanes.

Diane shows them a ruler and a measuring tape and explains that they are now going to go outside and learn about measuring distance. There is excitement about going outside. The partners stay close by because a number of the special ed students have fears and physical challenges in walking down the flight of stairs. Again the peer educators support and coach and their caring elicits trust and the triumph of having everyone make it downstairs with no mishaps. Outside, Hunter shows where the line is from which they will sail their airplanes and has his partner and then Diane's throw their planes to see which will go farther. They demonstrate with a measuring tape how to measure the length. All of the students then clamor to throw their planes, measure the length, and write it down. For some of them the measurement has conceptual meaning, for others it is a visual perception, and for all of them it is bonding with the PEP students who show them love and companionship—a success on many fronts.

A year after the class, Diane comments, "That was an awesome chance for me to be able to work with Hunter. He is a really great guy. It was really cool for me to be able to work with him because I was younger and in that class he was one of the mentors. I always looked up to them so much."

The lesson is emblematic of the established relationship that PEP has with all of the special ed students in the school. A few years before, when PEP students noticed that some other students in the school were belittling and playing jokes on the special ed students in the cafeteria, PEP decided to ally itself with the special ed students. Most days PEP students, many of whom are the "stars" of the school, with their friends eat lunch with the special ed students. Hunter underscores their connection with special education students. "Most people forget that they are humans and that they have feelings. Just because they have Down's syndrome doesn't mean that they don't have feelings. They still have feelings and all they want is companionship." Diane remembers as a freshman seeing the Peer Educators "hanging out with the special ed kids" and it impressed her. "It connected for me that they didn't just go to Peer Education and think that peer education stops in the classroom." PEP's alliance with special education has made RHS a safer and happier place for many of the most vulnerable students, and it has deepened the power-from-within of both groups of students.

PEP partnerships span the school community. In the 1999 school year, PEP's alliance with the school's Junior ROTC (JROTC) program to heighten awareness about the disastrous effects of teenage drinking and driving offered them experience in organizing for change. With the JROTC students at RHS, PEP discussed strategies for raising awareness at their school about drunk driving. Together the groups came up with the idea of a mock funeral for a teenager supposedly killed in a drunk driving accident. The JROTC students, dressed in black pants, white dress shirts, white gloves, and black berets, served as pall bearers. The students recruited a high school teacher who also is a minister to dress in his black cassock and white surplice to preside at the mock funeral. They borrowed a coffin from a local theater company and placed a full length mirror on top of it.

At lunch hour, which is a free period for most of the school, they held the mock funeral in the library. It was attended by numbers of curious students. After the funeral, they formed a procession, which took them through the halls of the school and into the school cafeteria. A hush came over the hundreds of students there as the procession made its way in and the coffin was placed on a table with the pall bearers standing at attention around it. After the initial shock wore off, the hum of chatter arose again and curious students went over to look. As they gazed at the coffin, they saw themselves reflected in the mirror. Their response was horror. The hope was that the shock of seeing their own faces reflected raised their consciousness as well.

In allying themselves with the JROTC students, who did not customarily follow their democratic style of decision making, PEP ended up educating their peers beyond the lesson of drunk driving. JROTC fulfilled part of its mission in trying to improve responsibility among students. Akamine sees sharing power-with totally different student populations as critical for preparing students for the challenges of leadership in more diverse communities. She also sees the crucial importance of connecting the school with the community.

PEP's partnership with the RHS special education students is an example of how they learn to share power-with across differences and to extend the relationship into the community. The connection between these two groups of students has developed into an ongoing partnership around the Special Olympics in Hawai'i. This experience Hunter saw as magical for both PEP and their Olympic partners, for it connected their bond out in the community and made them understand another way in which the boundaries of school could be transcended. This partnership took place after the school year had ended and proved an assertion of King's: "Young people are capable of taking more responsibility for themselves in and out of school. They should be given that opportunity. They are prevented from doing that a lot of times by adults. Students can do a lot more than we give them credit for." For King, the most important lesson is that an endeavor like this "really gives them a taste of what they can do to make positive change in the school and ultimately in the world."

Peer Mediators: Negotiating Power

Mediation Workshop. September 25, 1997, 9:00 A.M.–2:00 P.M. This is the second of the traditional two days at the beginning of the school year that Akamine uses to create their *'ohana* (see the Peer Supporters section). On September 24, they engaged in team building on the athletic field. Today they are in one of the few air-conditioned areas in the school, the library, learning mediation skills. The PEP students are huge football players and female athletes as well as both males and females who are just about five feet tall. Amid them, Akamine is closer to the five-foot-tall younger students. Maurice, who is now four years out of RHS and is still remembered as a football hero and member of PEP, as well as a 1996–1997 volunteer in PEP, has taken the day off work to assist Akamine in the mediation training. His commitment sends a signal to the students of the importance of their project. After Akamine's introduction, he gets a hero's welcome.

Akamine gathers the students in a group around a TV monitor and underscores the importance of the training on which they are about to embark. She begins by showing the students a front page story from the day before in the *Honolulu Advertiser* focusing on the mediation program at Nanakuli High School. A student asks, "Why isn't the story about Roosevelt? We trained the kids at Nanakuli." Akamine points out that Roosevelt has gotten its share of media attention and that it is important to show how the program is spreading. She then screens a 10 minute Department of Education "how-to" video on mediation that features the program at Roosevelt. They like seeing Roosevelt in the video.

Akamine then asks the students to spread out to the nine large library tables in the center area. They do this with a minimum of confusion. Akamine walks in and out among the tables as she begins the process with a brief reflection on the team-building exercises the day before.

> In class this morning, Jeanne praised Oli for coming over yesterday and telling her that it was okay that she touched the rope and the team-building exercise had to begin again. Oli told her not to feel bad about it. That's important and that makes me feel proud. Mari also praised Koko, who helped a lot of people in the human ladder exercise. It's important to notice these things. When people really help out, it's important to recognize that.

She pauses and asks, "Anyone want to add anything?" Diane reflects, "I thought that the way that everyone worked together as a team and supported each other was great." Akamine adds, smiling, "Yeah, it wasn't even visible that it was really two classes. We're an *'ohana*. You people did a great job."

Akamine connects and weaves, showing the students how to build love, respect, and trust. The smiles on their faces indicate that they enjoy praising each other and see themselves as a community that is building bonds.

Akamine distributes an Office of Instructional Services book written by King, *Secondary Training Manual for School Mediation* (1995), and begins reading the essentials of the process:

> Mediation is a voluntary process, in which two mediators help the parties in dispute find ways of resolving their problems. In mediation the disputants are
> - asked to tell their "story" about what happened
> - helped to clarify the issues involved
> - encouraged to understand how each other feels about these issues
> - helped to find some resolution which each party agrees to which can work and for which both can share responsibility, and
> - finally, if and when an agreement is reached by the disputants, they are helped to write and sign an agreement. (1)

Learning these mediation skills will help all the students be better listeners, allies, learners, and educators.

As Akamine reads, a few students get restless and start chatting. She concludes the reading and says, with a tone of genuine concern in her voice, "I worry about all of you folks who are not paying attention. If you're not paying attention to learning this process, then you should take this opportunity to go back to class." The students immediately refocus. Her expressed concern has no hint of power-over in tone or affect.

Akamine approaches a table in the middle of the library area and asks the students where they think disputants should sit around a table. The experienced students who know the answers hold back while the new trainees, who are very lively and have suggestions, engage. Akamine, pointing to two students, then asks, "Shall we have these people be the mediators?" One student says, "Yeah let's shine the spotlight on them."

"Okay let's begin. I'll play a disputant." Akamine picks up a book and walks toward the table where the mediators are sitting. She slams the book on the table and shows attitude. "Is that okay?"

A resounding "No" comes from the class.

"Why?" she asks.

The students point out that they have got to keep respect going among the disputants and toward themselves. Akamine is pleased. She moves to another table and uses them for her demo. This dispute involves a girlfriend-boyfriend issue. Akamine asks, "Who should speak first?"

Vernon jibes, "The man."

Akamine strikes a pose and looks at him, as all of the students laugh. Another boy, Taylor, says, "That's sexist." Akamine says, "That's right." Within the first month of the school year, Akamine has forged, among a diverse group of 40 students, a community that is comfortable and accountable, loving and challenging, playful and highly motivated. Watching her move through this opening segment, I am aware of the enormous amount of energy required of her to maintain the electricity and enthusiasm in the room. I note as well the ways in which the students, particularly the experienced members of the program who are already peer educators, appreciate and facilitate Akamine's work. They do not answer questions that newcomers should address.

For the next hour, students engage in simulated mediations as Maurice and Akamine move from table to table listening in, answering questions, and cheering on the new mediators. They praise good work and make suggestions to improve poor practice. At each table they are fully engaged with the participants. In the evaluation before their potluck lunch, students raise questions about difficulties that they encountered and Akamine gets them to problem solve together. A feeling of camaraderie continues to swell.

At lunch break, they go to the PEP classroom, which is a refuge for many students at Roosevelt. On a flip chart stands the sign-up sheet reminder for today's potluck meal: main dish, salad, rice, drinks, dessert, and paper goods. These students have organized their celebration—an unbelievably sumptuous spread. Students put out the food as Akamine adds some finishing aesthetic touches. Within 25 minutes they consume all of it.

They return to the library and do a fishbowl simulation involving a breakup of a girlfriend and boyfriend. The boy, a second-string basketball player, is jealous of his girlfriend, who is a first-rate player on the girls' basketball team. He wants her to quit playing basketball. The girl wants to break up with the boyfriend but is afraid that he will beat her up if she does.

Diane, who with Keanu is mediating, calls a time out on the mediation and asks Akamine, "Doesn't this have to be reported to school authorities? Isn't this in the category of life-threatening?"

Koko, who is role playing the boyfriend, answers, "No, this is not life-threatening. If I beat her, that's just beating. I didn't say that I'd kill her." A silence hangs in the air. All of the students look to Akamine. She is standing still, a model of compassion and determination. She is compassionate toward Koko, who knows immediately that his role playing went too far and that he has uttered something that shocks the other students. Akamine is determined to draw the students into deeper thinking on the topic. She says, "We don't always know what is life-threatening and we have to trust our instincts. What we need to look at is imminent danger. Abuse can lead possibly to death. That is serious." Then Akamine speaks directly to Diane and Keanu, the mediators. "You folks are caring. You could have just gone on with the mediation, but you cared about the issue and stopped us. In a real mediation, you could extend that caring about the girl and carry on after the session with a referral to counselors who could also assist."

The mediation resumes with Diane and Keanu interviewing Koko to get his side of the story. After a few minutes, Koko says, "She's better than me at basketball and that's why I want her to quit. 'I'm the man.'" Diane does another stop action and asks Akamine, "Isn't what he's saying really pretty male chauvinist? If he said that to me, to quit playing basketball because 'I'm the man,' I'd walk." Akamine opens up the discussion. The students agree with Diane and a number of them point out that it's a male ego thing and that he's just jealous. Akamine nods. She has set the tone of seriousness and caring in the mediation and in this exchange she does not need to speak.

This, the most highly charged of all of the mediations of the day, focusing as it does on sexism and abuse, sobers the mood of the peer mediators and focuses their attention as no other issue has. They all are riveted on this mediation and keep their attention focused on what is happening. As the mediators lead the disputants individually through the process, they underscore the rights of the girl to have her own life and to play basketball. They do not mention sexism and instead focus on fairness. When the girl says that she wants to break up with the boy but is afraid, the mediators listen and tell her that she is being quite reasonable in not wanting to quit the basketball team. When they speak with the boy separately, they listen to his desire that his girlfriend quit the team and interrogate the fairness of that wish. When the two disputants are brought together, the mediators encourage them to write and sign an agreement respecting each other's pursuits and pledging that if tempers flare, they will come back to mediation. The mediation concludes and all of the students seem emotionally drained from the tension.

Akamine ends the day with a reflection, praising them for their seriousness and intelligence in dealing with difficult issues. She reminds them that they will have support and that if they get into a mediation that feels too complicated or beyond them, they can always ask for help, and that in fact knowing when to ask for help is very important. "What did you see today as the biggest challenge in dealing with some of these issues?" A student replies, "The answer is not always just black or white. It's not clear."

"Yes, that's a key thing to understand," Akamine points out. She cautions them, too, "There is a blur between peer support and peer mediation and you have to be the ones pulling that into focus. It's complicated but I know that you are a caring group and I think that you can do it. We'll work together on this all year."

This last mediation has made them think deeply about what happens in a mediation when one disputant, such as the girl, clearly needs peer support and further dialogue about her issues, and the mediators are pushed to be fair in the mediation. It's not always black and white, indeed. But the earnestness with which these mediators approach the issue is inspirational. Confidentiality issues make it impossible to observe actual mediations, but these simulations based on actual high school cases make the mediation process come alive for the students, as well as for an observer like her.

Akamine concludes the day, explaining how they will all designate their free periods for the semester to set up a rotation of available mediators. When students come seeking mediation either from a referral or in self-referral, she will then know who will be available to mediate at designated times. Her parting words to them are "You've been great today. You did some very hard work that is draining emotionally. Good thinking. I'm proud of your work." Throughout this whole day Akamine is really pressured to be fully present for these students in this large area in the library. Maurice's support and the leadership of seasoned mediators have been invaluable and she leads the gathering in a round of applause for them.

Throughout the mediation simulations, students have noticed who has the most power or control among the disputants. While not naming it as power-over, the students nonetheless identify it as a fairness issue. In listening carefully to both disputants lay out their claims, mediators come to understand competing claims and also learn that parties in a dispute are not necessarily "equal." Diane's recognition of sexism and other students' recognition of class and race differences indicate their understanding of how power operates in the world. They can disentangle what may be considered "accepted practice" from what is just and fair.

In showing the concern that they do about the issues of disputants, they demonstrate that they care about their peers. They establish a climate of respect and trust in which disputants are empowered to solve their problems and commit to the solutions in a signed agreement.

Shifting Power. Giving students the tools of learning how to offer peer support and how to resolve conflicts shifts an enormous amount of power to them and makes it possible for them to become positive forces in creating a healthy school climate. Akamine finds students so committed to the process of peacefully solving problems that she feels once the training is done, "students don't really need us anymore." She believes that students long for peaceful solutions to problems and want to avoid tension and violence. "If we died, the students would still go on with mediation."

The culture of sharing, listening, supporting, and facilitating problem solving totally captures the minds and hearts of students in PEP, and they take their roles and responsibilities very seriously. Having peer supporters who will listen to them is enormously comforting, and offering that to their peers becomes their mission.

When Hunter, as a freshman, and an RHS school secretary trained by King mediated a grade dispute between a student and a teacher, new ground was broken. The teacher, who was willing to resolve the dispute in this way, deserves high praise for his faith in a democratic process, especially since tradition granted him autocratic autonomy. The teacher's actions taught far beyond what any of his words could say. When Akamine herself mediated a dispute between two departments at the school, a message also was sent to all of the faculty. Rather than filing grievances and setting up a situation in which an administrator would solve a faculty issue, the faculty spoke with each other and listened, and Akamine helped them heal a misunderstanding. When teachers feel powerful in their own lives, it is easier for them to facilitate the development of power-from-within for students.

King has a vision for teachers that could transform schools. "I'd like to see all teachers trained in mediation, so that if they had problems in the classroom, they would be able to use the techniques to resolve them. I see it as a way of enabling teachers to be better communicators with kids rather than being so autocratic. Maybe encouraging them to listen to kids more." Maurice, responding to the tension created in many classrooms by teachers who operate exclusively in the power-over mode, declared, "My dream is that I could train all teachers out there in mediation." Life then would be easier for everyone in classrooms he believes.

Adults needing to hold onto power often feel threatened by student empowerment. For the student government, the honor roll students, and the model athletes to have power stretches the limits of many educators' imaginations. The real challenge, however, is to support the average and below average academic achievers and those once seen as "outsiders" as they take on democratic responsibilities in the school. Shifting those paradigms decenters power.

REACHING OUT: COMMUNITY SERVICE AND COMMUNITY ACTION

Parent Night, February 8, 1998
From the first time that I spoke with him, Hunter told me that I would not

really understand the power and significance of PEP unless I went to a Parent Night. There, he claimed, I would see the power of the bond among the students in PEP and the kind of effect that PEP has even on the community. On February 8, 1998, I got a chance to see what he meant.

As with all of their activities, students plan Parent Night with those who have been a part of it before guiding the newcomers. The process is an exercise in community organizing. To begin, they discuss in class the significance of the night and then they make up a flyer to go home to all parents and guardians of peer educators. On the flyer, the parents are told, "A peer educator will be contacting you soon." As an invited adult, I learn how the PEP Posse works. A peer educator calls me 10 days before the night to remind me about it, and then 2 days before the event she calls and asks whether I need directions to the Lincoln School Cafetorium, where it is to be held. The peer educator exudes poise and self-assurance on the phone. Every peer educator talks to another student's parents or guardians. They take nothing for granted in making sure that all of the people they want to be there will get there. This lesson in organizing is critical for students intent on changing the world.

On the night of the event, the students, masters of the art of the potluck, provide a spread that is magnificent. A team of students arranges a photo display that covers all of their activities thus far in the year. They artfully display brochures and flyers from all of the programs that they put on. As parents come in, they are greeted by students, given name tags, and walked through the display. Teenagers make the adults feel comfortable by introducing them to each other. The poise that is required for all of this is considerable, and the students rise to the occasion. Dinner is a flawless and fun event as students sit with other students' parents and talk with them about the program.

When everyone is finished eating, a male and a female student go up on stage and take the microphone and thank the group for coming together on this important night. They explain that each student will have an opportunity to come up on stage with the adults whom they have invited and honor them. Maurice, a year before, explained to me the challenge. "It is really hard especially if you are not getting along with your parent or you hardly see your parent or your parent is not getting along with you." In families who rarely show the openness that PEP students have become accustomed to in their school 'ohana, the challenge is profound. Maurice described the poignancy of the moment. "You have to go up and say, 'I am thankful because you have done this for me.' And this is something that parents may go their whole lives without hearing." Parents also get to observe how other families operate, and, Maurice added, "They get to see other kids tell their parents, 'this is why I care about you.' So they get a good look at their own child." As the evening progresses, just as Maurice predicted, about two-thirds of the students admit that they have never before told their parents that they love them. Hunter had told me that at a previous Parents' Night, "One student just got up with her parents and started crying and the parents caught it. They knew everything. They all knew what each other was thinking. It was amazing." Expressing their love for adults in public is very important, and it is impressive to see the effect on the boys, in particular, who in their gentleness and thoughtfulness defy all "tough-guy" posturing that is so common among male teens.

Koko, a star male athlete, whom I had last seen role-playing a tough guy in the mediation training, goes up on stage with his grandmother. Koko wears a baseball cap, which he has pulled down to cover his eyes. He begins to speak and cries. He introduces his grandmother and says that when he and his two younger brothers were abandoned, it was she who took them in and now takes care of them. His grandmother is radiant and clearly very proud of him. Having observed Koko in class a number of times, I never would have guessed his plight or imagined the depth of his emotion. Koko presents his grandmother with a *lei* and Akamine takes a photo of the two of them, as she will of each family, crystallizing the moment. The photos that will be hung in their classroom are a poignant reminder of the night.

The stories of pain that many of the students tell provoke me to think about the complicated and difficult lives that many students lead. To teachers this pain is not always obvious. After Diane has told her dad that she loves him and appreciates him now that they are getting along much better than they did before, she wipes away tears. She talks directly to him about the hard times that they have experienced over his rules and her reluctance to follow them, even though she knows that she needs them. She thanks him for being a great dad for her and for always being there for her. Later, Diane and I chat and she tells me that PEP has turned her life around. "I don't know what I would have done, if I hadn't gotten into PEP. It saved my life." I ask her what really is different about PEP. "In other parts of school we are competing," she observes, "but in PEP we work together. There is so much love and support between everyone in this program." Diane's analysis points not just to Akamine but to her peers, who are so key in creating and sustaining this pocket of hope.

One hour into the event, Leonardo, whose mom has not arrived, keeps looking toward the door. She finally arrives and is clearly not very happy about being there. He shows her to a table where he and I are sitting, and she barely speaks to him and hardly has any affect at all. When it is their turn to go on stage, she will not look at him as he expresses his love for her. Later Akamine tells me that she has abandoned him and that Leonardo has been taken in by another student's family. Their pain is obvious, but in a small way, she has come through for Leonardo, and he has had an opportunity to express his love and gratitude to his mother.

I speak with a parent who is here for the second year and she tells me that she would not miss this night for anything, because this is one of the few places in the world where she sees the genuine love and appreciation that teens feel for their parents but rarely express. Her first experience at Parent Night left her floating on a high for weeks, she tells me. Hunter points out that returning parents who experienced Parent Night before act like "they're part of the program. They go and mingle with other parents. I think that's how parents end up loving the program. It's word of mouth from other parents." The tears that their parents, parole officers, guardians, or siblings who take care of them share with the students create a feeling of openness in the space that transforms the energy. The students are taking bold steps at opening up new lines of communication with adults that, Akamine later tells me, often transform relations.

Another parent e-mails me later. "It was a very moving evening and an opportunity to renew my appreciation for Amy [Akamine]. It also was an opportunity to be reminded of how lucky my family is. We have certainly had our share of sadnesses, all families do, but I was reminded how resilient people can be." The stories of the students touch everyone and build solidarity among them. Most significantly this parent saw how committed these students are to changing themselves and the world. "Here were some very, very stressed students but they still chose to use their energies to help others. How unselfish is that?" Parent Night opens up an opportunity to raise consciousness on many fronts, not only to educate parents about the work of PEP.

Before the evening ends, the student emcees explain that they want the adults to understand the collaborative way that the PEP Posse works together, and thus, they are throwing out a challenge for adults and students to work together on a group project. Groups are arranged so that everyone meets new people. Each group is given a card that prompts them to create a community visually on a large poster board with magic markers. The project demands careful listening, cooperation, planning, leadership, and support—skills that the students are very good with but not necessarily the adults. It is impressive to watch the students attempt to bring their skills to bear on the group. After all of the groups have completed their tasks, they one by one go up on stage to do a show and tell about their project and how they completed it. Although the presentations tend to be filled with good humor and laughter, the challenge clearly provokes the adults to think about the dynamics of their group.

The intensity of the emotion of this night and the instructive quality of the group interaction create enormous goodwill. At the end of the night, the students honor Akamine and each one presents her with a *lei* until she is barely able to see out of the ring of them around her neck and face. She removes some of them momentarily to address the parents and tell them how much she enjoys working with their children and how proud of them they ought to be. Ironically, she has to tell them that if what they have experienced this night makes them feel enthusiastic about PEP, she would appreciate it if they would contact their state legislators because in the new budget, PEP has been eliminated for the third year in a row. The irony of this seems just too perfect. What has clearly raised hope for everyone in the room about what happens in school is an endangered program.

DEMOCRATIC PRACTICE

Going to the Legislature
PEP, originally funded by both the Department of Education (DOE) and the Department of Health (DOH), often becomes a political football around the time of budget cutting. In Hawai'i, the legislature acts as the school committee for the state, funding programs recommended by DOE and DOH that it deems worthy. Over the four years that I followed the program, beginning in 1995, PEP lost and then regained and then eventually lost DOH funding. Each year the program struggles through lobbying to maintain its presence in the schools with DOE funding.

In 1998, at Parent Night, when Akamine announced that the DOE had cut the funding for PEP because the legislature had not given DOE enough funding, a few students and parents knew what they had to do. As one parent said, "PEP had been down this road before so when they called out the troops—the troops came. Several schools with PEP programs brought advisers, students, and a very small handful of parents to testify before the legislature." That they gathered on a Saturday to save PEP funding indicates their level of commitment.

Akamine's advice to the students when they went to the legislature was "speak from your heart. Just be honest. Tell them what you think about this program." She later speaks proudly about their eloquence in testifying, "They did well. They really did because it's a belief they had. They realized how important it is to make your view known and they are willing to do anything to help save the program."

Jasmine, a ninth grader and first-time lobbyist, recalls her experience. "I remember toward the middle of the school year, when the Peer Education

Program's existence was being threatened that we all had to go down to the state capital to give testimony about why we think PEP should be kept. All the adults listened to us and took to heart what we had to say." Jasmine thinks about what she said and then adds, "Just by the way that they listened so intently to us, proved that we were making a difference. That was the difference that we as peer educators have the ability to make."

Although the committed parents who showed up at the legislature understood more of the political machinations of the funding, Jasmine and the other students took some important first steps in the democratic process in the larger community. Students whose power-from-within has been nurtured in a program like PEP find it possible to go to the Legislature to testify and lobby—an important lesson in democratic practice that few people ever learn in this democracy. Confronting those in power, even our elected representatives, is a daunting challenge for the large majority of U.S. citizens. This is not what democracy should look like.

The Politics of Education

PEP survives because of persistent lobbying by students. Administrators, teachers, and parents have played their roles, but the students' impact has been the most dramatic, making the news each year. Akamine and the PEP teachers in the 26 programs statewide can rest assured that their students "have a belief in the program."

Teachers and students also lobbied for King's statewide Conflict Resolution Program when it was threatened. Twice they were successful; then they failed. As Hawai'i faced an economic downturn and revenues dried up, the two-person team at Hawai'i's Department of Education was lost: King's position as State Resource Teacher in Conflict Resolution was eliminated at the same time her supervisor in the program retired. Hunter and Akamine were part of a cadre of students, teachers, and administrators prepared to testify at the legislature to save King's position and the larger Conflict Resolution Program, but budget hearings ended abruptly with a negative vote. Akamine comments, "When Janie lost her job, I thought, 'Oh wow, that's going to be the end of us.'"

But, Akamine explains, King had laid such a firm foundation in terms of all of the training that she had done that mediators and peer educators were empowered to continue her work. The alliances established through the annual statewide conferences as well as through promoting inter-school efforts such as Roosevelt students' training students at Nanakuli remained. Further, the important alliances that she had built in the community, with groups such as the Neighborhood Justice Centers and the Hawai'i Bar Association, assured that when she left her DOE position and returned to a school, the networks were sustained because they had a firm foundation. King, who in five year's time had established or shored up mediation programs in over 80 percent of the intermediate and high schools in the state, remained philosophical about the dismantling of the DOE program. "I always had that thought in mind that I wanted to work myself out of a job. I wanted everybody to learn the process of mediation...give them the seeds...show them how to plant the seeds." Her understanding of power and her overarching desire to help shape democratic school climates make her, according to Akamine, an extraordinary leader and ally.

Nurturing the Grass Roots

With King's return to a high school, one more secondary school now has a program in mediation. At the new King Kekaulike High School in Kula, Maui, where King currently works as a guidance counselor, she is engaged again with peer mediators and in the vanguard with a new National Education Association (NEA) effort to have teachers mediate disputes between teachers. When she attended her first faculty meeting at King Kekaulike, the principal passed on a request from the Student Government for a mediation program at the school. Some of the students requesting the program were from an elementary school where King had previously done the training and assisted in setting up a mediation program.

In November 1998, I observed King's two-day training of 3 faculty and 20 student mediators at King Kekaulike, building trust, honing listening skills, simulating mediations, screening clips of recent examples of conflict in the world and on Maui, and creating the conditions in which students could analyze power relationships and negotiate solutions to conflict. Of course, she screened the videotape made at Roosevelt on mediation. The grass-roots work continues, and King is firmly there, even as she ventures into new cutting edge challenges in conflict resolution among faculty.

King's most recent work with NEA and the Hawai'i State Teachers Association (HSTA) allows her to use her talents to influence the creation of more democratic spaces within schools for teachers. In encouraging teachers to develop their power-from-within in solving grievances among themselves, King is helping to create alliances that will build power-with and it is hoped offer teachers more skills for creating democratic spaces within schools.

In the past few years, Akamine and her students in PEP and King and her mediators from King Kekaulike have been part of a coalition working on the statewide mediation conferences now sponsored by the Hawai'i Bar Association. For King and Akamine building alliances, modeling for students how to share power-with peers, resisting power-over, and nurturing more democratic school climates are a lifelong mission. The grass-roots movement inspired by alliances such as theirs is taking hold every time one of their students has the courage to be an educator of peers, a supporter of other students in need, a mediator for students in crisis, a partner sharing power-with peers, an active participant in our democracy testifying before the legislature, and a teen capable of sharing love, respect, and trust with family and community. In PEP, I found a remarkable group of students engaged in a project that puts feeling, service, and community building at its center. In this program students are developing an inner life, cultivating courage and integrity, and building a capacity for love.

There are always bridges to cross. In crossing them, these students and teachers are changing the world.

CHAPTER 4

Moving from the Field of Terror to the Field of Hope: Project 10 East, a Gay-Straight Alliance

Eileen de los Reyes

> Maybe someday my mom will be able to see me as my friends do: opinionated, verbose, feminist, bookworm, writer, philosopher, actress, and idealist who also happens to have a crush on Melissa Etheridge. Maybe someday she will realize that my lesbianism is just one part of a very complex whole—something that has contributed to my identity and broadened my horizons. Whether or not "someday" ever comes, I know that I have the strength to continue to be who I am. So, on my first day of the fall semester, listen for my contagious laugh and look for the rainbows I wear with pride.
>
> —Joy C., quoted in The Phone Call (1996)

THE MEANING OF SUCCESS

Al Ferreira, the former director of Project 10 East, a gay-straight alliance at Cambridge Rindge and Latin (CRLS) High School in Cambridge, Massachusetts, speaks proudly about his school's fulfilling its mission to create a safe environment for all students. As an example, he tells the story of a young man, Sam, who was a cross dresser. Sam's father, who knew of Project 10 East, decided to send him to CRLS so that he might have at least one good year of high school. After a successful year, Sam made plans to attend the high school prom. Ferreira was concerned because his own schedule would prevent him from attending. He notified the security staff of his concern for Sam's safety. Sam arrived at the prom dressed in a gown and with a male date, but the night went off without a hitch. Not only was Sam not harassed, other students went up to him and commented on his courage to be who he is.

Ferreira describes the prom night as a "flawless" event. He concludes that "when somebody like Sam can be in an urban high school setting, [and] be simply who he is, and have as good a time as everyone else, then we have succeeded at what we are doing."

Principal Edward R. Sarasin points with equal pride to the fact that in one year CRLS welcomed three self-identified transgendered youth who enrolled at the school because they could not survive at their own high schools. During the first visit of one of these youth to Principal Sarasin's office, he tells of reassuring the student, reiterating that "this is your school, you have [the same] rights as everybody else." Without dismissing the difficulties and the constant work required to make CRLS a supportive environment for all students, Sarasin celebrates the arrival of these students, who find in CRLS the only space where they can be accepted and nurtured. Respect for all students, he argues, is the most fundamental value at the school.

How do teachers, students, and allies join in a movement to transform their school? How does Project 10 East provide a pocket of hope—a safe space—for GLBT youth? How are students educated for democracy and social change? This chapter focuses on trying to answer these questions and, in doing so, illuminates a path for other schools that share CRLS's commitment to safety and respect for all students.

For the past four years, I have had the privilege of working with Al Ferreira, students in Project 10 East, members of the project's staff, and Principal Sarasin. I have visited Cambridge Rindge and Latin and Project 10 East's office, joining students and staff in their weekly meetings and interviewing participants. I also accompanied Ferreira and students from Project 10 East to a high school in Massachusetts for a community meeting concerning a new anti-bias curriculum. Ferreira and students from Project 10 East have presented in my courses and, most recently, collaborated with me in a presentation about their project at The Principal's Center, located at the Harvard School of Graduate Education.

THE OUTCOME OF A SCHOOL'S COURAGE

Project 10 East, which was created in 1988, defines its mission as "building bridges between gay, lesbian, bisexual, transgender and straight youth." Organized as a gay-straight alliance, it extends membership to anyone who is interested in ending homophobia and intolerance, regardless of his or her sexual orientation. Two fundamental beliefs propel the organization's work: (1) teaching and learning respect and tolerance are necessary if we are to live in a just society, and (2) alliances across differences are necessary for social transformation. The project advocates for the needs of GLBT youth and provides a structured and safe environment where students can meet; talk about their lives; analyze issues of power, gender, and sexuality, as well as class and race; and develop the leadership skills they need to engage in projects of social change. In addition, Project 10 East works with teachers to help them enhance their curricula to be more sensitive toward all forms of diversity.

By educating student leaders who value respect, safety, and justice, Project 10 East has transformed CRLS into a place where GLBT students—so often marginalized and suicidal during their teen years—know that they are free to explore their identities and express who they are. During their meetings and their free time, Project 10 East members work on a variety of projects, including planning for guest appearances in high school and junior high classes, organizing events such as National Coming Out Day, preparing presentations for conferences, and organizing around political issues from gay rights to the death penalty.

In 1997, Project 10 East at CRLS created a second, community-based, nonprofit organization called Project 10 East, Inc., which serves the needs of homeless GLBT youth and replicates the work of Project 10 East at other area high schools. Although it remains closely connected to the gay-straight alliance at Cambridge Rindge and Latin, Project 10 East, Inc. is a separate organization.

The research for this chapter took place at CRLS from 1995 to 1999 and primarily focused on the work of Al Ferreira, the founder and, for 10 years, the director of CRLS's gay-straight alliance. During the period in which this research took place, the staff included not only Ferreira, but also co-director Chris Markowski, communications specialist Jay Laird, and Cambridge Public School System parent liaison Emmy Howe. In part the larger staff became necessary because of Ferreira's national reputation, which took him all across the country to speak about the necessity of creating safe schools for GLBT youth. Ferreira has been honored with numerous awards, including the Anti-Defamation League's World of Differences Teacher Incentive Award and the city of Cambridge's Peace and Justice Award.

In 1997, Ferreira had a heart attack, which forced him to take much of the year off from school. It is a testament to Ferreira's success as a democratic leader that Markowski, Laird, and Howe were able to sustain the project in his absence. After attempting to return to work with a less stressful schedule, Ferreira left the director's position in 1998 and became the chair of the CRLS Art Department. Jay Laird is now director of CRLS's Project 10 East and Markowski is executive director of Project 10 East, Inc.

Project 10 East has evolved from its early days as a support group for high school youth to a respected and influential organization. The journey has required the courage and vision of adults and teens who, believing in equality, justice, and dignity, committed themselves to creating a safer world for future generations of GLBT youth.

From Personal Courage to Collective Action

Planting the seeds that grew into Project 10 East took immense courage, because it required individuals to break their silence and take the risk of "coming out." At the time, there were no legal protections for gay teachers, who had long lived with the fear of being fired for revealing their sexual identity. Students, too, hid any interest in same-sex relationships, knowing that homosexual desire was an invitation to harassment and abuse.

The first steps were taken by a student who reported that he had heard a teacher make homophobic comments about the only "out" gay teacher at CRLS, Arthur Lipkin. The student respected and admired Lipkin and was distressed by the disrespect inherent in the straight teacher's remarks. Lipkin had the courage to take the issue all the way to the school superintendent. Asked what he thought would be an appropriate remedy, Lipkin requested that CRLS faculty and staff be required to attend a meeting that focused on the situation for GLBT youth and teachers at the school. Lipkin also suggested a more extensive series of voluntary workshops for those who would like to explore the subject more thoroughly. The student's decision to take action— to report the homophobic comment—as well as Lipkin's decision to ask for schoolwide education rather than disciplinary measures against the offending colleague moved CRLS closer to becoming a safe school.

Prior to the incident, a support group for gay teachers, organized by Lipkin, was already meeting after school. The offensive remarks against Lipkin galvanized the group into action. The workshops provided the vehicle for these teachers to take the lead in transforming the school. Lipkin left CRLS in 1988, but it was his willingness to take the risk of challenging homophobia that provided the impetus for Project 10 East.

Around the same time that Lipkin challenged the homophobia of his CRLS colleagues, Ferreira, a much-loved photography teacher who had himself graduated from CRLS, heard about the suicide of a former CRLS football star who had recently won a scholarship to the college of his choice. The suicide of this bright, athletic young man, who according to Ferreira believed he was the only gay teen among CRLS's 2,000 students, pushed Ferreira to embark on a personal journey that would take him from fear of exposure as a gay teacher to political and collective action. Concluding that his silence contributed to this student's isolation and death, Ferreira decided that he either would come out or would quit teaching. He could no longer collude with a system that caused enormous pain to other gay and lesbian faculty and students. Finding his inner strength—his power-from-within—Ferreira chose to struggle for the rights of GLBT teachers and students to be safe and respected.

Sarasin supported Ferreira's decision to come out. Thinking that it would be less painful, Ferreira decided to use the opportunity of the mandatory training for faculty and staff to reveal his sexual identity. His story moved many of those present to begin examining their own actions. But this same meeting reminded him that, for some, his coming out of silence would never be acceptable. The refusal of a teacher to get on an elevator with him foreshadowed the painful journey he had chosen to undertake. That relatively small slight from a colleague was followed by death threats as Ferreira became more public as a gay teacher supporting GLBT students. Ferreira describes these days as "a field of terror" and his work as "life threatening." But his commitment to his students sustained and inspired him in his journey from silence to action.

By challenging the beliefs and values of their institution, the student who made the initial complaint and Lipkin, Ferreira, and Sarasin opened up the space at CRLS to consider the plight of GLBT students and faculty, who lived in daily fear of exposure. Through their courageous actions, these four individuals invited others to take up the struggle to create a safe place for GLBT teens both within and outside the school.

Paving the Way with the Help of Allies

By coming out, Ferreira created a safe space for his students to come out as well. Recognizing the need for a more formal support system, he suggested that they schedule a regular meeting time. With Sarasin's support, the group began meeting every other week.

One of Ferreira's first actions was to take students to Harvard to hear Virginia Uribe, founder and director of Project 10, a dropout prevention program for gay and lesbian teens at Fairfax High School in the Los Angeles Unified School District. Virginia Uribe's program provided a model that Ferreira and his students could consider in creating their "safe school." After the presentation, they were so excited about what they had heard that they asked Uribe whether it would be possible to call their group Project 10 East.

Using the Project 10 model and claiming the name gave the CRLS group a broader vision. They could collaborate with other schools in creating similar projects that would support GLBT youth around the country. Ferreira describes their dream of a network of projects that would be like "a railroad…[that] would meet in the middle of the country and shake hands with the support systems and schools interconnecting [across] the United States."

Each year, Project 10 East in Massachusetts and Project 10 in California get closer to transforming this dream into reality as more schools look to them for guidance in creating their own gay-straight alliances.

During this initial phase, Ferreira also paid a visit to Kevin Jennings, an openly gay teacher and activist at a private high school in nearby Concord, Massachusetts. Jennings confirmed Ferreira's idea that creating a gay-straight alliance would eliminate the additional burden for adolescents of having to identify their sexual orientation in order to become involved in the project. As a result of the conversation between Jennings and Ferreira, Ferreira and his students defined Project 10 East as a safe space for all young people, regardless of their sexual orientation.

Both Uribe and Jennings, by sharing their experiences and knowledge with CRLS, played key roles in the creation of Project 10 East. In forming the alliance, the three teachers strengthened their shared commitment to safety and respect in schools and established the groundwork for future collaborations. This provided a strong foundation on which to build Project 10 East.

In addition to external allies, Ferreira needed allies within the school system who would support his work by taking concrete actions that would make it possible for him to dedicate his time to creating a safe place for GLBT students. Initially, he planned to continue teaching while working with students to organize the project, but the project demanded all of his time, energy, and focus. He asked for a reduced teaching load, and, in a show of support, Cambridge School Superintendent Mary Lou McGrath and Principal Sarasin agreed. But Ferreira says it was still too much: "I was down to one class and I was going to the class not prepared." In addition to teaching his one class, Ferreira was preparing and conducting workshops, providing faculty support for the new student organization, responding to students' crises, and doing home visits. Once more, the superintendent and the principal signaled their commitment to the project. In 1993, Ferreira became the full-time director of Project 10 East.

CREATING A "COMPLETE FREE ZONE" IN AN UNSAFE SOCIETY

Project 10 East is a safe haven within the safe haven of CRLS. While many pockets of hope struggle to survive within hostile institutions, the administration of CRLS has supported this pocket of hope since its inception. Principal Sarasin is clear that CRLS should be a place where all students are able to learn. He explains that he sees CRLS as "the students' safe haven," where students should feel protected and respected.

Creating a safe, supportive, and comfortable environment for students from dozens of different countries, speaking 35 languages, representing all races, sexualities, and abilities, isn't easy for the administrators and teachers of CRLS. Sarasin describes his vision of a successful school as one where the differences in each individual student are respected. He sees CRLS as a "giant mosaic [with] these 2,000 pieces and they are all different. But you've got to match it just right and if you [do], you have this beautiful mosaic." When the problems faced by GLBT teachers and students were brought to Sarasin's attention, he followed two fundamental principles: students should be able to feel safe in their school and everyone should be treated with respect.

Although the administration has demonstrated a strong commitment to ensuring the safety of all students at CRLS, the school still operates within a larger heterosexist and homophobic social context. During my first visit to CRLS, I was immediately struck by the contradiction between the school's commitment to creating a safe community and the unsafe society in which it is situated. As I was about to enter the school to interview students in Project 10 East, I overheard a group of students speaking with each other. Away from the watchful eyes of teachers and administrators, the mood was relaxed and friendly. Jokingly, one student said to another, "Oh, don't be such a faggot." The word "faggot" did not seem to anger anyone, or if it did, no one said anything. Mulling over the casualness with which these students expressed their homophobia, I entered the school, registered to visit with the students, and, eventually, after a few wrong turns, found my way to the Project 10 East office.

Countering Institutional Definitions of Time and Space

As I crossed the threshold into the Project 10 East space, I was overwhelmed by the lavender color of the room, which was so deep that it looked like black raspberry ice cream. The room was crowded with photographs of families, posters, books, a computer, a desk, a refrigerator, and a small table and chairs. It felt more like the family room at an old friend's house than any classroom I had ever been in. When students started arriving, book bags seemed to sprout everywhere. The space, which used to be a storage room, was overcrowded, but the interactions, the laughter, and the conversations confirmed my sense that the occupants considered this space their home.

For Ferreira "symbols of affirmation" are very important; he believes that in the United States countless practices celebrate "who we are and the culture we're from." He admits that this is the reason he has "gone overboard in painting the furniture in the office and the door." Understanding the significance of the space, Ferreira focuses on ensuring that every detail in the room from the art to the furniture conveys the message of inclusion, respect, and recognition. The transformation of the space into a community begins with the visible and proud acknowledgment of GLBT students' presence in the world.

Students at Project 10 East connect their space to the learning process. Asked, "How would you describe Project 10 East?" a student explains,

> Well there's the space. There's a room where anyone can come and people come and hang out…. It's like a little community; there's pictures up on the walls and we have meetings and…anyone else?

Other students respond to her request for more details, adding, "It's a place you can go and talk about whatever you might wish to talk about and have people give you input on the subject." Two students comment that they have a library, and they can "ask people questions and talk and find out more about things."

Students in Project 10 East talk to each other about sexuality, violence, fear, relationships with family and friends, dances, and dates. The range of their concerns and ideas can be found in the project's scrapbook, which since 1997 has offered students a place to write, draw, and respond to other students' comments. For example, a student writes, "I told my mother last night that I was never going to school, ever again, too bad I am here. Why are people so mean?" Another student chooses to motivate her peers to find strength in who they are: "Gay is A-OK. Work hard. Be yourself. Do the right thing." The multiplicity of voices, feelings, and dreams constitute Project 10 East's "little community."

Ferreira believes a strong learning community is one that recognizes the students' humanity, giving them the time to relax, learn, and enjoy each other's company. He observes that students are subject to an "inhumane schedule," which asks that they move from one class to the next in three and a half minutes. Depending on where they are in the building, students may not have time to go to their lockers, which means that they carry around books for all of their classes. Lunch, a time where students could relax, is a 20 minute rush to get in and out of the cafeteria. If students have jobs or after-school activities, the "run" continues until they go home late in the evening to do their homework.

Entering and leaving Project 10 East resembles getting on and off a conveyor belt. Outside in the hallways students are always moving as quickly as they can; once they cross through the doorway and get off the conveyor belt, the pace changes and the demands to be constantly moving stop. The homelike space seems to operate "outside time," providing students a chance to relax, sit, eat, and have conversations. The result is that students are "hanging out" all the time, even when they are not in scheduled meetings. When they need to get off the fast track, they know where to go. A pocket of hope, Project 10 East provides a comfortable and safe place for students to discover themselves and build a learning community.

Moving from the Margin to the Center

In 1997, students need to adjust to moving from their safe "home space" into a more central location. Ferreira knew that as long as they remained in the small lavender-colored storage closet, they would continue having difficulty making Project 10 East known across CRLS. Divided into five separate schools, CRLS doesn't easily sustain schoolwide organizations. Students from one school rarely cross the boundaries into other schools, and most identify more with their school-within-a-school than with CRLS. As Ferreira describes it, "We're tiny little villages living separate realities and nobody knows what the other people are doing." Ferreira worked hard over many years to ensure that all students, regardless of their school, felt welcome at Project 10 East. Nonetheless, he explains that a move to a larger, more central location made a difference, opening up the door to students passing through the school's main corridor. He reports that "[t]his is the first year I've had students I've never met before come in and ask questions about gay and lesbian civil rights issues. They're doing papers and research in their classes, so I think they're beginning to see it as a resource center."

The move, which Ferreira welcomed, was not easy to accept for some students, who felt threatened by the more central and visible location. Ferreira explains that initially a student asked whether they could close the door, to which he responded that he wanted to have an "open-door" policy. But Ferreira agreed to close the door until this student felt more comfortable. Eventually, he notes, "instead of [this student] coming in the room and hiding over here—not hiding but moving away from the entrance of the door—she now is willing to have a conversation with me right in the doorway or out in the corridor."

The new space, although more central, is no less unique than the lavender-colored storage closet. Painted yellow like the hallways outside, the space still reflects and celebrates the students. The most important piece of furniture in the room is the large round table in the middle of the space, on which brownies or cake sent by Ferreira's partner often sit, waiting to be consumed. Everyone who enters the room converges at the table, where someone always seems to be sitting and speaking with either Ferreira or other students.

Although eight students can sit comfortably around the table, I have been in meetings where two circles of students have sat around the table. When more students show up for meetings, the group moves to a larger space, but the "center of operations" continues to be the yellow home space. Here, students prepare to share, with anyone who is interested, their understanding of how to create a more caring and nurturing teaching and learning environment within a school context that is often structured in dehumanizing ways.

A "Complete Free Zone"

The homelike atmosphere of the Project 10 East room immediately conveys the message that this is a "safe haven," a place where students will not hear what I heard as I was coming into the school. Though CRLS is committed to safety for all students, it is a big place. Outside the Project 10 East space, there is no way to guarantee that GLBT students and their allies will not be harassed and abused.

As I interview students that first day, they confirm that what I heard entering the school was not unusual. Erica explains her reaction to "name calling" in and outside the school:

> I just block it out. Whenever people are [saying], "Oh, that's so gay, you faggot," I don't know why, [but] I don't [respond].... Wendy is always like, "Why are you saying that? That's not cool." But I don't do that as much.... It doesn't really feel safe.... Because I hear it a lot, I [think], "Oh yeah, they're not homophobic, they're just insults."

A student writing in the Project 10 East scrapbook explains her recent experience at the school:

> Today I was called a "*little fucking dyke*." What is that? Where is that coming from? That's not what I've known all my life.... It feels strange & foreign & like something that's not supposed to be here. I don't want it here. This is CRLH.

Lucia also comments on the name calling: "A lot of gay students don't feel the school is safe for them, because they're not out and people will say 'fag' all the time." Students are afraid to challenge these comments because it could be interpreted as "coming out." It is not clear to them that speaking out would make them safer; on the contrary, they fear that it might further endanger their well-being. As a result, they endure the demeaning and insulting words and accept that at their school, as in the larger society, they must be careful to protect themselves.

Referring to the compromises students make every day, a male student explains how some spaces and classes are safer than others:

> The whole school feels pretty safe in general. I feel less safe in the locker room, I think. In one class, it was just very easy to see homophobia; I watch what I say pretty much. But I feel generally confident about not getting attacked anywhere, myself. Most of the time, people who are homophobic are a minority, at least in my classes.

That a student thinks about whether or not he will be abused in this manner reflects the day-to-day fear and vulnerability that characterize GLBT students' lives. Feeling "less safe" in some places, this student watches what he says and feels "generally confident" that he won't be attacked. He seems to have reached a compromise with the school and his peers, in which he accepts that he will never be completely without fear. The school offers a level of "limited safety" within which he can function. This student contrasts the "limited safety" of CRLS to Project 10 East, when he says: "I think...here it's great because it's a complete free zone. We're even encouraged to talk about this."

In Project 10 East, students sense that they have a "complete free zone"— an empowerment zone—where they can be themselves and speak about their concerns and fears without compromising their safety. No longer on the defensive, these students, guided by their teacher, use dialogue to begin to analyze power and powerlessness in their lives, envision alternatives for teaching and learning, and imagine new possibilities for a more just school and society. Project 10 East, thus, emerges as a pocket of hope that sustains a vision of psychological well-being, acceptance, and justice that is often elusive in the larger world.

THE POWER OF DIALOGUE

Creating a Safe Space for Dialogue

Ferreira argues that to address issues of homophobia, racism, sexism, and classism, teens need to engage in dialogue in a safe space, a space that welcomes, supports, and celebrates who they are. His deep understanding of the power of dialogue generates the pedagogy that sustains the project. But Ferreira contends that the kind of focused dialogue that takes place at Project

10 East is not necessarily a relaxed, comfortable conversation. As he puts it, "You never lose sight of the fact that everybody has to feel safe. But not everybody has to feel comfortable." He refers to this as "having a dangerous dialogue in a safe place."

Ferreira identifies four things that must be present for difficult dialogues to take place. Participants must (1) accept that they can disagree (2) not be afraid to say anything (3) get away from "political correctness," and (4) be willing to take risks in order to create change. In the final analysis, Ferreira believes that "if all you do is share your hopes, then I think after a while, that becomes a very Pollyanna type of thing. You also need to share your fears and your anxieties and your nightmares."

Ferreira argues that the teacher cannot remain safely distant in these dialogues. If the teacher isn't willing to take risks, the students will refuse as well. According to Ferreira,

> In order for me to see you as somebody that I can have compassion for and sympathy and empathy, then you have to reveal to me something inside of you that I can connect to as a human being and that means vulnerability. If you remain on an intellectual level, then I can dismiss you and shut you up like a television set. The minute you have a face and a personality, a heart, a soul, and a spirit I cannot hurt you anymore. That's why it is important to do that kind of sharing.

An example of Ferreira's willingness to expose his biases and fears so as to teach his students can be seen in a conversation in one of their meetings. Students listen attentively as Ferreira tells them about his recent experience with a Latino group at the school.

> I have to say, I was very anxious going to the Latino group to do a presentation...because I had a lot of stereotypes about that group. I was most concerned about the young men in that group; I anticipated a hostile reception. So I brought a lot of my own cultural baggage to that meeting. Thankfully, they couldn't see the baggage, but I still brought it with me, so the anxiety was internalized.

Ferreira also willingly shares what he learns from these Latino students: "What was amazing about that experience...was that it was the exact opposite of what my anxieties were and every stereotype that was inside of my head was broken." A simple act of kindness moved Ferreira to reconsider his preconceived ideas about young Latino men:

> In fact, when I got a dry mouth from talking, it was a young man who offered to get up and get me a drink. That sort of graciousness and sensitivity to my being uncomfortable was something I would have expected maybe from a young woman but not from a young man.

Through his example, Ferreira shows that meaningful dialogue is possible only when participants are willing to share their fears and anxieties. By allowing himself to be vulnerable, he presents students with an authentic invitation to join the conversation. Because of their willingness to put all they know and feel on the table, they can collectively build a meaningful understanding of "dangerous" topics.

In sharing their stories, Project 10 East members begin to see patterns of discrimination that affect their lives. Individual experience is reconceptualized as a social issue. This provides teens, who are angry and frustrated from dealing with the daily abuse of relentless stereotypes, with the opportunity to regain hope and strength through developing power-with other oppressed youth. As they come to understand how their experiences are shaped by social and political forces, the teens at Project 10 East realize that those forces are subject to change. They have the opportunity, through collective action, to create a better world for themselves.

Sharing Ideas in a Safe Place

Students describe Project 10 East as a place where anyone can come in and join in the conversation. To participate, one only needs to sit at the table. This simple act allows students to speak and to be heard. Even if they come only once, or are unable to show up for an extended period, the group always welcomes every student.

Kareem, who went to Brighton High School in Boston until senior year, when he moved to Cambridge, explains why it is so easy to become part of this community. The story of how he joined the project is similar to other students' stories:

> I knew about Project 10 about a year before I came, because I had a couple of friends who went to Rindge and a couple of friends who were in Project 10. I would hear them talk about it. Then [one day] I was supposed to meet a friend outside of

school, but I heard she was in Project 10, so I went inside the school to look for her. When I showed up in Project 10...I sat down in the meeting and introduced myself, and that's how it all started.

Kareem participates in regular meetings and often represents Project 10 East at conferences and other public presentations. Although, while at Brighton High, Kareem was not a typical Project 10 member, his participation was always welcomed. In fact, the students in Project 10 East are always reaching out to those inside and outside the school who may need Project 10 but either don't know it exists or are afraid to come. Many meetings are dedicated to coming up with ideas for making Project 10 East better known in the school and in the community. This reflects the students' commitment to being inclusive as well as their concern for those who may be alone and scared.

Kareem captures the essence of Project 10 East's mission and pedagogy. He says,

> [Teens] can basically come here and not be judged. They come here and give their opinion and talk about what they're going through without someone talking down to them.... So they can find something in common with someone and that can help the coming out process...make it easier for them.

Students repeat over and over again that everyone is heard and no one is judged. As Joshua explains, "[Y]ou don't have to worry about people saying, 'Oh, that's a stupid idea, why are you saying that?'" Students speak up because they don't have to worry about appearing "smart." Here students know that everyone is invited to participate in the dialogue in whatever way feels comfortable. They can let go of self-protecting defense mechanisms that interfere with learning.

Ferreira understands that students need to find a space where dialogue is encouraged. He explains that the voices of teenagers are often discounted:

> When I listen to what they have to say it affects me really profoundly, but they are acutely aware of the fact that their voices are not heard by the adult community, particularly in the area of sexual orientation and human sexuality. This is an issue on which they are either dismissed or they are preached to. Very

rarely do they have an opportunity to engage in an intelligent dialogue with adults who they respect or care about.

Ferreira firmly believes that students are capable of engaging in intelligent dialogue and making significant contributions to discussions of sexual orientation and human sexuality as well as any other topic they choose. Because of this fundamental belief, everyone sitting around the table feels that his or her contribution is necessary to gaining a deeper understanding of the topic at hand.

Michaela, a longtime member, elaborates on Ferreira's observation that adults do not listen with respect to what teenagers have to say. She argues that teachers are "condescending" to students in spite of the fact that "teenagers are vital to the earth." Clearly, she explains, if adults understood this, they would pay more attention to what teens have to say.

By contrast, Michaela asserts that at Project 10 East, "when we have discussions [and] people say things, they're given the utmost respect and, I think, Al and the adults here, actually listen.... They just really realize that teenagers' viewpoints are important and, sometimes, they'll bring up something that you've never thought about." Michaela acknowledges and welcomes the leadership of the adults, who, by listening carefully, bringing up new ideas, and challenging students to think critically, engage in a teaching and learning process that respects the students' intellect. These teachers receive the utmost respect from their students.

At Project 10 East, teens talk with each other about serious issues that affect their lives and those of other teens. In a discussion about how to ensure that all students feel welcome, the conversation turns to the subject of fear. Everyone listens attentively and speaks with great honesty about his or her own experiences.

> *First Female Student:* I think that's really important that we talk about that [fear]. How do we break that fear down, because I'm sure Jean was anxious about coming in, too.
>
> *Second Female Student:* What's remarkable [is that] Michaela came in the eighth grade. Coming up to the high school is scary enough as it is, never mind coming to a Project 10 East meeting. I think [it] is quite amazing. But [speaking to Michaela] you recognized the need for support and you weren't getting the support that you deserved at the elementary level.
>
> *Third Female:* I was contemplating coming here before, maybe once at the beginning of the year, and I was [thinking], "Why

am I putting this off?" My head was really like a fog bank all year.... I don't remember anything that was going on inside my head the whole year. I finally just made a decision.... I still feel kind of cautious coming in the door because if you look in here, it screams pink triangles at you, through the doorway, but heah.

This conversation on fear is the context the students establish for their ongoing discussion about how to make Project 10 East a welcoming space for all students. They are especially concerned that youth of color may not feel comfortable joining the project. Although some students of color attend meetings regularly, the group revisits the issue often and plans a variety of actions to promote diversity. After some discussion, a student proposes that although they need to continue focusing on making Project 10 East a welcoming space, they could also spend time visiting other student organizations at the school. Ferreira agrees that fear is less of a barrier if they visit other groups, instead of asking individuals to take the risk of coming to the Project 10 space. They decide to establish more formal collaborations with Latino and African American groups in the school, organizing joint activities and sharing resources.

This is by no means the final conversation on this topic. The students settle on a plan for action, but that is only a beginning. In the future, they will revisit the issue and analyze the results of their actions, in order to determine whether, in fact, they are succeeding at their goal of creating an inclusive organization.

The Project 10 scrapbook provides another source for ongoing exchanges between students. Often written exchanges become the source for meetings. For example, a student shares his sense of confusion and his search for answers,

> Being gay is incredibly confusing and sometimes annoying. Many times I feel like I am at a dead end with nowhere to go. I constantly strive for answers about my life, but the answers are not there. Oh, what to do, what to do? Life is hard, especially if you are gay.

Students respond in the next couple of pages. One student provides these words of encouragement and support: "When life gets tough: Be strong; Be Brave; Hang in there; Fight it out; Don't give up." The support the student receives is personal as well as political. Students use words such as "strength" and "courage" to acknowledge what is required from each one of them to confront homophobia. Individual survival, however, is not enough. Homophobia, a topic of ongoing discussion at Project 10 East, moves students to seek justice through action. For example, each year Project 10 students organize a celebration of National Coming Out Day at their school. The event provides them with a public opportunity to celebrate who they are and, through peer education, reclaim for themselves and others respect, dignity, and a safe space at their school.

A student explains in the scrapbook why she is making the personal decision to come out on this day. She also shares her dream of what she would like to see happening in the nation:

> I am going to come out on National Coming Out Day because I would rather people know that I'm openly gay and not have to come out to people individually and make it a big deal. It should be a federal holiday because there are so many gay people in all the fifty states (like it or not) and they should all have a chance to nationally celebrate who they are and what they are proud of about themselves.

As students in Project 10 come to terms with their identities, they learn to embrace their social and political responsibilities. Dialogue inevit-ably moves toward action. As one student explains,

> I think we are here to educate. Unlike racism, gay people are in every family.... Maybe gay people have a responsibility to help others deal with differences.... I am here for the good.

Ferreira participates in all of conversations at Project 10 East—whether about gay bashing, going to the movies, or political action—with equal enthusiasm, always asking questions, explaining his views, and providing room for students to do the same. He understands that constructing a safe space for dialogue is a circular process. Believing that students have important and intelligent insights to contribute to the dialogue, he provides them with the space to speak, listen, and contribute their thoughts. Knowing that Ferreira expects this kind of deep and insightful dialogue, they seize the opportunity and engage in powerful discussions. Every time Ferreira listens to his students, he finds new evidence to support his belief in the power of the students to co-construct knowledge. Contrary to being in the circle of despair, where teachers expect little and students give them just what they expect, Ferreira and his students function in a circle of hope, where high expectations of the power of dialogue and the ability of each member to contribute preserve and nurture the circle.

DISCOVERING POWER-FROM-WITHIN; DEVELOPING POWER WITH OTHERS

Project 10 East embraces students as complete human beings. Their pain, fears, sorrows, what makes them angry or happy, and how they make sense of their lives are at the center of their democratic space and of their dialogue. It is through these conversations, which explore the interlocking nature of oppression and its impact on their lives, that students discover their power-from-within and prepare to engage the world.

Teens recognize that Project 10 East, which provides them with the time and space to discover themselves, is unique. It is a pocket of hope that they must protect, nurture, and sustain for future generations of GLBT and their allies. In order to take on this responsibility, teens must learn how to organize, express dissent, and implement new ideas that strengthen the project. Observing Project 10 East teens engage in this process, I witnessed the birth of strong leaders, ready to take an active role in their community.

Transforming Pain and Fear into a Source of Individual and Collective Power

The message on the answering machine at Project 10 East serves as a reminder that many GLBT students face serious problems with their families, schools, and communities: "If this is an emergency, call...." A list of resources follows. This message reflects a crisis recognized in the 1995 Massachusetts Department of Education report Massachusetts Youth Risk Behavior Survey Results. According to the report, students who describe themselves as gay, lesbian, or bisexual and/or who have had same-sex contact are more likely than their peers to report being threatened and/or involved in violence-related incidents. These included being in a physical fight in the past year (62.3 percent vs. 37.3 percent); not going to school in the past month because of feeling unsafe at school or on the way to school (20.1 percent vs 4.5 percent); being threatened/injured with a weapon at school in the past year (66.7 percent vs 28.8 percent); carrying a weapon in the past month (43.5 percent vs 19.0 percent); attempting suicide in the past year (36.5 percent vs 8.9 percent).

Ferreira receives hundreds of calls from GLBT teens as well as teachers and parents who need help dealing with serious crises and life-threatening situations. Audible from all parts of the room, the answering machine announces that this is a space not only for sharing food, stories, and experiences but also for saving lives.

Joshua explains that at Project 10 East adults and students who can help are always around. "If people have problems [they] can talk to Al or Chris or any of the other students here that they feel comfortable with. And as much as possible, we try to help each other." Lucia is more direct than Joshua and is the only student who ever mentions the issue of suicide: "The way I see it is we're a presence in the school, so if some kid is [thinking], 'Oh my gosh,... I'm attracted to my best friend,' instead of going and hiding in the basement and killing themselves, they say, okay, maybe I'll [go] down to Project 10 and talk to people about it."

The burden of knowing that GLBT youth who do not come to Project 10 East may consider suicide is always hanging in the air—a reminder that Project 10 East is an island of safety floating in a dangerous sea. Inevitably, this sense of danger and impending crisis gives the conversations at Project 10 East a seriousness and urgency rarely evident in other classrooms. Students who are laughing and giggling like typical teenagers transform themselves into very serious young adults when engaged in discussions of the abuse they suffer and the confusion they feel. For some, their relationship with family members is very difficult and painful. Not being able to share who they are and who they dream of becoming saddens and angers them. Forced to lead a double life, these teens arrive at Project 10 East searching for a space where who they are is accepted and celebrated. They find peers who are compassionate and supportive and who understand their experience. Slowly, with the support of Project 10 East, these teens transform their private pain into a source of inner strength as well as collective power.

The feeling of danger and insecurity GLBT youth experience can generate anger and even rage. Ferreira believes these feelings of rage should be part of the dialogue.

> Part of what we've dealt with here [is] rage and anger in the group, and students are quite surprised that I don't automatically throw students out because they have a lot of rage and anger. I just say, "That's part of all of our lives."

Denying students their anger denies the injustice of their situation. Ferreira meets students where they are, even if this means working with those who, in their rage and frustration, may not behave appropriately. Knowing the deep need to be accepted, Ferreira refuses to discard even the most difficult teens. He works patiently with the whole group, engaging everyone in discussion and holding everyone accountable for his or her actions. The objective is to gain the trust of disaffected teens so that they choose to become involved with the project in positive ways.

Students relate a story about three students who were kicked out of a meeting because of their behavior. The adult who took this action was not, at the time, completely familiar with Project 10 East's pedagogy. Students relate this as an example of a low point in their experiences with the project.

One of them explains this was unacceptable because "it had never happened before. No one had ever been kicked out of the meeting. And some of the people didn't come back after that." She makes the point that this was not the project's way of doing things. She also explains that there is a process for involving participants in these kinds of decisions. She says, "I think we were just really mad because [the adult facilitator] didn't ask us at all. She could have…just not done it then and later talked about what was good in a meeting and what wasn't."

Understanding that for some GLBT youth this is the only place they can go to find the support, safety, and the knowledge they need to make sense of their lives, the students are particularly disturbed by this incident. Students point out that this authoritarian approach to education, which is typical in other classrooms, is unacceptable in Project 10 East.

The Power to Act, Dissent, and Contribute

The ways in which Project 10 East encourages democratic participation became even more evident, when, in the course of the research, students, who believed the project was drifting off course, twice organized and presented their grievances. In both cases, students used dialogue as a tool to redirect the path of the project. In the first instance, the students were concerned that too many adults were showing up for their meetings. Kareem explains what happened.

> I guess the problem [students] had with that…was that they felt like they weren't being heard or they felt like they weren't being very involved in Project 10. We had all these volunteers and all these adults doing all this stuff, whereas the students could have done something.

To resolve this problem they "all sat down to have that discussion…so we could write down the problems we were having with Project 10, just to get them out in the clear, in the open, so there wouldn't be any miscommunication." His assessment of the outcome of this meeting is that things are going "fairly well with the adults now. It had to go through a little disorganization at first. I think now it's back on track."

Ferreira views this kind of student organizing as a necessary part of the learning process. When this particular action took place, he says, the process was "very collaborative." He confirms that students are "constantly working on it together and they are very involved in the operation [of the project]." The students' request for change indicates that members of Project 10 East feel they have the right and the responsibility to organize and dissent. In this case, students asked for more participation in the project. I ask Kareem, "You mean to tell me, students wanted more work?" He answers, laughing, "I guess so."

A year and a half after this first action, the students again gather to present their grievances. This time, I am there to interview them, but they are focused on how to present their case. I ask whether I can attend the meeting and they agree, as long as I don't tape the conversation.

Erica comes to the meeting with a written agenda that lists a series of problems they have identified and want to see resolved. The students are also prepared to present possible solutions. For example, students want to post all events in a calendar so that everyone can check what is happening at Project 10 East and plan for upcoming conferences and different social and cultural activities. They recommend that they receive more training to ensure they are doing a good job welcoming new members and conveying the message that this is an inclusive and supportive community. They also request more power to plan and run the meetings, including having a students' steering committee. Finally, they recommend moving the health and human sexuality unit of the CRLS curriculum to take place earlier in the year. As peer leaders, Project 10 East students make guest presentations during this unit, which falls at the very end of the semester; they argue that students would benefit more from this information earlier in the school year.

Ferreira takes notes and comments on each proposal. In some instances, he remarks, "I had thought of that; I am glad you brought it up." In others, he explains that he has never thought of the point in the way they are presenting it. Ferreira summarizes the issue several weeks later during an interview: About the big calendar, he says, "It's true, I carry a small calendar and I couldn't live without that.... They also have very busy lives to plan around." On providing training on creating an inclusive community, he acknowledges that he may have been "a bit too cautious." Through their action, he notes, the students signaled that "they want a solid set of ideas of how to welcome new members." He considers the idea of rotating student facilitators "really good" since it "empowers young people." Finally, he defines a course of action to address the students' recommendation of moving the human sexuality section to earlier in the semester. He will bring this recommendation to the curriculum coordinators in order to begin the process of dialogue.

Reflecting on the same meeting, Michaela explains how students know they were heard:

> We were trying to figure out how to make it better. I know that
> Al really listened to what we said because he has been acting
> upon it, and people have been trying to change what we

thought were problems and they didn't pass it off, [saying], "Yeah, that's a good idea, but we're not really going to do anything about it."

The organizing skills the students demonstrated in developing a list of grievances and making a serious and credible presentation provide a powerful example of students' sharing their power-with each other so as to make positive changes in the world around them. In commenting on their decision to take action, students who participated in this meeting acknowledged that it was a difficult moment, particularly for Erica, who took the lead in presenting the group's grievances. Yet, they pointed to their success: they were able to shift the path of the project so that it would continue to address their needs. Again, the students demanded more work and more participation.

Although many teachers feel that their students don't care to work hard at learning, Project 10 East students appear to love their work, to value the knowledge they gain, and continually to seek new opportunities to participate. What makes these students want to know more, do more, and contribute to what happens in the classroom? As students describe their experiences with and expectations of the educational system, they offer remarkable insights into the kind of teaching and learning that works for them.

An Education for Life

Students, so often thought to be disengaged and sullen, are, in fact, very demanding; they have high expectations concerning how and what teachers teach. Michaela expresses the concern that I have heard countless times from students in Project 10 East and other classrooms: "I don't know if people can ever learn from a school situation how to function in society. I know that I can't. That's not what taught me how to function in society."

Working with Project 10 East, Michaela finds the kind of learning environment that she is looking for. Here students resolve actual problems in "real" time. She feels empowered by the democratic and collaborative teaching and learning process, and thus, like other Project 10 members, she embraces the hard work of ensuring that the project continues to carry out its goals and objectives. She sits on the project's steering committee and often does public presentations for the project.

Students in Project 10 East have advice for their teachers, who they believe have the ability to create empowering and transformative learning environments. Michaela attributes immense power to teachers. According to her, teachers have the power to transform the world, but first they must understand their students:

All the teachers need to realize is that they need to accept their students for who they are and accept that they have other differences in the way that they can learn, the way they survive, and the way that they live in the world. I think the most important thing is teachers putting themselves on the same level as their students, which hardly ever happens. If every teacher could do that, I think it would completely change the world.

Michaela holds out some measure of hope for the potential of education to change the world. All it would take is for teachers really to know their students, to understand how they survive and live in this world. If teachers took the time to know their students and to engage them as equals in the learning process, students would respond. Michaela is quite clear that the democratic classroom, where students make decisions about their education, is the starting point for effective teaching and learning. As she explains, students want two things: respect and an education that is relevant to their lives.

"DO YOU REALIZE WE ARE MAKING HISTORY?"

Project 10 East prepares students to live in the world—as Michaela argues all education should—by giving them the tools they need to become active participants in a democratic society. Rather than shunning the idea of teaching students how to become social activists, Project 10 East embraces the notion that students need to be educated in the practice of democracy and political participation. This understanding of education opens up the doors of the classroom to the school and to the larger society, where students can experience and experiment with ways of living and participating. Ferreira begins the process of educating for social action by modeling for students his vision of what it means to be an effective agent of social change. At CRLS, he works tirelessly to create safe and respectful conditions for all students. Project 10 East students observe, and then join, his efforts. Together, they move beyond the school context to "make history" at the community, state, and national levels.

Modeling Transformative Work at CRLS

As an agent of change at CRLS, Ferreira has paid particular attention to school policies and curricula. By institutionalizing changes in these areas, he believes, Project 10 East can have a long-term and structural impact on the school. Ferreira argues that "when a policy gets established, it is easy to melt the policy into the language of the curriculum and into the language of the bureaucracy or the structure that exists. The result is that it becomes a part of the fabric within the structure." For example, one of the first actions Project 10 East undertook was to change the school policy addressing sexual harassment, which had had the unintended outcome of re-victimizing the victim, who was required to identify why he/she was being harassed. The new policy protects students by giving them control over what they want to disclose.

Project 10 East has had a transformative impact on the school curriculum, as well. Ferreira has actively collaborated with the comprehensive health team and the physical education teachers, assisting them in adding values clarification and stereotyping exercises to the standard curriculum. The objective of these exercises is to get students to focus on how they treat each other and how certain actions may be threatening to others at the school.

To further efforts to create a more inclusive environment, Ferreira and Project 10 East peer leaders visit classes to talk about GLBT issues. The peer leaders lead discussions about homophobia, sexism, racism, and classism in health courses on a regular basis and in other courses when invited to do so. Together with Ferreira, Project 10 East members join in doing the work necessary to making their school safe for all students.

Transforming their school prepares both Ferreira and his students to think about ways to contribute to their communities. They know, because they have experienced it, what it means to bring change to an institution. The hard work necessary, the frustrations, and the joy are part of their daily lives as committed agents of social change.

Moving from the School to the Public Arena

Ferreira's pedagogy moves easily from the classroom to the public arena. Asked to make presentations before a wide variety of local and national audiences, Ferreira tries to take his students along as often as possible. This, too, is part of the teaching and learning process. Ferreira's belief that his students are capable of making intelligent contributions to state and national discussions of sexual orientation and sexuality shines through. As in his practice in Project 10 East, Ferreira creates the conditions for meaningful dialogue by sharing his own experience. In allowing himself to be vulnerable, Ferreira presents the students and the audience with an authentic invitation to join the dialogue.

I have observed Project 10 East make several public presentations. Sometimes audiences have been receptive and other times hostile. Always Ferreira has taken the lead, opening the discussion with a short introduction about who they are and the goals of the presentation. At a presentation in front of an angry high school audience in Massachusetts, I noted that the students from Project 10 East, Lucia and Noah, were unusually quiet. This high school was considering introducing a new antibias curriculum that many of the town's residents found objectionable. The superintendent had invited Project 10 East to share their experiences in order to provide the community with a better understanding of what it means to create a safe school environment for all students. The high school students, upset that they had been ignored in the pitched battle between parents and the school administration, were not ready to hear from Project 10 East.

Ferreira positioned himself slightly in front of Noah and Lucia but in a manner that allowed him to keep an eye on his two students to see whether and when they wanted to intervene. Noah and Lucia took their time. When they finally chose to speak, they did so eloquently and with great dignity. After Noah and Lucia finished, Ferreira asked for questions and took the responsibility for answering them. Noah and Lucia understood that if they took the initiative to answer, Ferreira would immediately yield the floor to them. During this particular presentation, Ferreira showed through his physical location, the way he took questions, and how he closed the session that he was very much in control of the process. By creating this space of safety and respect for Noah and Lucia, Ferreira ensured that his students had the choice of speaking or remaining silent, taking or avoiding the risk.

After this public presentation, Ferreira, Lucia, and Noah were scheduled to have a press conference with local newspapers and parents. This discussion was even more tense as adults took the floor to express their frustrations and disagreements. Ferreira was brilliant in his efforts to continue the process of building bridges and creating alliances. Eventually, Noah and Lucia took over the presentation, answering questions themselves and pointing out the importance of Project 10 East in their lives and what it meant for them to have a safe school. At the end of the conference, Noah and Lucia had emerged as powerful voices in the debate.

One parent of an elementary school child was very upset about the possibility of presenting families with two fathers or two mothers as "normal" to elementary school children. She believed that this was a violation of her rights as a mother and argued that it was her sole responsibility to teach this topic when she felt it was necessary. The responses that Lucia, Noah, and Ferreira gave did not satisfy her and she continued to be visibly upset. Instead of feeling that their work was done at the end of the press conference, Lucia sought out this mother and sat down with her to continue the conversation. Lucia's commitment to the process of dialogue was strong enough to weather the most intense and antagonistic discussion. The mother, recognizing Lucia's courage and conviction, sat with her, listening, speaking, and trying to make sense of such a profound point of disagreement.

Referring to their participation in these presentations, students are very proud to explain that "Al never tells us what to say." Knowing that Ferreira trusts their ability to have a public dialogue and will honor their opinions, the students speak honestly and openly. The presentation becomes a collaborative event. As in the classroom, teacher and students engage in the creation of transformative knowledge, which, in this case, they share with the audience. The trust, respect, and love they have for each other are palpable, making their presentations all the more powerful.

Ferreira could easily occupy center stage during these presentations. His personal narrative inevitably captures the attention of his audience. Yet he always finds a way to create the space for students to speak, while he gracefully moves to the background. Each one of these students becomes a powerful teacher and visionary leader who, like Noah and Lucia, is willing and able to take the risks necessary to create a safer world for GLBT youth.

Enlarging the Circle of Safety

The most powerful example of Project 10 East's success was their participation in the Governor's Commission on Gay and Lesbian Youth. The commission recommended and eventually successfully lobbied for an antidiscrimination bill protecting the rights of Massachusetts gay and lesbian students. Bill No. H3353 Chapter 282, which passed the legislature on December 10, 1993, is the first of its kind in the nation. Backed by a set of recommendations from the state's Board of Education and the Massachusetts Department of Education Safe Schools Program, the bill encourages school districts to establish policies that protect gay and lesbian students from harassment, to educate staff about gay and lesbian issues, to offer in-school clubs for gay and lesbian students, and to provide support for their parents and friends.

Ferreira recalls a moment in the long process of lobbying for this bill that helped him realize what this kind of action means for Project 10 East students:

> I didn't fully realize the power of the experience until [I saw] that poster up there advertising the new civil rights law.... There is a young woman hiding behind the two women on the left. She was a Cambridge Rindge and Latin student, a young lesbian whose mother said, "If you come out as a lesbian, your grandfather is not going to pay for your college education. So if you want your college education paid for, you better stay in the closet. So she stayed in the closet but she refused not to be an activist.... At one point she said to me, "Do you realize we are

making history?" I hadn't thought of how powerful it is for those young people who have been involved in changing a state law and who will be able to look back and say, "I helped change the direction."

In this moment a student recognized that history is for the making: it is not fixed, finished, or immobile. The student experienced her ability to change the law and, in doing so, to transform public education in the state. Importantly, the student crystallized for Ferreira the importance of this kind of active community engagement, which he now views as fundamental to the students' classroom and school experience.

Ferreira believes in the importance of community activism, but he is careful not to define what these activities should be for the students. Each generation of students shares the legacy of past successes but is encouraged to define the project and their activities in their own terms. Ferreira begins each year by creating what he calls a new knowledge base because, he argues, "Every year new students arrive with their own experiences, knowledge, and dreams." Contributing his own experiences and understanding, Ferreira listens intently to his students, and together they define the field of action for the coming year.

Lucia explains how her generation of students decided that Project 10 East should participate in rallies against the death penalty. Together with a group of friends, they decided to bring the Project 10 East banner and hang it up at a rally so that "people...connect us with other things." Their picture with the banner made the local newspaper. Ferreira celebrated their initiative. He points out, "There are times when [we] can take our collective voice to other issues."

Ferreira's emphasis on democracy in the classroom and collaborative learning should not be misinterpreted. His refusal to take center stage does not mean he abdicates his leadership role. Without Ferreira's careful direction, the students could be flailing about without the tools necessary to engage in the difficult and new practice of democracy. Ferreira has intentionally and methodically created the space where students can collaborate in the construction of knowledge that will allow them to engage in transformative actions. Feeling confident that Ferreira is capable of charting a path, of guiding them with questions and answers, of changing policies and direction, of advocating for them at the school, students occupy the space and rise to the occasion. As they become capable leaders who have the skills, knowledge, and vision necessary to plan and take action they begin the long-term challenge of carrying on the struggle for justice into the 21st century.

CONCLUSION

Schools such as CRLS, which define their mission as creating a welcoming, safe, and respectful learning community for all their students, should be recognized for their commitment to the well-being of our youth. The story of Project 10 East also illustrates that it takes tremendous commitment, of administrators, teachers, and students, to overcome obstacles and transform a school.

Many factors have contributed to Project 10 East's success. The project was blessed with the extraordinary leadership of Al Ferreira, who contributed courage, vision, and a commitment to democratic pedagogy. Ferreira understood the importance of building alliances that gave him the personal and institutional strength necessary to bring about transformative change. He also understood that a gay-straight alliance would provide both a safe place for students to explore their sexuality and a stronger voice for change within CRLS. Most important, Ferreira knew that students needed a place where they could share their thoughts, feelings, and secrets with adults and peers who would listen respectfully and provide support. By providing a safe space for "difficult dialogues," Ferreira opened up enormous possibilities for students at CRLS. In cultivating student leadership skills, he nourished a new generation of student activists ready and able to become full participants in a democratic society.

Project 10 East grew into a truly transformative project because of the tremendous support Ferreira received from the superintendent of schools, Mary Lou McGrath, and CRLS's principal, Edward Sarasin. Institutional support helped to sustain this pocket of hope and allowed the project to focus on its goals rather than the struggle to survive. The administrators and teachers who embraced Ferreira's vision and changed policies and curricula to reflect the school's diversity have ensured that what could have been a momentary response to an "unfortunate" incident has become a proud legacy for future generations of teachers and students.

In this pocket of hope, GLBT teens who experience verbal and physical abuse on a daily basis find safety, respect, time, and space to discover their power-from-within. They are joined by allies who believe so strongly in justice that they are willing to risk harassment for associating with "queers." All of these teens deserve credit for their courage. Crossing the threshold into Project 10 East takes strength, determination, and hope in a society in which the hatred of gays and lesbians is still condoned by institutional silence and inaction. Teens in Project 10 East model for adults who may still be comfortable in their silence what it means to stand up for justice.

Project 10 East provides a "home space"—what the teens call a "complete free zone"—where members can "simply be teenagers." Typically, there are laughter, fun, food, and joy in being together and talking about things that matter. The lives of the teens are at the center of the project's content and pedagogy. Teens gather to make sense of their world and to dream about their futures. They gather to get an education about and for life.

The primary mode of teaching in this pocket of hope is dialogue. Teens engage in discussions that are serious and sustained about issues that matter to them. Why are GLBT youth harassed? Why are teenagers so afraid to challenge strict gender roles? What do I do if my family rejects me because I'm queer? How do homophobia, racism, sexism affect our lives, opportunities, and dreams? How can students help teachers educate other students about GLBT issues? What do we need to do to organize the next dance? All these questions are discussed in an environment that encourages difficult dialogue about issues that usually remain hidden in a culture where silence about GLBT issues is tolerated, even encouraged.

Project 10 East members educate themselves about issues of gender, sexuality, sexual orientation, as well as other forms of oppression such as those related to race and class. This requires that teens listen with respect and compassion to each other's stories. When they understand that others are listening to them they reciprocate by giving their undivided attention to their peers. As they begin to see commonalties in their experiences, they develop insights into the structures of oppression that affect their lives. They make well-thought-out contributions to the discussion and prepare to take action in the public arena. They begin by educating other teens in their school, but soon they are ready to engage in struggles for social justice in their communities. Contrary to teens who are detached bystanders in the unfolding drama of the teacher, these high school students request more and more responsibility for defining the direction of their project and fulfilling their objectives. When they feel adults are intruding, they organize to redress the "imbalance in power." They envision themselves as active agents in their own education, an education that they see as preparing them to reshape the world in which they live.

Creating the conditions for this democratic pocket of hope to emerge and blossom has been long and hard. Yet, Ferreira is the first to assert that to teach in this environment of safety, respect, and deep and engaged dialogue is a joy. Functioning in a circle of hope, where high expectations in the power of dialogue and the ability of each member to contribute preserve and nurture the circle, is the dream of any teacher. Seeing his students take the stage and become leaders themselves, creating their own field of action and hope, allows this wise teacher to move to other spaces to create and re-create other pockets of hope. This, too, provides a source of joy and a sense accomplish-ment in a job well done.

CHAPTER 5

Aloha ʻAina

Patricia A. Gozemba

Aloha ʻAina, love for the land, is at the heart of Hawaiian culture. Taking care of the land, which is considered sacred, is an honored spiritual practice. On the 45 square miles of the bomb-scarred island of Kahoʻolawe, and on the once abandoned, trashed, and overgrown seven acres of farm land at Castle High School on the island of Oʻahu, special education students, the largest percentage of whom are Hawaiian, are healing their land, revitalizing their culture, and following dreams of political and personal sovereignty. On their farm, the students have a bold yellow sign proclaiming *"Aloha ʻAina"* over a beautiful emblem of taro plants signifying a return to the roots of their culture. On Kahoʻolawe they see signs of the colonizing U.S. culture that warn of danger from unexploded bombs, missiles, grenades, and mines. In both places, Hawaiian culture sustains them in their search for hope.

Immediately after the bombing of Pearl Harbor in 1941, the U.S. Navy seized the Hawaiian island of Kahoʻolawe to use it as a target for bombing practice. Assurances were offered that it would be returned at war's end. The navy, however, did not honor its promise to the then colonial Territory of Hawaiʻi. Motivated by *aloha ʻaina*, native Hawaiian activists engaged in civil disobedience and occupied Kahoʻolawe, beginning in 1976, to protest the continuing desecration of the island by the military. The constant bombing of the island destroyed its vegetation, turned the higher elevation of the island into hardpan, and, tragically, broke the water table. Goats that remained from a ranch, active until the island was seized by the U.S. Navy in 1941, destroyed whatever vegetation the bombing had not. By 1981, the activists, who then called themselves the PKO, the Protect Kahoʻolawe ʻOhana (family) had won the right in court to have monthly access for religious and cultural purposes, thus bringing periodic respites to the bombing, which would not end until 1991.

On one of the first legal accesses to the island in 1981, Pi'ikea Miyamoto, a native Hawaiian special education science teacher at Castle High School, took one of her students, Gary Reavis. From a boat about 100 yards off the rocky coast of Kaho'olawe, they helped swim in to shore the large *'ohia* logs that would be used to construct a thatched *hale* (building). Eighteen years later the *hale* still stands and Miyamoto, now a respected *kua* (leader), still takes her largely working-class, special education Hawaiian students to heal the island, to learn about their culture, and to test themselves for five days in the unchanged rugged conditions of Kaho'olawe. They still swim in their "luggage" in trash bags and buckets. They form a human chain and pass in the five-gallon water jugs that they each have brought. They camp out and survive, with no electricity and no running water. Having participated in an access, the students automatically become members of PKO.

Miyamoto's students, who work their own farm at school as part of their Plants and Animals of Hawai'i special education science class, understand, perhaps better than many other young members of PKO, the importance of taking care of the land so that it will take care of them. Their taro *lo'i* (irrigated terraces), covering an acre, produce the staple crop for *poi* (pounded taro corms), marking both a political return to the culture's roots and healthy native diet. Their connection to nature is alive and ongoing; it is their love for the land—*aloha 'aina.*

Keawe, a sophomore, when asked to envision a future for Kaho'olawe, reflects with his classmates and Rebekah Luke, a Hawaiian community ally who has been to Kaho'olawe with them many times: "My dream would be to start our own village. This is one area [he points to Hakioawa on a model of the island on the classroom wall]. Can make your own houses or whatever.... We need to know our culture and preserve it because it is dying out. Even if the whole culture dies, you know that at least on one of the islands, the culture is still living." William chimes in, "Two, Ni'ihau [a privately owned island where native Hawaiians continue to speak their language]."

Keawe continues, "You see like what they are doing on Ni'ihau. That's good. You only have so many Hawaiian islands and so many of them are being taken over. You know what I mean. Look at Hawai'i, how much it's overpopulated with so many people. More tourists...." Kaleo pipes up, "Than natives."

Keawe pushes the dream, "Start your own farm. Just like we have done here. We've got all the experience already." His classmates add in turn, "Taro." "Corn." "Pig." Keawe continues, "They [the PKO] have some really smart ideas—like with the check dams and how they can conserve water.

Like that whole system. That's all good ways of conserving the rain. That's the natural environment. We can use the natural environment to help us live. Whatever we have to do." His confidence, based on what he learns in his science class, comes through: "It's almost like doing something with whatever you've got. That's the best way." Significantly, he recognizes the importance of his ʻohana, as he gestures to his peers, "We have all the experience to do this kind of stuff."

Luke challenges the group about whether they could "rough it" for very long. Bronson reminds her that his Hawaiian family is part of a strong native movement and has camped out in protest to have ceded lands returned to Hawaiians. "Yeah, I could. I did it for two months already. Survive on fish. I did it here. Two summers ago up at Makapuʻu. Didn't have fresh water." Kimo adds, "I know a lot of Hawaiians who would do it. Like the kind of people living on welfare. They're living in small houses or they're living at the beach. Plenty people would go there." Donovan continues, "They can just restore their own sanity. They could just grow their own foods and get on their feet."

Luke persists, asking whether they truly have the confidence to do this. Keawe responds that he has confidence that among his classmates in that room there are the knowledge and the desire for the culture and the island to flourish. "The people that I see who are really into the Hawaiian culture and stuff like that are right here in this class.... We did everything. Like we did the two loʻi. Planted some stuff."

Kaleo reminds him that the government has got to "take out all the bombs. Clean it up. Restore the Hawaiian artifacts so that everyone could see what a real Hawaiian island used to look like." When Luke asks, "What do you think made the U.S. government and its allies feel that they could continue to bomb Kahoʻolawe until 1991?" Kaleo responds, "They thought that they were higher than the Hawaiian people."

For Hawaiians, Kahoʻolawe is perhaps the ultimate modern symbol reminding them of how the United States has devastated so much of their culture: a language nearly lost, homes disrupted, people debased, rights to water taken away, fishing rights curtailed, and a land depleted and scarred.

INTRODUCTION

The sustained vision of Miyamoto over nearly 20 years links her special education science program in Plants and Animals of Hawaiʻi and the farm at Castle High School to the Hawaiian community's project on Kahoʻolawe, creating the conditions in which generations of students can forge their own visions of their lives and their culture. Miyamoto, who grew up in a well-known and very accomplished Hawaiian family, models for her students a way of claiming pride in one's culture. *Aloha 'Aina* is a project in which students—many of whom have extremely challenging problems, ranging from learning disabilities to emotional impairment to family issues, to substance abuse problems—are experiencing school, culture, and politics as an integral part of their lives.

Some of these students have parents in jail, are in families who have no stable place to live, and have negative reputations with the vice principals, police, counselors, and, of course, other teachers. Their lack of success in school often fuels their desire to find status through forms of resistance that bring them into conflict with the rules of school and society. Like all young people, they seek direction and approval from whatever sources are available to them and, in this regard, teachers like Miyamoto, who make themselves, their creative energies, and their work available to students, fill an enormous need. Her classroom and the farm have become spaces where students participate with their teacher in shaping an *'ohana*—an extended family—that is there for them even when the school day ends. Students gather at lunch and after school in Miyamoto's classroom and outside on the farm, "safe spaces" they consider their own. A student carved a sign for the classroom that says simply, "Our Place."

This pocket of hope, existing as it does within the confines of the conventional authoritarian high school, offers students the opportunity to participate in experiences aimed at developing their power-from-within. As they become grounded in that power, they learn how to use power-with others, both in the school and in the community. In nurturing aloha 'Aina in her students, Miyamoto continuously nurtures hope even in the face of the ignominy of living in a colonized land.

Like Kaho'olawe the public school system today operates as a legacy of colonialism, largely ignoring Hawaiian culture and Hawaiian ways of knowing and, thus, further oppressing Hawai'i's native people, who make up approximately 20 percent (200,000 people) of the population. Of the 1,600 students at Castle High School, 48 percent are Hawaiian, yet only 4 of the 145-member faculty are Hawaiian. Close to 80 percent of the special education students are Hawaiian, a statistic that speaks to the ineffectiveness of the education offered to the indigenous people. In a land caught up in a joyous Hawaiian cultural renaissance and in a political movement led by Hawaiians seeking self-determination, sovereignty, and nationhood, most of the public schools seem out of step. Mainland U.S.A. models of education dominate. Indeed the Hawaiian epistemologist Manu Aluli Meyer (1998) astutely questions whether it would even be possible within the colonial model of schooling for a Hawaiian way of knowing to flourish. She notes the contradiction of fighting "for a Hawaiian identity in a structure that is set up to assimilate it into a larger hegemonic context" (145). As true as this might be, some people in the public schools, such as Piʻikea Miyamoto, are struggling to imagine, create, and sustain pockets of hope steeped in the values and traditions of Hawaiʻi's indigenous culture.

As a participant-observer over a four-year period in the *Aloha ʻAina* Project, I have sat in on many classroom discussions, gotten into the mud of the *loʻi*, and planted and weeded, picked potatoes, accompanied Miyamoto and her students three times on the rugged trip to Kahoʻolawe, protested at Waiahole over water rights, welcomed voyaging canoes back from their trips to Tahiti, and observed the students as they worked with the adults in an *ʻohana* firmly committed to seeing each of them become a self-actualizing individual. As a *haole* (white person) who has spent a substantial amount of time over 20 years in Hawaiʻi, I am still learning about this culture for which I feel admiration and passion. In interviewing 15 students, each of whom I observed and worked with over at least a two-year period, I came closer to understanding the project from their perspective. As my understanding of pidgin (the Hawaiian creole that they speak among themselves) improved, so did their trust in me as an ally. In comparing interviews conducted by their teacher and separately by a community ally, I checked my perceptions. The essence of the project emerged in multiple ways, but the voices of the students give the most telling testimony of their understanding of education, culture, and politics. I take friends disillusioned and disgruntled about education to the *Aloha ʻAina* Project, and to a person they wonder, as do I, Why wasn't school like this for me?

DREAMING AND BUILDING THE FARM

> To others who have not known fishers and planters it is impossible to convey even a hint of the quality of mind and sensory perception that characterizes the human being whose perpetual rapport with nature from infancy has been unbroken. The sky, sea, and earth, and all in and on them are alive with meaning indelibly impressed upon every fiber of the unconscious as well as the conscious psyche. (Handy and Handy, quoted in Meyer, 1998, 33).

Miyamoto, first a planter and then a fisher, with a "perpetual rapport" with nature, serves both consciously and unconsciously as a force who can show others the wisdom of opening their hearts to nature. As a teacher of over 25 years, "Miya," as the students call her, confronts every educational challenge believing in the power of the natural world to touch and transform people. Some of the worst-behaving and persistently truant students in the school have been turned around (sometimes only temporarily, but that is a start), when given responsibility for baby chickens. Her courses continuously unveil opportunities of hope, connecting her students to a world that is physically outside but very much inside them in a cultural and spiritual way.

Getting the Land and Finding Allies

In the early 1990s, having lost the school's agriculture teacher and besieged by complaints from abutting neighbors about the rundown condition of the overgrown farm, Castle High's principal offered Miyamoto the school's back seven acres as a lab for her science classes. She took up the challenge.

Miyamoto, realizing the advantages that having other adults involved in the *Aloha 'Aina* Project would give the students and her, recruited Rebekah Luke, her high school classmate and a native Hawaiian activist, and Tet-Choi Fung (known to all as Choi), a 73-year-old banana farmer and longtime ally of Hawaiians.

For the three adults, the satisfaction, as Choi describes it, is in seeing "the kids show a little pride in themselves.... And I think with the team [pointing to Miyamoto, Luke, and himself] plugging along with them, we get frustrated occasionally, but I think in the long haul, it is very satisfying." Luke adds, "I think that Choi and I do it a lot to support Pi'i.... Teachers need support.... And it's kind of nice to have community people come in and contribute. I've been honored to participate, if only on the fringes."

The most important part of all of the work that the team engages in is creating the conditions in which the students come to understand who they are as Hawaiians or allies to Hawaiians in the Hawaiian struggle to reclaim their culture and sovereignty. As a Chinese American, Choi's connection with Hawaiian activists like Miyamoto and Luke, serves as a living example of what should be expected in an alliance.

Miyamoto is fortunate in having a strong institutional ally in Vice Principal Beverly Barnard, who concerns herself deeply with making Castle High School more responsive to the large Hawaiian community it serves. The *Aloha 'Aina* Project, she says, is "looking at learning through the Hawaiian lens, a view of agriculture from the perspective of Hawai'i's history or culture." She adds that it is more than an academic program because it involves "caring about others, values, and behavior—so a lot of counseling occurs, as it does in any classroom, but in this setting [it is] more culturally compatible."

Barnard, herself part Cherokee, understands and articulates well the reality of what has happened to the very large Hawaiian population in the area Castle serves. Eight generations of Hawaiians, she says, have been denied water rights in this area and the skills of taro farming and farming in general have been eroded. So Miyamoto's project "is providing an opportunity—not just for those kids, other ones, too—but it means it's there for them, that it's specifically learning taro, and that is so needed in this state." Barnard further underscores the importance of the project, noting, "We're living in Hawaiʻi. This is the culture's home and the learning should be compatible to the culture. To not have this program is unconscionable in my estimation."

Barnard understands well the challenge of the project. "It was difficult to work with some of these kids. Some of them didn't want to get dirty and they're used to doing nothing. Doing something was suddenly very difficult. It was a matter of incorporating Hawaiian cultural values." Significantly, she notes, it also meant recognizing the skills and the cultural understandings that students take with them to school.

The commitment of an administrator such as Barnard makes it possible for this public school to address community needs and aspirations for an education that is not at odds with the culture of the land. Without the critical support of such an administrative ally, this pocket of hope, like many others, would not likely survive.

With allies who share her cultural values and students who learn to dream and make possibilities become realities, Miyamoto has dreams for the farm, for Kahoʻolawe, and for the sovereign nation of Hawaiʻi that are expanding.

Radical Tarorists: Going Back to the Roots

A T-shirt that is popular with the students who often refer to themselves as "Radical Tarorists," has a beautiful design of taro corms clumped together with their majestic leaves upright, nearly the same design that is on the *Aloha ʻAina* sign at the edge of their farm. But the T-shirt also says, "Without One's Roots, One Becomes Ruthless." The wisdom of this slogan resonates with the students and expresses succinctly the imperative of this project: the importance of knowing one's culture and, for those who are not indigenous, knowing the culture of the place in which you live.

The *ʻohana* at Castle feels that psychic and spiritual link with their taro. The students' cultivation of the taro connects them with a movement back to the roots, which is a dynamic metaphor for the cultural and political resurgence of the people. When Brianne, the first girl to join the program and work in the *loʻi*, takes home to her grandma a bag of *poi* made from the taro that she has planted and tended, she cultivates as well a synergy that connects her and her grandma to their Hawaiian roots.

Sione, a male Tongan student, points out to Miyamoto that Hawaiians and Tongans, both Polynesian cultures, share a great deal in common culturally in terms of the way they approach farming. "My father thinks the farm is like a certain part of like church." That cultural philosophy guides the work of *Aloha 'Aina.*

Building the Lo'i. Miyamoto, in her first attempt with her students to build a *lo'i*, ended up getting the tractor stuck in the marshy land near the stream. This crisis confirmed for some of the doubters at the school, unwilling to assist her, the problems she would have in attempting to transform the rundown farm. This defeat, however, was short-lived. Miyamoto and her students had studied together how to build a *lo'i* and they had gone out and talked with experts about what had to be done. They were determined. Miyamoto recruited a part-time teaching assistant, who, happily, had some experience with *lo'i* but, unfortunately, did not have any experience in working in a democratic classroom. Miyamoto recalls that he had a "dictatorial" style of teaching, "never being clear with the students about what his plans were or why they were doing what they were doing." In essence, Miyamoto says that he tried to "use the kids as laborers." Despite the expertise that this assistant teacher gave to the endeavor, a pedagogy such as his could only be short-lived with the Radical Tarorists in the *Aloha 'Aina* Project. With his dismissal, Miyamoto and the students geared up to achieve their goals. Working collaboratively, they came up with solutions, but it was only when Choi joined them and offered his expertise that they successfully built two additional *lo'i.*

Unlike the teaching assistant, who never could try any pedagogy other than one based in using power-over the students, Choi became as resourceful in his ways of teaching as he was in his ways of using all of the resources that were presented to him on the farm. He had to learn how to relate to the 1990s student, and, Miyamoto says, "He had a real hard time because the kids couldn't deal with his non-communicative style. He was into pointing, thinking they could read him and then he'd blow up because they couldn't understand. But then, you know, they came around." But Choi came around, too: "I didn't expect the next person to change and I wouldn't change. That's not fair, that kind of attitude." So Choi changed to relate to the students and keep the reciprocity of teaching and learning alive for all members of the *'ohana.* He listened to their ideas more and presented them with problems, allowing them to use their problem-solving skills in math, science, and agriculture to figure out how they needed to approach building a new *lo'i.*

As they started work on the two *lo'i*, problems cropped up, but Choi felt that they should go ahead and the students should do the troubleshooting and learn from their mistakes. When it became apparent that the levels in the *loʻi* were off, the students suggested calling in the industrial arts teacher to survey it. Sure enough, as Choi suspected and the students learned, there was going to be a problem with water levels and flow. They were, however, fast approaching the night the students had decided that they would plant the new *loʻi*. Miyamoto muses on this particular learning experience: "After months of working on this project, we were impatient, so we let the water in and we could see that it was not right because the ground was too hard.... I was equally as impatient as the kids. And so we just went for it and then we learned that it wasn't the right way." Despite the problem with the *loʻi*, the students' plan to plant at the full moon, as their ancestors did, took precedence.

Students Seize Their Culture. The decision to plant by the full moon, wearing traditional dress, was an enormous cultural leap for the students. Choi and the all-male group of students wore *malo* (loincloths), and Luke and Miyamoto wore *kikepa* (sarongs). The pride was palpable, and, Choi reflects, "If you have that kind of pride, more than likely you're going to be all right."

Word of the ceremonial planting spread throughout the school, and the cultural pride that the students felt dissipated as some of the boys were teased about wearing the *malo*. Kimo says of the teasing: "At first, yeah, we were shamed but after that we just blocked it out." Bronson reasons that his ancestors wore the *malo* as regular clothes and trying to make them feel shame is just an attempt at regulating them. Miyamoto reflects with them: "How are people made to feel ashamed? How did that all come about? Why do we feel shame about our cultural practices?" Keawe answers, "Because we've been Westernized for so long and we haven't had enough experience of doing this Hawaiian culture like wearing *malo* and stuff. This is in our minds, 'Oh well, I look different because everybody is wearing a certain thing and I'm wearing a *malo*. Like I become ashamed because I'm the only one....' But they can laugh all they like because it really doesn't phase me." Kimo, Bronson, and Keawe articulate cultural pride, nurtured in an *ʻohana* where strong cultural mentors play an important role. The resistance that they mount to those who attempt to put down their culture becomes a powerful lesson.

Getting It Right. A short time after the ceremonial planting, the students determined that they really wanted to get the *loʻi* right, and, Keawe recalls, they "stopped the water. Drained it. Dug out some more dirt and filled it again." Choi, in thinking over the whole experience, points out to Miyamoto how impressed he is with what the students eventually accomplished. Comparing the Radical Tarorists to some other students he has observed at the school working half-heartedly on a project for grades, he says to

Miyamoto, "With your kids, it was purely 99 9/10% motivation." He then adds, "Pi'i is motivating them not just to do the work but to change their thinking, to not be self-pitying, to get something done. That's different for them, you know." The Radical Tarorists recognize the difference in how power operates in their 'ohana and acknowledge their motivation. Kaleo says with pride, "You come to Miya and you do more." Richard contrasts this with what happens in another teacher's class. "He doesn't push us. He just says, 'You don't want to do it. Take an F.'" Kaleo confirms Richard's observation of this teacher and notes another characteristic abuse of power that some teachers engage in. "Yeah. Yell at them. Yell. Yell. Yell. Even from the other side of the school."

The 'Ohana: A Hawaiian Style Empowerment Zone Emerges

Understanding the fear that resides in the hearts of many of her special education students as they confront or are confronted by academic work, a teacher like Miyamoto, along with her allies, models important lessons in the positive uses of power. Vested as Miyamoto is with institutional power-over her students, she has the power to create the conditions in which they can banish fear from their hearts. By focusing on creating an empowerment zone within which her students, her allies, and she can develop their power-from-within and share power-with each other and the community outside school, she changes the dynamics of "power as usual" in the school. The students speak of this empowerment zone as an 'ohana. Here they confidently use all of their academic, cultural, and interpersonal skills; work collaboratively with adult and student allies; feel capable of challenging received knowledge; and co-construct knowledge. All of this occurs in a space where students, teachers, and allies do not feel self-conscious about having hearts that are open to each other.

Alliances among the adults model the democratic processes that are at the foundation of this 'ohana. Within this context, the students look to the adults not for all the answers but for a caring, perceptive dialogue that will lead them to their own answers as, for example, in building the lo'i or figuring out how best to grow ti plants or irrigate dry land taro. Luke comments that Miyamoto "told me that she wanted the students to realize that this is an 'ohana. That we are all one 'ohana." She then adds poignantly, "I'd bet that school is probably the center for a lot of students—the one thing that is constant year after year." Then Luke recalls that "when one student ran away from home and his mother didn't know where he was, she knew that every day he'd be in school." "Yeah. She knew he'd be with me," Miyamoto adds. "I got a very nice letter from his mother thanking me for caring about him and taking the time with him." The mother acknowledged how important it was to have "other adults caring about him and taking him here and there."

Love, Respect, and Trust. In creating and sustaining an *ʻohana* among the students in a class, Miyamoto shifts that nexus of power-over and, gradually, as the school year progresses, comes to share more power with the students. She models this with her community allies, Choi and Luke, making palpable her own reliance on others. A circle of love, respect, and trust becomes visible, and the students expand that circle through their work in it. The acknowledgment of what happens is significant. In a conversation with the students about their class, Luke reflects on her own education and remarks that they are lucky to have Miyamoto as their teacher. The students respond, "Yup," "We know," "I know. We love her." This acknowledgment from a very tough looking group of what the school regards as "at-risk" students speaks volumes about the power of a loving relationship in a classroom. Keawe muses about their connections and declares, "It's perfect. A bond between the teacher and the students and...the culture, too."

The love that is shared in this classroom is visible. Brianne says that it's clear that the students care about Miyamoto: it can be observed in "the way that they act towards her. What they do in class. She tries to like everyone and she tries to pay attention to everyone too.... Some teachers don't want to help you but Miya helps us, but she tries to tell us to do it on our own first. She doesn't baby students. She treats them equally." Above all she does not patronize the students. She pushes them, and, as Kaleo observes, "If we just act dumb, then that's what makes her mad." The students know that her challenges are from a place of love and respect.

While some teachers recoil in fear about an open, loving relationship in the classroom setting, Miyamoto demonstrates the ways in which it can inspire the process of teaching and learning. But the love is grounded in respect, Miyamoto says. "My kids respect me, because I respect them. They know that I have fun with them, but they don't go overboard. I mean they don't treat me like some of them treat their own parents." Teachers who do not respect students or the cultural knowledge that they take with them to school miss an enormous opportunity to transform teenage alienation. In Miyamoto's classes, the students feel pride in themselves and in their culture. For example, Richard, a big Hawaiian boy who was very shy, entered the *Aloha ʻAina* Project already knowledgeable about taro and maintaining a *loʻi*. The project became so important to him that he even returned to work there when he was no longer in the class. But he had not always liked working in the *loʻi*: "My dad just dragged me in around the sixth or seventh grade. I never did like working in it. You get muddy, that's why." At school, being in the mud of the *loʻi* took on another whole dimension for Richard. When the dignity and importance of his knowledge and work were honored at school, that affirmed his culture. While many students hate school because it undermines their culture, in Miyamoto's classes students come to prize the knowledge and practices of their families and communities. Ultimately most of these students become more engaged in school.

Miyamoto's students understand clearly why her classes "work" for them and other more traditional classes don't. Al keys in specifically on those all-important first impressions. "When you come to class on the first day and the teacher says, 'We notice your attitude,' they forget that we notice their attitude, too. Students do the same thing." He gives every teacher a chance. "I come in open-minded every first day of school. I do. I don't say nothing. I just watch to see how the teacher acts." The power-over authority that teachers have can be opened up on that first day of school, or it can be established as the controlling force that will serve to replicate an undemocratic way of teaching. Many classrooms are spaces where no love flourishes and a repressive atmosphere prevails. Teddy asserts that there are teachers with a bad attitude who "pick on you all the time." Al agrees and says that students are very keen at sensing those attitudes. "You just know that they don't like you." What neither Al nor Teddy looks for is a permissive atmosphere. They want mutual love and respect.

Al understands why Miyamoto's class works for him. "Well, you know, we got punks in every class. Every class. She don't take nothing from the punks. She shows them who's boss. I think that's bad [good] because after that they respect her and they don't say nothing.... The punks can wreck a class.... She cares about us." Brianne offers advice to how beginning teachers ought to be with students: "Treat them with respect and the students will treat you with respect, too." Miyamoto works from the very beginning of the year to create an 'ohana where nobody, neither student, teacher, nor ally, "can wreck a class" for anyone else. Everybody feels responsible and everybody cares.

Love and respect engender trust. Choi recalls that as a high school student, he had a teacher who trusted him with taking care of their farm when he went away on trips. That kind of responsibility, he feels, was critical in developing his own sense of feeling competent and useful in the community. Al reflects the same attitude about his school experience, 60 years after Choi's, when he assumes responsibility for the project's 1,000-pound pig, Norman; Safi, the pygmy goat; 20 or so chickens; and 5 tanks of fish while Miyamoto is on vacation. With obvious pride, Al recalls, "She trusted me with her pig. She trusts us." Al knows, just as Choi does, that the ultimate in trust is to be given responsibility for plants and animals.

Miyamoto is the open-hearted adult with whom the students talk-story about problems with their girlfriends or boyfriends. They worry about a friend of theirs who is into drugs. They talk about the brushes that they have with the law. They think about the consequences of becoming a parent as a teenager. They share the problems of being in alcoholic families. In short, they can discuss their real lives with a respectful, trusting adult who always engages them in a way that makes it clear to them that she cares about them. These kinds of conversations happen as they work in the *loʻi*, weed on the farm, rest in their little *hale* that shades them from the sun, or spend time in "Our Place" before, during, or after school.

Even after they finish with Miyamoto's class, students like Richard and many others go back to "Our Place" because, as Miyamoto sees it, "There is a close bonding…and there is still an interest in the taro that they planted." Most significantly, there is Miyamoto's unconditional love. Vice Principal Beverly Barnard acknowledges that the students reciprocate the love: "They do. That's all of it in a nutshell, right there. Exactly. They're not afraid of that." She notes, "Piʻi does not go easy on the kids…. There also is a very firm line about what the behavior is to be, but there is always this strand of love and caring that goes through it all…. She doesn't let them get away with stuff…what always comes across in working with the kids is the caring. 'I care about what's going to happen to you. You can't do it this way. You've got to learn to take care of yourself.'" A circle of love, respect, and trust holds this *ʻohana* together.

The Learning Community

Aloha ʻAina is an organic learning community that continually reinvents itself as new students appear each year and, with the guidance of Miyamoto, choose new academic problems to focus on and struggle with. Teaching such as Miyamoto's, focused as it is on a challenge, puts neither her nor the students at the center of the pedagogical practice. Instead it puts collaborative effort in the forefront, as they explore uncharted territory for all of them, replicating what thinking and doing are all about in the real world. The challenge may be a new *loʻi*, the cultivation of native plants, or the design of a landscape.

Al sees what he is learning in this science class as distinctly different from that of other classes that he takes. "This class. Oh, I think it's way better because we can learn real things that you really have to learn to go out in the world." His classmate Teddy interjects, "Not teacher stuff." Al expands on Teddy's critique of the teacher-centered class where the subject matter is of little interest to the students and the pedagogy is culturally incompatible both for special education students and indigenous students: "It's all the time in the books. You know what I mean?"

Choi understands their point. "We all have different learning styles. Some people can learn by doing, others by seeing, or others by listening. If you put all of your senses together, you will learn faster." Miyamoto recalls how she was bored by just listening to lectures and can understand why her students feel the same way about many of their classes in which the lecture method prevails.

Al and Teddy agree that the balance of work on the farm and in the classroom makes their Plants and Animals of Hawai'i course in the *Aloha 'Aina* Project effective. The "book work" becomes relevant when connected to projects on the farm. There they put their classroom knowledge to work in planting crops and nurturing many native plants. Al reflects on the education that he is conceiving and receiving: "I think that other kids would be jealous if they knew what we do. Before I came to this class, I never knew how to do corn or taro, until Miya taught me." Al, who is Portuguese, says that he sees "planting, harvesting, and caring for the land" as spiritual practice, and his friend, Teddy, who is Hawaiian, nods at him in agreement. This project offers students an opportunity to learn the science and culture of the land in which they live.

Finding a balance in activities to keep students engaged is an art practiced by great teachers. When Sione tells Miyamoto, "Your class goes out live," he pays tribute to the spontaneity of it and the organic nature of the relationships between the teacher and her students. But a "live class" compared to a "canned" one that has been rehearsed for years, requires enormous planning by the teacher. Miyamoto speaks to this: "Any time you have a bunch of kids, no matter what kind they are, you have to have a plan...otherwise we'd be sitting under the mango tree talking story every class period." But the kind of plan that a teacher like Miyamoto makes is more like a start to a dialogue. As she describes it, "It is almost always a negotiating session." Allowing the students to negotiate with her opens up democratic practice and holds to a traditional cultural value of respecting those with knowledge whether they are old or young. Learning to negotiate with the teacher, who in most classes holds total power-over them, opens up opportunities for Miyamoto's students to experience another way of power operating in a classroom. It teaches them decision-making skills and hones their ability to express their opinions and argue their points of view.

In assigning areas on the farm to specific students, Miyamoto gives them the independence to dream about what they would like to do with their piece of the *'aina* and then dialogue with her about feasibility. Experiments are always encouraged. On one planting rotation, students decided that "they wanted to plant a variety of crops" rather than the standard one or two. They experimented with this method and, in Miyamoto's words, discovered "it became overwhelming." But a lesson was learned by all of them.

The sense of ownership that students have over particular projects excites them. Brianne, the only girl in the project during one semester, recruited Amber. Although Brianne didn't mind being the only girl working on the farm, she wanted the companionship of another girl. When she and Amber teamed up, they became the most devoted workers in the biggest *loʻi*, and, Brianne says, "That's why Miya calls us 'the taro patch girls,' because that's our taro patch. We're the only two girls who go into the taro patch every day." They, like many other Hawaiians and their allies, are no longer ashamed of working with the soil a process that for many in the working class, in particular, conjures up memories of plantation life. *Aloha ʻAina* opens up the space for these students to practice their culture and connect with their community. The Plants and Animals of Hawaiʻi course becomes a bridge to cultural revolution.

ACTIVISM IN THE COMMUNITY

Miyamoto's genius in promoting alliances and creating an *ʻohana* where love, respect, and trust ground students in a deep sense of caring and commitment emerges as a powerful pedagogical strategy. She proves year after year that the most challenging students in the school can learn basic science and agriculture skills, become active participants in democratic processes, and develop a strong commitment to their community. Her democratic practice is slow and deliberate, and day by day, she calls upon enormous reserves of energy in order to be fully present and involved in work with the students. Her style is characteristically Hawaiian, and she acknowledges that her cultural values deeply influence her way of being with her students. She observes carefully and listens intently. She is not a big talker. She is a worker, a doer. Above all she takes action and sticks with difficult projects in a way that is so joyful that her students want to collaborate. As a strong and resourceful woman who can drive a tractor, fix the weed-whackers, show students how to make *poi*, teach them how to feed baby chicks with eye droppers, or explain reproductive cycles of fish, Miyamoto is a strong role model for male and female students in her classes.

Within the school itself, she connects her students with allies like Choi and Luke. But she consistently pushes the boundaries of her students' educational experiences by connecting them with Hawaiian culture in the community. The Radical Tarorists' skills were never meant to be used only on "school work," nor was their commitment to cultural and community work meant to be contained on a high school campus. Miyamoto's dreams of how they will change the world are far bigger. The *Aloha ʻAina* Project engages students with the world, opening up a path to understanding why it is important to participate in shaping their communities.

Keawe, Kaleo, William, Bronson, Keola, Kimo, Sione, Brianne, Amber, Donovan, Al, Teddy, Beau, and Richard are representative of the hundreds of Radical Tarorists who in their science class have prepared for and engaged in cultural and social change projects. Miyamoto's lifetime of commitment and her willingness to share her life's work with students make this possible for them. When Miyamoto honors a student by inviting him or her to join the PKO on an access to Kahoʻolawe, the honor and the challenge are understood. They have been part of the transformation of their own farm, and on Kahoʻolawe they get to see the enormity of other projects of transformation.

Kahoʻolawe

> "It was disgusting. I saw there were targets, I was so sad.… To me as soon as I got on the top [Moaʻulaiki, the second highest point on Kahoʻolawe], I thought Kahoʻolawe was a human itself you know and it's like, like so abused."
> —Sione

Opening One's Heart. Sione, like every visitor to Kahoʻolawe, signed beforehand the U.S. Navy Release of Liability, which warned him that he might encounter live explosives in the waters and on the land. Even the stark release form, however, does not prepare one for the devastation. Videos and photos that the students study in advance pale beside the reality that they confront on the island. Sione's reaction to the abuse of Kahoʻolawe gives eloquent testimony to the sense of culture developed in him and the understanding that Miyamoto's students give to each access. Big, tough boys are brought to tears when they see the devastation. Wanton destruction made visible in mounds of bombs and missiles tells a story of oppression. Land, devoid of most vegetation and windswept into hardpan, washes into the sea, giving the island a muddy aura.

After he had witnessed the horror of the bombing, Sione, a Tongan, came to see the peace of the island. Participating in healing ceremonies for the land and working on cleanup and restoration projects prod these students to think about the island in a more spiritual way. In reflecting with his classmates and Miyamoto about his feeling for the island, Sione made important connections about the healing that he saw taking place there: "I think this from the bottom of my heart. When I saw whales around Kahoʻolawe, I knew that they knew that they were protected by this land.… The reason they stayed there is that they can get their own peace around that island. It's like that island is their mother."

Perceptions such as Sioneʻs resonate with other students. They realize that in taking the risk of going to Kahoʻolawe, they have found a source of cultural inspiration and spirituality within them that they are often blocked from feeling in the frenzy of their everyday lives. In reflecting on their experiences with them, in what Westerners would call "dialogue" and Hawaiians would call "talking story," Miyamoto lovingly acknowledges their transformations.

In monthly accesses to Kahoʻolawe, Hawaiians work on revegetation projects and cleanups at historic sites on the island. The *Aloha ʻAina* Project, because of Miyamotoʻs long-standing work with the Protect Kahoʻolawe ʻOhana, has the honor of being invited to the Opening and the Closing of *Makahiki,* the season that honors Lono, the god of fertility and agriculture. On Kahoʻolawe, this season, which begins in November and ends in January, takes on special meaning. The rituals of *Makahiki* give important life sustaining transformations to both the people and the land. Although the Radical Tarorists may not be the most academically successful of the students who gain access to Kahoʻolawe, they do have a training that has prepared them well to participate in ceremonies healing and restoring the land and asking for a plentiful harvest in the next year. In choosing to go to Kahoʻolawe, they show their *aloha ʻaina* for the most devastated land in the Hawaiian archipelago.

Getting There. Kahoʻolawe accesses are deep cultural experiences. The journey to Kahoʻolawe for the Radical Tarorists begins in Honolulu on Oʻahu with a 20-minute flight to the island of Maui and then a one-hour bus or truck ride to Makena Beach, where they spend the night. At daybreak, they depart for Kahoʻolawe on the fishing boat *Pualele.* For many of the students, this is their first trip to any other island.

The trip across the seven miles of the ʻAlalakeiki Channel to the base camp at Hakioawa Bay can be rough. The *Pualele* can go to only within 200 yards of the rocky coast. All in turn transfer from the boat to a rubber raft that carries them in another 100 yards, then they jump into the ocean and become part of a human chain that will swim in all of their supplies—five-gallon water jugs, double-bagged heavy-duty trash bags or five-gallon buckets sealed with duct tape that contain their clothes, food, and minimalist camping gear—to shore. The ocean floor, covered with coconut-size chunks of lava, rumbles in the pounding surf, making it difficult to gain a steady footing. The human chain demonstrates *laulima* (cooperation) in action. Coming up on shore early in the morning, one feels as if an enormous journey has been completed and, in a sense, it has. Arriving on Kahoʻolawe, the students step back in time to a culture quite different from what prevails on Oʻahu. The journey, however, just begins to unfold on that first day.

Challenges. Being chosen to go to Kahoʻolawe bestows on a student a certain prestige but at least one first-timer always backs down from the challenge before the departure day arrives. It is easy to lose one's resolve in the face of the well-known rigorous demands of an access: swimming in rough seas, camping without electricity, being vigilant about live explosives, walking barefoot over jagged lava rock, hiking 16 miles, and sharing one's heartfelt thoughts with a large group. The challenge of making it on Kahoʻolawe is formidable. For five days, from Wednesday to Sunday, activity begins between 4:00 and 5:00 A.M.

Within the first few hours on the island, the U.S. Navy briefs everyone about the unexploded ammunition, bombs, missiles, and grenades and makes sure that everyone signs, for the second time, waivers holding the navy and the state of Hawaiʻi blameless in case of injury. At the Opening of one Makahiki, the Radical Tarorists posed on a U.S. Navy tractor for a group photo. Two months later at the Closing, they passed by the site of the photo and observed that, within 10 feet of where they posed, recently discovered live ordnance was cordoned off.

While on the island for the Opening and the Closing of Makahiki, participants work on small reclamation projects, but their primary purpose is participation in cultural rituals at historic sites. In procession, all participants walk barefoot to the sites, sometimes over extensive areas of jagged lava rock. Everyone endures the pain and moves quickly, never even considering stopping or breaking the line of the procession. The seriousness of purpose that everyone has in enacting rituals directed at healing the island are so all-consuming that any deviation from the path would seem as if one were pandering to a need that hardly matched the needs of the island. And yet no one has ever said, "Don't fall out of line. Don't stop to tend to bruised feet." On the longest procession, which goes 16 miles across the island, participants can opt to wear shoes. When that procession arrives at the base camp on Kealaikahiki Channel, everyone races against the impending sunset to bathe in the ocean, quickly lays out his or her sleeping bag on the beach, changes into ceremonial clothes, and participates at sunset in a final ceremony asking for a good harvest and the blessings of fertility for Kahoʻolawe.

Although everyone on the access always goes the first three miles for a ceremony at Moaʻulaiki the highest point on the island, some because of age, physical condition, or fear back off the 16-mile procession across the island. For the Radical Tarorists, some of whom admit that they do not walk two miles in a day, the challenge to join the procession is greater than for others. They know that Miyamoto, now in her late 40s, was in the first procession that the navy allowed across the island. Choi made his first crossing at 73 and Miyamoto laughs, recalling the students' reaction to his strength. "We were about eight miles into the hike and the kids are moaning and groaning and saying that they were tired and their feet hurt. I just pointed to Choi and there he was plugging along. That ended the complaints." Mutual challenges and mutual support undergird this *ʻohana*, always offering opportunities for physical and spiritual growth in an important cultural context committed to seeing everyone succeed.

The physical challenges on land are always eclipsed by the dangers on the ocean. The PKO counts among its members many very experienced water-safety people, but, in the face of pounding seas and gusts of wind, many need help both in getting out to the boats and in getting back in to shore.

Keawe recalls a time on Kahoʻolawe when the Radical Tarorists helped others escape danger. The Castle group arrived on the first boat in the morning in relatively calm seas. Then at 10:00 A.M. another boat with students from Waiakea on the Big Island arrived and, after swimming in their gear, they proceeded to go back in to the water to participate in a ritual cleansing to prepare for a ceremony. Then the ocean kicked up and many of them got caught in a strong current. He recalls, "It was slamming everybody against the rocks and we saw it and we ran." Kaleo adds, "Over rocks and thorns…about 200 yards." They ran from the kitchen area where they were helping to set up. Bronson continues, "All of a sudden, we just saw them up on the rocks. Like the waves would be coming just like this [shows them breaking in sets]. And this lady was getting pushed up on the rocks." Donovan shrugs his shoulders and shakes his head, remembering the scene and thinking of this near-death experience: "Oh wow, she was just…." Keawe continues, "One of our students had to jump in and save them and[as it] ended up we had to save him, too." William who had jumped in and rescued some of the students and then had to be rescued himself, says, "I thought I was never going to get off that rock." Keawe recalls how the students from Castle and Waiakea bonded and how it drew the Castle students themselves closer together. They dropped everything that they were doing to put their lives on the line for others because, as Keawe says, "We have so much *aloha* [love]." This dramatic rescue brought honor to the Radical Tarorists. The entire PKO paid homage to their quick thinking and their bravery.

For many of those who do go, the experience transforms their lives, building their power-from-within by making clear to them what they can endure physically. As the students act together as a group and as part of the PKO they experience power-with others committed to the struggle to reclaiming their culture.

Consciousness Raising. Part of the work that must be done for *Makahiki* involves cleaning around the women's and men's *heiau* (place of worship, shrine), which are large stone enclosures, and cleaning the trails that lead to them. These gender-segregated tasks offer an excellent opportunity for consciousness raising. The energy of the students makes these tasks enjoyable, but it is the willingness of the elders to share their *mana'o* (thoughts, wisdom) that infuses all of the activities with meaning. As males and females attend to their respective *heiau,* a leader engages the group in sharing some of what coming to Kaho'olawe has meant for them and how caring for the island is important. Often elders share stories of their awakening to a sense of pride in their Hawaiian culture. These conversations in which everyone participates elicit some of the most profound expressions of awareness of cultural and political connections. When Kealohakina, a *kua* (leader), speaks of the early accesses to the island when she took two of her children as babies, she conveys the deep-seated sense of her commitment to having her family know the reality of struggling to gain back rights. She shares her experience of working as a waitress at one of the most luxurious resorts on Maui, where tourists spend thousands of dollars a day, noting that the workers are not unionized and that she is the only Hawaiian. Her comments lead everyone to think about colonization and the ways that it is still in process in Hawai'i. Many of the students talk about their feelings of resentment toward *haole* (white people); they get affirmation and are pushed to think even more deeply about the roots of their oppression in colonialism. Above all, adults and students, ironically, share their feeling of peacefulness on this island that has been so abused.

Brianne speaks about the peace that she finds on Kaho'olawe, which is not in her home, and how it reminds her of the stories that her grandma has told her. For the Radical Tarorists, this ceremony often becomes one of the first times that they are able to hear other Hawaiian adults, outside their project, talk with passion and love about culture, spirituality, and politics, linking them all. The adults take care to bond with the youth, taking the time to listen intently to what these students have to say.

Rites of Passage. On the first full day on the island, everyone rises at 4:00 A.M. for *hi'uwai,* an ocean purification ceremony. They line up on the walkway leading down to the ocean and, from a coconut shell, sip *limu kalawai,* freshwater algae symbolizing forgiveness, and *olena* (turmeric) for cleansing. Then in the moon-lit darkness, they take off their clothes and wade into the water, meditating on purifying themselves for participation in the ceremonies honoring Lono. They rid themselves of anger, negative energy, and frustration and focus on positive healing for themselves and the island. Away from the distractions of 20th-century Hawai'i, they actually have a chance to focus inside themselves, and this becomes a key part of their experiences on the island.

For the teenagers who are the least bit self-conscious, undressing in public, even in the dark, is an activity they would like to avoid, but their elders have explained to them the importance of the purification. They make the choice. Sione recalls his feelings of uneasiness: "Kaleo, he's the one who told me about *hiʻuwai*. He told me 'give what you got and don't let anybody judge you by the way you look.' That's what got me to go in the water." Kaleo deserves credit for supporting many of the Radical Tarorists and helping them believe in themselves.

In making five accesses, Kaleo, who once felt clearly self-conscious in all aspects of his life, has become remarkably self-assured. He tells me, "I'm comfortable with myself. It shows more." As Kaleo moves to build the confidence and pride of others, he strengthens his own power-from-within and makes possible stronger alliances with his peers and with his own teachers and mentors. Choi speaks of Kaleo's growth over three years, "He's more assertive. He's taking an interest in learning how to read now. He's feeling a good kind of power, not the 'I can bust you up kind.' And that power is having confidence in yourself. In this program we are slowly trying to have them earn back their pride and pride is that power."

Honors. On every Makahiki access, some students will be further singled out by the *moʻo Lono* (priests of Lono) to present *hoʻokupu* (ceremonial offerings such as banana or taro wrapped in a *ti* leaf bundle) at the shrines. Participation in this ritual will require them to memorize a protocol in Hawaiian. Although most of Miyamoto's students are Hawaiian, none of them speaks or understands the language, which was banned from the public schools for nearly a century. Although today they could study Hawaiian at school, as special education students, they do not. They know words and phrases and concepts from their work in the *Aloha ʻAina* Project and their trips to Kahoʻolawe. In both projects, words like *laulima* (cooperation), *kokua* (help, assistance), and *lokahi* (unity) take on significance. The students routinely incorporate words such as these into the pidgin that they speak—a language of convenience, but also a language of resistance.

When Beau, who is Filipino, and Brianne, who is Hawaiian, are chosen to offer *hoʻokupu*, they must learn how to prepare the *hoʻokupu*, and then face the most difficult challenge: memorizing in Hawaiian their three-line presentation speech. "*O Beau koʻu inoa./ I noho au Waimanalo./ Eia ka maiʻa mai Luluku mai no Lono.* (My name is Beau. I am from Waimanalo. Here are the bananas from Luluku for Lono)." In the formal ceremonies, they will have to recite these lines four times over two days—at the *imu* (underground oven) where the *hoʻokupu* will be baked, then later at the women's shrine, at the men's shrine, and a day later at Moaʻulaiki on the top of the island. Although the lines that they are required to memorize seem relatively simple, for these students the task proved formidable.

As Miyamoto teaches them how to prepare the *ho'okupu,* she helps them recite the lines. They practice for over an hour and a half. Two hours later, they seek her out in the community space that she has constructed outside her tent and practice again. Both of them have forgotten the lines. Brianne begins to worry and she goes back to her tent reciting her lines. Later she tells me that she kept repeating her lines before she fell asleep. "As I was sleeping, I kept seeing it in my head." So obsessed with the process of memorizing, she sleeps through dinner. About 10:00 P.M., after almost everyone has retired to a tent or to sleeping in the open, Al and Teddy go to Brianne's tent to have her come help Beau memorize his lines.

At 11:00 P.M., he runs to his teacher. "Miya, Miya. I got 'em. I got 'em." Miyamoto struggles to awaken herself. "What Beau? I'm asleep." Beau is not to be silenced; he recites the lines loud enough for all of the Radical Tarorists to hear. His peers come running from about 100 feet away down to where Miyamoto is sleeping and they all break out in applause. Miyamoto gets up and praises him, "Yeah, Beau, you've got it. *Maika'i* (good). *Maika'i.* Good work. I knew that you could do it." General celebration hails Beau's flawless recitation of his lines. The students had pulled together to make it happen.

Brianne recalls how she felt the next morning as the group prepared for the *imu* ceremony. "I was getting all nervous as if I wouldn't remember it, but when I was walking I was saying it in my head. Saying it. Saying it. I was like ohhh hoping I would remember it during the whole procession." She did remember her lines, but Beau forgot most of his. As Beau's partner, Brianne remembers how she ached for him. "He started his lines, but then he was like stop and then he pause, pause, pause." He remembered parts of his lines at each of the three sites at Hakioawa, but when he got to Moa'ulaiki, he remembered them all, to the joy of all of the Radical Tarorists and Miyamoto.

The lack of success that many of these special education students have in school can be readily understood from this example of the chore of memorization. So much of school is based on memorizing; for students unable to accomplish the task, the knowledge they do have—which is often based in cultural and spiritual understandings—is disregarded. For other students on Kaho'olawe accesses, this task of presenting ho'okupu is minimally challenging. Those who speak Hawaiian or are learning it have little difficulty mastering the few lines. The learning difficulties that many of the Radical Tarorists have, as well as the fear that they experience about public performance, make one admire them all the more for being willing to take up the challenge and accept the honor.

Reflection on Kaho'olawe: Kukakuka. At a traditional *kukakuka* (a gathering where people share their ideas and feelings) on the evening before departure from Kaho'olawe, David Duncan, a respected leader, pays tribute to Miyamoto before the 90 people there. Miyamoto's work with the students from Castle reminds him, he says, of the old Crosby, Stills, Nash, and Young song, "Teach Your Children Well." She is assuring the connection between past generations and the young, exposing them to the meaning and beauty of Hawaiian culture and giving them the opportunity to shape the future. He tells the group that he especially appreciates it, because as someone who himself went to public school in Hawai'i (the state with the highest percentage of students in private schools), he sees that she is helping students who often are neglected and not afforded privileges, such as going to Kaho'olawe. The students hear this, and later Al says, "We're lucky to go there. 'Cause how that guy [Duncan] was saying about how he never got to go because he went to public school. And there's only a few of us who get chosen."

At a *kukakuka* session, Beau shares that he never knew that he could meet so many nice people and that he will return to the island as often as possible. He makes a special point of thanking Miyamoto for all that she does for him. Keola has a poignant metaphor for the island that all of the access members love. "This is a little island but it's got a big heart," he says, breaking out in tears like many others in the session. Keola would later sum up the feeling that they all had and mention it as his most outstanding memory: "The love. Everybody had love. *Aloha.*"

Al, too, felt the love. When it is his turn to speak, he says, "I had one speech planned but I just forgot it. I want to thank my teacher, Miya, for bringing me here. But I want to say that I love everyone here and love this island and care about it and I'm coming back." Kaleo thinks about participating in *kukakuka* on five accesses and still shakes his head in disbelief. "I didn't really want to. Not that I didn't like them, but shame a little bit. No can talk. Nervous. And if I do talk, then I cry." For many of the boys like Kaleo and Keola the idea of talking and then crying in front of a large group of people about their love for the island would have been unimaginable before they went to Kaho'olawe.

The *kukakuka* session provides an opportunity for adults and students to reflect about what has significance in their lives and to share their thoughts and their feelings with each other. The intergenerational sharing that occurs here creates a powerful force for action and for validation. The opportunity for students to speak out in a large public forum of supportive adults and peers offers them a chance for leadership and affirms the dignity of their thoughts and feelings. An *'ohana* grows.

Reflection at Castle High. As is typical of learning experiences with Miyamoto, the students enjoy themselves. Keawe captures it: "That whole trip was memorable. There wasn't one dull moment the whole time that we were there. There was always a new activity that we had to do every day." This is strong praise from a turn-of-the-century teenager bereft of CD players, TV, video games, organized sports, cars, and entertainment centers. In place of the comforts of home and pleasures of technology, they find themselves enjoying sleeping on the ground, walking barefoot over lava rock, hiking across a desert island in the midday sun, and engaging in work that tests their physical limits.

Miyamoto injects humor into their recollections, "What's memorable for me is the two biggest guys, Donovan and William, sleeping in their tent and the wind blowing it down and their just continuing to sleep in a collapsed tent." She jokes with the students as they reflect, but she has spoken individually with all of them assessing how they met both their expectations and hers.

That not all of the students meet the demands of being on the island reveals more about the overwhelming majority who do. Miyamoto looks for signs of behavior change: better attendance at school, a willingness to work in classes, a stronger commitment to work on the farm, passing grades, a greater sense of maturity, and, in some cases, a turning away from drugs and alcohol. For the most part, her expectations of success are met, but for those who fail in any way, she continues to hold out hope simply by believing in them, giving them her unconditional love, and sharing her wonderful sense of humor. In this nontraditional program, with strong mentoring from Miyamoto and other allies, the students begin to find their culture and themselves within the borders of the school, and that discovery affects their lives.

Miyamoto and Luke agree that "things worth doing involve taking a risk." The students themselves are very open to risks, but often of the sort that endanger their well-being. Luke reflects that "with the trips and the kids, it was risky, because we didn't know what the outcome would be. In some cases it was wonderful. In others less than wonderful.... But I think they're worth taking."

What thrills many of the leaders in the Protect Kahoʻolawe ʻOhana is the faith that Miyamoto shows in taking Hawaiian students, who are often among the most marginalized and most difficult in the public schools. The students themselves are well aware of their position. When Miyamoto shares with them a bad report on their behavior that she heard from someone at Kamehameha School (a private school for Hawaiians), Kaleo reacts defensively to the elitist attitude of the exam school: "They only take the smart kids, not the Hawaiians who are stupid." His comment speaks volumes about his understanding of his class position and his lack of success in much of his school life. But David Duncan has followed Kaleo's growth over four years and sees him as a great success on Kaho'olawe. "He proved everything that Pi'i already knew and what some of us were hoping for and, lo and behold, he just blossomed into such a terrific guy. He became the veteran of those guys."

In taking to Kaho'olawe students who are most in need, Miyamoto faces a challenge on each trip. Duncan admires the way she works with the students. "Pi'i is a genius, and she can kind of eyeball a situation. She just has even a greater faith and the students just emerge. And if they don't, fine, and if they do, swell. Well, maybe she's that cool. It doesn't seem like she sweats over it."

Miyamoto's generosity of spirit influences the students. They do not wait to be told by adults what to do, especially if they have been on the island before. In a debriefing conversation with some of the students who have just returned from Kaho'olawe, Miyamoto asks what they learned about sustaining the 'ohana spirit there when they saw tasks that needed attention. Beau replies, "Do it without asking." In a similar debriefing a year later, Miyamoto asks Al whether he was aware of how the Castle students impressed the elders on Kaho'olawe. He seems surprised, "No, they wasn't telling us anything. We were just doing what we had to do, not to impress nobody." The spirit of *laulima* (cooperation and working together), which infuses every activity on the farm, influences their behavior on the island in everything from making dramatic rescues to scrubbing the kitchen pots down at the ocean side.

Inspired Dreams of Pedagogy

The Radical Tarorists' ability to dream and envision the future is one of their most powerful assets. Just as they could dream of a plan for a village on Kaho'olawe, so too they imagined an even closer connection for themselves. In talking story with one of her classes, Miyamoto shares that she has been invited by the PKO to serve on a committee that will plan more connections between the schools and Kaho'olawe. She asks the students for ideas.

William quickly points out that they really need to be there more to tend to plants. Keawe, clearly a leader in the 'ohana, once again articulates a vision, this time for a study-abroad program on Kaho'olawe. He comes up with the idea that they should live there for one or two quarters each school year and commit themselves in a broader way to the revegetation project. They could learn in the old ways of Hawaiians. "It would have to be from experience. Like if you go fishing, you take your son with you and you show him the ways.... You know that Hawaiians, they never used to have school books. They were just taught by moms and dads and their gramps.... Pass it on generation to generation." Implicit in his suggestion for a more hands-on 'ohana-based education is a critique of what he is experiencing generally in school.

He suggests that they could try something besides the routine of "Read Chapters 5 and 10." William adds, "There's other ways of learning that are more meaningful."

Miyamoto presses them to think about the proposal in more detail. Immediately, they respond that they could learn math figuring out the watering system. They suggest that navigators could teach them the stars and they could learn as their ancestors did how to plot trips to the South Pacific. They show enthusiasm about learning true Hawaiian history from other Hawaiians. They adamantly believe that they could learn a great deal from talking story on the island. One of them recalls how they learned a lot about the history of gaining access to the island from talking story with Emmett Aluli, the first named plaintiff in the ultimately successful suit against the navy that gave Hawaiians monthly access to the island for religious and cultural purposes. Keola reflects on the whole experience of learning on Kahoʻolawe: "It's fun. You learn stuff while you are there. You meet different people."

Adults who share their love, history, and wisdom with young people and who want to hear what the young people have to say make an enormous impact on them on Kahoʻolawe. Keola recalls, "The first time that I went to Kahoʻolawe, I was getting into trouble and stuff but when I came back I used my head and started thinking." Beau acknowledges the difference that going to Kahoʻolawe made for him but bemoans the fact that it is difficult to keep the values of Kahoʻolawe on Oʻahu because there are so many distractions.

In reflecting on her dialogue with the students, Miyamoto notes that the most important lesson that they learn is the need for an awesome amount of commitment and patience over years of struggle to bring about change. And from her they also learn that they have the power to bring about change—to act effectively in their community and to enjoy it. The pedagogy of the farm, of Kahoʻolawe—of all of the work of the *Aloha ʻAina* Project—encourages all of the participants to believe in their power to bring about change.

Making Connections

Miyamoto feels that the traditional compartmentalized nature of education fails many students and that teachers ought to be looking at that failure and determining how we can do better by students. In the *Aloha ʻAina* Project, students make connections between their work in school and life in the community in an ongoing way that makes sense to them more immediately. Becoming active agents within cultural and political spheres creates opportunities for them to understand their place in society and in history and, most significantly, in the creation of history. For example, in April 1995, a number of students, Miyamoto, Choi, and Luke, wearing traditional dress, were part of 300 Hawaiian marchers carrying bamboo torches who made their way 12 miles through darkness to a ceremony marking the 200th anniversary of the Battle of Nuʻuanu Pali. In following the route that King Kamehameha used to fight his last great battle in uniting the Hawaiian people, the students relived history and created their own. At the ceremony on the Pali, the students joined in offering *hoʻokupu,* in chanting, and, most significantly, in giving witness to a part of their history that is rarely acknowledged in school. On an island with nearly 1 million people, these students are in the vanguard of a cultural and political movement.

In reflecting with Luke about the meaning of their experience, they make connections. Donovan, Keawe, Kaleo, and William talk about how the Pali March is connected to a unified Hawaiian cultural movement, the accesses to Kahoʻolawe, and sovereignty. Donovan notes that sovereignty to him means "getting the land." Keawe adds, "Reuniting Hawaiians with the land." Luke expands the argument: "Sovereignty to me is self-determination of native peoples. We should be able to decide for ourselves how we're going to live." William agrees and says it succinctly: "Self-government."

William adds another dimension to the conversation, suggesting that there are ways that they can protest some of the assaults on their culture. "Write to Governor Cayetano, who's trying to get rid of King Kamehameha Day in Hawaiʻi." He points out the irony of two front-page newspaper stories, one talking about the Pali March and another discussing cuts in state funding to the Kamehameha Day Celebration. "They're trying to get rid of all of this kind of stuff." When adults sit and talk story with them and, most importantly, listen to them, the students make political and cultural connections easily and with poignancy. This practice of reflection and dialogue allows them to clarify the uses of their education in the present rather than having a teacher tell them "the connections will come later."

CONCLUSION

A democratic teacher like Miyamoto, committed to sharing power, building an *ʻohana* that operates as an empowerment zone, forging alliances within the school and the community, and actively engaging in projects of social change with students creates "an arch of social dreaming" (McLaren & da Silva, 1993, 68). Her sense of evaluation and assessment reveals her values. She listens deeply and constantly urges students on to achieve more and expect more from themselves and the world. The students thrive on the *ʻohana* relationship; it comes first to their minds when they talk about how they behave as a group. Keola and Kaleo respond in unison when asked how they get along on Kahoʻolawe, "One *ʻohana.*" Beau confirms their view, "Yeah, like one 'ohana." The cohesiveness of this 'ohana, Luke suggests, may come from experiences like going to Kahoʻolawe, where they have only themselves to rely on in some fairly challenging and threatening situations.

When they go to Kahoʻolawe and experience the true 'ohana spirit of the Protect Kahoʻolawe ʻOhana, the circle of love expands. Al says it clearly: "The best thing was...all 63 of us were all hugging each other, kissing each other, you know we were all family. It felt like you're loved by everyone.... With 63 people and you don't know a lot of them, just your teacher and friends." What amazed Al and Teddy were the love and attention that the adults gave to the young people on the island.

Respect in this project goes further than respect for people and the capitalist notion of respect for property; at the basis of all is aloha 'aina, a deeply spiritual concept that informs all of the work of the participants. When students are asked what kind of work they do with Miyamoto that would make them good caretakers of Kahoʻolawe, Teddy answers that their ability to work as a team is really important. Al responds matter-of-factly, "Respecting the farm. Same thing as respecting the island.... Yeah, loving the island and respecting it most of all." As an ally of Hawaiians, Al understands and appreciates the importance of the message that they learn and live in the project.

These special education students who are loved and respected and nurtured in an 'ohana that they feel responsible for having created and sustained emerge as socially and politically committed agents of change in their society. Luke points to the critical factor in their education: "If you can show people how their culture is being disturbed, changed, they understand what politics is and why it's important to be active and take a stand and defend the culture."

These students are making the connections on a day-to-day basis and forging a future. Keawe comments on the importance of participating consciously in their culture and seeing the bigger picture. "It's all connected," he says—the Pali March, the return of the Hawaiian voyaging canoes from Tahiti, going to Kahoʻolawe, and their work on the farm. Overwhelmed, Bronson, who comes from a politically active family, laments the situation they are in: "They're phasing out our culture." Keawe, however, remains optimistic. "There's more Hawaiian activity going on," he says to his peers, "more people are getting into the culture. They realize that once the culture dies, it's gone."

Miyamoto realizes that in teaching, mentoring, and loving these students, she and her allies help to create the energy that will assure a future for the Hawaiian culture and for Hawaiians and their allies.

CHAPTER 6

Spinning a Magical Web in Rural New Hampshire: The Appalachian Mountain Teen Project

Eileen de los Reyes

> Maybe schools would be better if they let you think about why the sea and the world are the way they are instead of making you learn by heart what they tell you to learn. Maybe teachers should help you discover what you really need and want to learn and do.
> —Danilo Dolci (1984)

The Appalachian Mountain Teen Project (AMTP), founded in 1987 by Donna San Antonio and Holly Manoogian, offers long-term support to youth and families throughout central New Hampshire. The project's mission—"to expand opportunities for youth and families so that socioeconomic problems (such as poverty and prejudice) and emotional challenges do not result in negative life outcomes"—is carried out through a group of programs designed for teens, parents, and educators.

Key to the AMTP's mission and success is its core program, the Teen Adventure Project, the subject of this chapter. The Teen Adventure Project empowers youth through a combination of intensive counseling; outdoor adventures that include hiking, canoeing, snowshoeing, cross-country skiing, mountain climbing, and other activities; and community service projects. By teaching participants to survive and thrive in the outdoors, AMTP has successfully turned around the lives of hundreds of marginalized teens who were headed toward trouble in their schools and communities.

Impressed with AMTP's commitment to poor rural youth and democratic pedagogy, I began observing the project in the mid 1990s. Over a four-year period, I sat in on AMTP parenting meetings, participated in outdoor adventures and mentoring classes, and experienced one of the longest budget meet-

ings imaginable. I interviewed teen participants and staff members, sometimes at the AMTP offices and other times at the Harvard Graduate School of
Education, where San Antonio is completing her Ed.D. in Community
Education and Lifelong Learning. During this time, I saw firsthand how the
directors and staff moved with ease between theory and practice. Every
action taken at AMTP is reflected upon, implemented, and reflected upon
again and again. This process generates an unusual depth of knowledge and
experience, which staff and teens generously shared with me, hoping to
inspire other teachers and students.

The level of deep thinking and engaged democratic practice that takes
place at AMTP is the subject of this chapter. In explaining what makes AMTP
a space of wisdom, respect, trust, and love, project participants—including
students, educators, and board members—illuminate how AMTP gives some
of New Hampshire's poorest teens the strength to face the challenges of economic poverty, disenfranchisement, and disrespect.

AMTP: CLASS, COMMUNITY, AND POLITICS

The Class Context

Towns in the AMTP service region are divided along class lines, generating a
structure of privilege for some and marginalization for many. As noted in the
AMTP mission statement, the youth and families that AMTP works with are
"over-stressed by difficult economic and physical conditions" generated by
the struggle to "achieve basic life goals such as economic security, social success, and physical and emotional health." Living in a state that shuns taxes,
poor New Hampshire residents have few places to turn for support. As San
Antonio (1995) argues, "in tax-free, live-free-or-die New Hampshire, people
are expected to make do without government services" (3).

Young people from rural areas face the brunt of New Hampshire's divisive
class structure when they move from elementary schools located in their own
towns to regional middle and high schools located in wealthy towns. Often
what await them are stereotypes, disrespect, and academic and social marginalization. To show how these forms of disrespect and marginalization
manifest themselves, San Antonio (1997) recounts the story of a girl from
Ossipee, one of the poor towns in the region, who ran for senior class officer.
Her posters were torn down because "kids from Ossipee don't become class
officers." San Antonio further relates how a teacher once asked her why she
chose to work with the "hopeless" and the "dregs" of society (3).

Teenagers from economically poor towns are conscious of how they are
perceived by their peers and teachers. They give examples of discrimination
that begin at a very early age. One AMTP teen believes that her kindergarten

teacher "didn't like me and my sister because we went to the day care center and we lived on Blueberry Lane," which was "a low-income housing place." Two teens describe clothing as the marker used to identify their class. One says that part of the problem was that "our mother made our clothes, she didn't buy them"; the other teen notes, people knew they were poor "because we bought our clothes at Ames Department Store and that was bad."

These youth from rural New Hampshire rarely have opportunities to achieve academic success, earn a college degree, or even find a decent-paying job. For many teenagers, the struggle at school continues at home. Their families, with few economic opportunities and alienated from an ever-shrinking social service infrastructure, find themselves living constantly at a dangerous physical and emotional edge. Living under these conditions of school, work, and family marginalization, these teens often suffer from low self-esteem and a lack of awareness of options and opportunities. Frequently, they end up using drugs and alcohol. The targets of peer harassment, they feel rejected at school and become accustomed to failure. When their despair and hopelessness end in violence, they end up in the criminal justice system. The AMTP often comes at the end of the line offering hope to teens who, for the most part, don't believe they deserve another chance.

Theory and Practice

A strong and clearly articulated progressive and feminist ideology sustains and guides the Appalachian Mountain Teen Project. Both San Antonio and Manoogian are veteran activists—San Antonio around labor and feminist struggles, Manoogian around environmental issues. They share a commitment to feminist and collective process, along with a profound love and respect of nature. Both love their work with families and youth in the community in which they live.

San Antonio and Manoogian agree that ending the culture of silence around issues of class, race, and gender can only happen in a democratically run, feminist organization that honors the voices of all participants. As such, they have given a great deal of thought to democratic leadership. Rather than exercising ownership over the organization, San Antonio and Manoogian see their roles as "guides, facilitators, mentors, translators, mediators and community organizers; [the organization's] structures, planning and implementation [processes are] as collaborative as [they] can make it" (San Antonio, 1995, 8).

I experienced AMTP's collaborative decision-making process in an eight-hour budget meeting that reflected the staff's careful consideration of its mission and goals. Because AMTP values dialogue, collective work, and consensus decision making, the staff were willing to take an entire day to work through difficult budget decisions, as opposed to relying on the top-down authority of San Antonio and Manoogian. Rather than "wasting time," the meeting resulted in a sense of unity and shared commitment. The staff's commitment to democratic process clearly underlay their ability to overcome their limited resources and generate a coherent set of programs that address the needs of rural teens in the region.

Shared decision making is only one aspect of the feminist ideology that guides AMTP. In a conversation about what it means to be a feminist organization, the staff and board identified various aspects of AMTP theory and practice. Joan Lovering, a board member, explained that a feminist philosophy stands for "probably the best of helping people be independent and whole, and…equal opportunities for both young girls and boys; women and men." Board member Jennifer Tapper described the philosophy as "inclusive," and staff member Jeff Martel tied the organization's focus on the development of relationships to their feminist ideology.

For San Antonio, other themes emerge as well. Of particular importance is an analysis of class and power. In recruiting staff, she emphasizes that AMTP is not interested in "social workers" with a missionary attitude. The AMTP is not about "helping" teens become "adjusted," but about empowering them to resist the very real oppression they face because they are of the "wrong" class, gender, race, or sexual orientation.

AMTP's belief in shared power and decision making, which guides their work internally as a staff, she explains, also guides their work with participants. Embracing democratic pedagogy, the staff creates a sense of community and shared responsibility by instilling participants with the knowledge and understanding that they each have something important to contribute.

The commitment to democratic practice both in AMTP's organizational structure and pedagogy strengthens AMTP's ability to carry out its mission. Although AMTP has had to struggle for institutional support, its success is apparent in the depth of community support expressed by the families it serves.

Responding to Community Needs

An organization that centers around supporting rural youth, AMTP has slowly and intentionally evolved by identifying the institutions and adults they need to work with in order to support the participants in the Teen Adventure Project. In addition to supporting the core project, the AMTP runs four other programs: a Parenting Skills and Support Course, which supports parents of teens in the organization's service area; the Riverland Education and Adventure Center, through which AMTP conducts a wide variety of outdoor education programs for local schools; the Mentoring Project, in which teens mentor children ages 10 to 13; and Professional Training and Consultation for school faculty and administrators struggling to resolve conflicts in their schools.

Through this array of programs, AMTP has created a network of services that respond to the needs of the communities with which they work. As a result, AMTP receives significant support from local communities and community activists in the region. Walking the streets with AMTP staff, it is common to stop and talk with parents and teens who have been involved with the project. The conversations are ongoing and never-ending.

Communities such as Ossipee and Alton publicly demonstrate their support for AMTP as long-standing allies. In Ossipee, for example, each time the AMTP has requested funding for services they will provide, the selectmen have refused to recommend funding for human services in their budget. Yet, each year in their town meeting, Ossipee residents have voted unanimously to approve the AMTP request for funding. The town of Alton, which has worked with AMTP for 10 years, joins Ossipee in their support for the project.

In addition to widespread support of families and schools in their region, AMTP has a number of important ideological allies. These allies include feminist leaders such as Kathy Kennett of the Women's Shelter and Joan Lovering, a longtime friend of San Antonio and a director of a feminist health center in Concord, New Hampshire, in the seventies. Other long-term allies include Arnie Alpert from the American Friends Service Committee (AFSC) and Judy Elliot from the AFL-CIO. The AMTP, AFSC, and AFL-CIO worked together to organize the spring 1999 conference Teens in the Workforce, which I discuss in detail later on in the chapter.

Working collaboratively with community allies, schools, and other progressive organizations, the AMTP has been able to create a network of programs that provide rural New Hampshire youth and their families the support they need to become powerful citizens with hopeful futures.

THE TEEN ADVENTURE PROJECT

The AMTP Teen Adventure Project works each year with approximately 35 youth between the ages of 12 and 18. These young people may be referred by the courts or a parent, teacher, or counselor who is concerned about their well-being. Teens need to commit to the program for a minimum of six months, during which they participate in wilderness adventures (1 to 30 days in length), engage in community service projects, join in cross-cultural experiences, and attend weekly counseling sessions. The outdoor adventures, which are the program's core curriculum, may include summer activities such as backpacking, mountain biking, canoeing, rock climbing, and ropes courses or winter adventures such as snowshoeing, cross-country skiing, sledding, and skating. Through these experiences, participants develop greater self-awareness and self-confidence, improve their communication skills and ability to resolve conflicts nonviolently, and have the opportunity to emerge as peer leaders.

During the initial six-month period in which teens are involved with AMTP, the staff members stay in close touch with the participant and the participant's school and home. After the six months end, the teens "graduate" from AMTP but are welcome to return as "members." The AMTP "open-door policy" is an open invitation to teens to return for outdoor adventures, discussions, or counseling when they face inevitable crises.

Experiencing an AMTP Adventure

Accompanying the AMTP Teen Adventure Project on a one-day canoe trip provides an opportunity to observe AMTP's highly skilled educators building a caring and respectful teaching and learning community. This community is the foundation of their pedagogy, which is further enhanced by a commitment to empowering youth through individual and collective problem solving. Throughout the day, the staff educate by posing questions, encouraging peers to teach and learn from one another, and providing opportunities for teens simply to have fun in a safe and healthy environment.

Creating a Peaceful and Stable Community. By 8:00 A.M. on the day of the canoe trip, participants are gathering at the AMTP's office in Wolfeboro. Manoogian arrives with two participants whom she has picked up on the way. AMTP doesn't want transportation to be a barrier to participation; thus, the staff members willingly pick up participants who live as far as an hour away. While Manoogian has been out on the road, San Antonio has been searching for a place to launch the canoes—there has been a lot of rain and many of the lakes in the region are flooded.

The conversation at the AMTP office is loud with chatter. Although it appears that the group of staff and teenagers are just "hanging out," waiting for the action to begin, closer attention reveals that Jeff Martel and Tim Moore, the two counselors who are going on this trip, are busy checking in with parents and teenagers. Each teenager is greeted and given individual attention; each parent who comes in also gets time with the counselors. Before we leave, Martel chats privately with two of the participants; he will continue to pay particular attention to these two teenagers throughout the day. As outsiders we're not privy to the content of these confidential conversations, but it is clear that the tone is serious. Nonetheless, Martel's manner is so quiet and unobtrusive that the rest of the group barely notices. The room feels relaxed and the sense of excitement about the forthcoming adventure never diminishes.

San Antonio and Manoogian set the tone for the day. Always relaxed, they create a sense of stability and peacefulness within the community that in turn generates a sense of comfort in the participants. Every step of the way, San Antonio explains the changes in schedule, showing her respect for participants who, given the circumstances, might feel aggravated and antsy. Her calm demeanor seems to rub off on the group, which adjusts smoothly to the changes in schedule. A sense of being a community that is about to share an adventure begins with the staff's careful attention to the morning's welcoming rituals.

Using the Outdoors as Content and Pedagogy. The process of teaching and learning begins with San Antonio's asking all participants to gather around and introduce themselves. The group consists of three male and four female participants ranging in ages from 15 to 20, three AMTP staff (Moore, Martel, and San Antonio), and Pat Gozemba and me. Some teenagers have been with the program a long time; for others this will be the first canoe trip. San Antonio explains the flooding problem, the weather conditions that led to the flooding, and why we are delayed. She also explains why it would be dangerous to canoe in some of the lakes. All the teens participate in the discussion, answering San Antonio's questions and asking questions of their own.

It takes us until midmorning to get permission to launch the canoes. When we get to the camp that has finally given us permission, San Antonio takes the leadership role. She gives instructions on how we are going to unload the canoes and explains that after we complete this task she will instruct us on how to use the canoes. Every task we are assigned requires teamwork, and teams of three form to unload the canoes and take them to the lake. The teens, having been instructed on how to care for the canoes so that they will remain in good condition, are careful not to scrape them on the sand.

The canoe lesson mixes practical information on safety and how to paddle with broader questions about nature. Participants are aware that what they are learning will affect their ability to enjoy the day. They give San Antonio their undivided attention as she asks: How far off the shore should we be? What happens if there is thunder? How far away is the front when you hear thunder? What do you call this part of the canoe? Susan, one of the participants who has been on a similar trip before, explains to others what she has learned from previous experiences. Her knowledge is impressive, but the others don't see her as a showoff; everyone is engaged in the discussion.

The outdoors presents almost limitless possibilities for teaching and learning. As San Antonio and others have noted, the natural world provides a metaphor for life's challenges. The physical challenges, the teamwork, and opportunities to experience success in situations that are sometimes risky and frightening can be powerful, memorable, and life changing.

After introducing participants to the environment we are about to enter, we get into the canoes and start paddling. I am in a canoe with Martel and San Antonio. Within the first five minutes, Martel observes that we will need to help one of the canoes. San Antonio agrees with Martel's assessment and we get closer. Sarah, the teenager seated at the front of the canoe, explains that they are going "all over the place." She is referring to her teammate, Anita, who is on her first AMTP canoe trip and has no experience paddling. Sarah is clearly frustrated. One of the suggestions San Antonio offers is that Sarah stop paddling, allowing Anita to do it by herself. Anita and Sarah agree and try this approach, which seems to work. When they try to paddle as a team, however, they still have trouble. Together they identify the problem: since Anita is not saying "switch" and Sarah cannot see her, they have no control of where they are going. Anita continues having trouble, leading Sarah to suggest that they switch positions, so that she can steer the canoe. San Antonio gently explains that a better strategy might be for Sarah to teach Anita how to steer, and Sarah agrees. Although it is clear that this is difficult for her, she does not challenge San Antonio. At one point, San Antonio asks Sarah, "Is this frustrating to you? I imagine it is." Sarah says yes but continues to work with Anita. They eventually begin to get the hang of it, but it is difficult for them to stay with the group. They finally agree to switch places, but only after Anita "gets it." Switching places, which is never easy in a canoe, is made more difficult by the teammates' size difference. They are visibly impressed when they accomplish the task. After working hard, they are able to integrate themselves with the rest of the group.

It took persistence and determination for Sarah and Anita to resolve their problem. San Antonio asks them not simply to resolve the situation, but to do so in such a way that allows Anita to learn from her teammate. Sarah learns in the process that being a teacher requires patience and fortitude. Without any recriminations or put-downs, these teens continue to work together until they are able to rejoin the group.

Empowerment through Success. The group, which has patiently waited for Sarah and Anita, sets off for the marsh. We were promised that this would be the highlight of the trip. The instruction to the lead boat is to set the pace but not to go too fast, keeping the group organized. Alice, a longtime AMTP participant who is now a board member, is selected to lead and is thrilled to be in this position. Later she explains to the group that she is amazed everyone follows her lead since this seldom happens in her life. The sweep boat takes up the rear, making sure no one is left behind.

San Antonio calls all the canoes together and poses a question to the participants. Given all the delays, the group can try to go to the marsh, or, she suggests, they could stop at a smaller marsh, have lunch, and go back. If participants decide to go to the smaller marsh, they will have time to swim later in the afternoon. San Antonio, the staff, and the researchers would love to go to the big marsh. The decision, however, is up to the teens. They choose the smaller marsh, so there will be time to swim.

The adults make no attempt to influence the teens' decisions; they feel that it is more important to allow the teens to make their own choice about how to spend the day. The staff doesn't worry that time will be "wasted," because an important element of their pedagogy involves encouraging the teens to build relationships with their peers and learn from one another.

On the way back, the group experiences success, with all the canoes moving at a steady pace and making great progress. As Alice explains later, she could feel the power of the group. Everyone agrees with her observation. Something great happens: each participant, including the adults, contributes to making the group work together and look good. Everyone, including the researchers, is proud of the accomplishment.

The experience of success—individually and as a group—is critical to AMTP's pedagogy. A great sense of pleasure comes from learning new skills and accomplishing physical tasks. The glow of success radiates through the group on the return trip as everyone realizes that his or her participation is essential to the overall success of the trip. Before these teens join the AMTP, they often see themselves as failures in the larger world; they feel marginalized and powerless, unable to take control over their lives. Experiences like the canoe trip provide tangible evidence that, in fact, they can access their own power and, thereby, experience success in the world.

Peers Educating Each Other. During swim time, a conversation between the female participants results in another teaching and learning moment, this one without any of the staff members present. Susan, who is 15, asks for a T-shirt to cover her bathing suit. She is clearly embarrassed about her body. Alice, who is 19 at the time, tells her, "I don't worry about that anymore." Susan says, "That's because you already have a boyfriend." Alice replies, "No, that's not it; I don't care about those things anymore; they're not important." Anita, who is the youngest at 13, has been listening; she says, "This is the first time I heard a girl say that." Everyone agrees and looks pleased with the conversation. The younger women clearly see Alice as a role model; their admiration grows as Alice teaches them a new way of thinking about themselves.

AMTP consciously builds leadership skills among participants. After a difficult adolescence, Alice has emerged as someone other participants look up to. This is the direct result of her having found at AMTP the rare opportunity to discover herself and her innumerable talents. She has made friends and has learned how to get the support she needs to overcome the obstacles in her life. She is now a confident young adult, able to pass on what she has learned. Her teaching during the day is as powerful as that of the AMTP staff. The dialogue between the young women confirms that the staff members were right to trust the teens in their decision to spend time on their own. Even when staff members are not present, the teens engage in a serious and respectful manner in discussions of issues that matter to them.

Commitment to Inclusion. Throughout the day, Moore and Martel concentrate their efforts on the two male teens—John and Steve—whom they appeared concerned about earlier in the morning. As the day progresses everyone begins to notice that John is quite disruptive. His first complaint is that he wants to paddle. Since three people are in his canoe, someone needs to sit in the middle and go along for the ride. Believing that John wants to take turns, one of the participants offers to paddle on the way over and John can paddle on the way back. But John insists that he wants to change immediately and bullies the other participant into switching. AMTP staff point out that this is not fair and, if John paddles on the way over, he will have to sit in the middle on the way back. John agrees to take turns as long as he is allowed to paddle on the way out. This kind of behavior continues throughout the day; AMTP staff must put a lot of effort into balancing this teenager's ability to participate in the group and the group's ability to function. This teen and the staff succeed in achieving this balance but only until the evening dinner.

At the end of the day, we return to the office and help prepare dinner. On the first floor of a two-story house, the AMTP is fortunate to have a large kitchen, which allows the staff and participants to enjoy meals together. Although everyone is expected to contribute to cooking and setting up the table, three students, including John, start trying to hide behind the house to smoke. Tension is evident among the staff members, who insist that the teens stay engaged with the group.

After dinner, San Antonio gathers the staff and participants to reflect on the day's experiences. This is typical of AMTP adventures. The physical activity often makes participants more open and able to communicate. In a paper titled "A Critique of the Appalachian Mountain Teen Project: Suggested Adaptations Using Ecological Theory," San Antonio (1995) explains, "We know that strenuous physical exercise over an extended period of time produces a bio-chemical response in the form of endorphins, which has a pain-reducing and relaxing effect" (5–6). Sitting on the floor of the AMTP office's porch after the canoe trip, it is easy to imagine similar conversations taking place around a campfire after a long, active day.

San Antonio begins the dialogue by saying that she is concerned because during the day she heard some people say things that were not nice and that she thinks offended other participants and staff. She proceeds to explain that this is not the way AMTP groups work and asks all the participants for their analysis. Alice explains that one needs to understand that some things are said to be funny and others to hurt people. She believes that on this particular day, people were joking. Alice tells the group that the wonderful thing about AMTP, for her, has been making friends with other girls. AMTP, she says, was the first place where people didn't tease and make fun of her. She acknowledges that it felt both "strange" and "good" to have people be respectful.

While most people are seriously engaged in the conversation, John again becomes restless and disruptive. San Antonio invites anyone who is tired of sitting to walk around. John gets up and walks around, releasing some energy. Though still needing to test the boundaries, he keeps returning to the conversation.

San Antonio picks up on the participants' comments and begins a discussion about the kinds of situations in which comments made by others are hurtful, but people ignore them. Moore takes the opportunity to speak about feeling hurt when he sensed that after we returned to the office a clear division erupted between participants and staff. He was disturbed by this antagonistic us-them relationship. He is referring specifically to John and the other two teens who chose to go to the back of the house to smoke rather than help with dinner. Both Martel and Moore had asked this group of teens to come back to the group with limited success. This antagonism, they observe, is not their vision of how groups work. Staff members explain that they expect to receive the same level of respect and trust they give all the teenagers. Further, they see themselves as part of the group and want to participate in that manner. More experienced AMTP participants fully understand and agree with this kind of reciprocal relationship. They add to the staff's observations with their own experiences, conveying in this manner the "AMTP way" of doing things. Newer members who are used to seeing "authority figures" as antagonistic are still holding on to old patterns; they seem to be wondering whether these people are "for real."

Although learning to be responsible for themselves is important, AMTP participants also learn that they must take responsibility for the well-being and success of the group as a whole. Although John has been difficult and disruptive throughout the day, everyone has worked hard to ensure that he is included in the group. San Antonio has extended that effort right to the end of the day, inviting those who are restless during the evening discussion to stand up and walk around. Although in more traditional environments John might have been asked to leave, the AMTP staff will remove a teen from the group only if the safety of the group is seriously compromised. Throwing away or discarding these teens—who have had that experience all too often—is not an option. The effort the staff put into helping John be a part of the group indicates their commitment to the principle of inclusion and group work.

The kind of day we experienced at the AMTP is the result of years of reflecting on and learning from their practice as democratic educators. The sharing of information and power with students, the commitment to reflective dialogue that guides the actions of the individuals and the group, the understanding of education as a process in which teachers and participants learn from each other, and the commitment to inclusion are all essential characteristics of a vibrant democratic community. Speaking with staff reveals much about how they understand education and why they choose to educate teens in the manner they do. Speaking with teens provides insights into how they experience the AMTP process, what they learn, and how they use the education they receive to understand and transform their lives.

Starting from Where the Teens Are

San Antonio imagines a good school to be one where "students really and truly have a voice in running the schools." Both San Antonio and Manoogian trust that participants "know best" what they need and, consequently, define the program on the basis of "what they have asked for." All outdoor activities begin with an introduction to the environment participants are about to enter, a discussion of issues of safety, and instruction on how to work collaboratively. But AMTP staff are attentive to the students' observations, needs, and requests, remaining flexible and willing to adjust plans to meet the teens where they are. Working within the boundaries of safety, respect, and trust that are fundamental to AMTP pedagogy, teens have the freedom to create an experience and engage in dialogues that they can call their own.

This philosophy applies to the counseling sessions as well. Many AMTP participants are facing crises at home and/or in school. The AMTP provides a safe, supportive environment in which to deal with their problems, which range from serious confrontations with parents to sexual abuse to harassment by peers to drug and alcohol abuse. For many of the teens and their parents, previous counseling experiences through mental health clinics have been disempowering and nonproductive. In these settings, counselors often try to exercise power-over and, thus, reinforce the feelings of inadequacy and lack of control that are already frustrating the teen.

San Antonio explains that counseling sessions in most mental health clinics focus on "behavior adjustment." The mission of the counselor is to figure out what is "wrong" with the teen and "adjust" the "problematic" behavior—preferably in the eight sessions that the insurance company will pay for. The AMTP approach to counseling is quite different. All AMTP counseling begins with what the teens define as their "truth stories." The counselors never challenge their truths, but rather asks questions that allow the teens to refine their understandings of themselves.

Actively listening to the teens' stories in an engaged and interactive manner, counselors ensure that teens feel they are being heard. The message teens receive from the AMTP counselors is that "I am a person who believes in your story." In turn, teens begin to see that "this is a person who believes in me." By gaining the trust of the teens, the AMTP staff create the conditions to begin identifying with them what needs to be done to resolve the problems that they both see as life-threatening. The experience of controlling their lives as well as the way the stories of their lives are told and interpreted transforms the teens' view of the counseling sessions, which become an important part of their lives.

The teen participants' understanding of who they are, the contexts within which they live, and what they need to survive and thrive are the building blocks of the AMTP's pocket of hope. A pedagogy of respect, trust, independence, and love supports and sustains this pocket of hope, countering the spaces of disrespect, distrust, and neglect these teenagers frequently inhabit. Here teens are able to rebuild their power from within by regaining their power to speak, listen, and act on their dream of a healthy and positive future. The AMTP objective is clear: to create the conditions for teens to re-engage in their schools and society as active participants. Understanding how the AMTP creates this pocket of hope requires listening to how these teens define themselves, the context within which they live, and their needs.

"I Was a Bad Kid": Narratives of Struggle and Survival

When the AMTP teens describe themselves and the circumstances that bring them to the project, they use words such as "losers," "bad" or "shy," "without friends." They also let you know that most of them are in serious trouble with drugs, alcohol, and violence. At the AMTP you sense they have found a peaceful space to reclaim their health and well-being. That space is important to them—some say it saved their lives. As young people with little control over their lives, teens find that this peaceful space exists only within the AMTP. Moving from the protected space that AMTP creates to the unprotected and often unsafe spaces such as school, work, and family, the participants recognize their own fragility and vulnerability.

Dan, who moved to New Hampshire from Massachusetts after his brother died in a car accident and his parents divorced, tells the story of how he joined the AMTP in his junior year in high school: "I was in special education at the high school; Donna and Holly, at that time, were doing stuff with that program." He explains that during a "ropes course," he began to understand the meaning of trust:

> There were logs you had to stand on and fall back. You had to trust that everyone was going to catch you…. And the look on people's faces when they [would] go up there…you were on a log that was three feet high. You know, there's nothing but ground. Normally, you wouldn't trust any of these people. They were the ones in high school people talked about [and] said, "Oh he's a druggie, a boozer."

This description fits both Dan's peers and Dan himself. Dan paints a clear picture of how he looked at the time. He was wearing "a leather jacket, jeans, and boots—typical thug. In my senior yearbook, I was the only one who was dressed like that; everyone else was dressed up. I was the only thug in the senior class."

During his senior year, Dan became a youth leader with the AMTP, helping with a three-day trip over spring break and a 20-mile bike ride. Ever since then, he says, "I have just been good friends with Donna and Holly." No longer a "thug," Dan sits on the AMTP board and is working full time. Along the way Dan has had difficult moments that might have overwhelmed him had he not been able to return to nature and to the AMTP for guidance and support.

Naomi, who takes her beautiful daughter Giullia to the interviews, describes what life was like for her in high school: "At school I was very insecure. I was very different…. I dressed like a boy, I got my head shaved and, then, I had the hair flopping over it and the rest of it was all long." People around her thought she was "a scum bag," she says. Even those whom she considered her friends were "really mean to me." Her assessment of why the school referred her to the program is that she was "very quiet. I guess they were worried about me, because the quiet ones are always the bad ones or something."

Naomi hated her first trip with the AMTP. Cold, homesick, unable to use snow shoes, and feeling she was on a trip with "weird people," she barely made it to the end. However, the spring canoeing trip was a different story. She explains, "I was hooked." Finding an outdoor experience that she enjoyed and excelled at began her long-term connection with the AMTP. After joining the project in the sixth grade, she continued to participate in AMTP activities for the next 10 years. Her dream is to work as a counselor for the AMTP.

Recently, Naomi spoke at a gathering of 200 funders. With great poise and strength, she delivered a clear message about the work of the AMTP. When San Antonio complimented her on her presentation, Naomi, who had previously collaborated with San Antonio in a presentation about the project at Harvard, responded, "If I can present at Harvard, I can certainly do it here." Naomi's journey has been long and hard, but with the ever-present support of the AMTP, she has become a powerful woman and mother.

Naomi analyzes carefully what the AMTP did for her, as well as the program's limits. In doing so, she identifies the treacherous journey these teens undertake as they move back and forth between danger and safety.

> [AMTP] can't stop…the pressures of school and your friends and everything.… I got into a lot of things I shouldn't have gotten into [and] it took me a few years to get out of it. I started smoking and drinking and doing drugs…that was just my way of trying to get through school. And I never did make it all the way through, just because I didn't like the school.

In Naomi's case, the AMTP provided a space for recovery and reflection, making her uphill battle more hopeful. She learned that there were spaces where she could be healthy: "When I went on the trips, I didn't need any of it [drugs, alcohol]; but when I went home, I felt I needed it. The trips were the adrenaline, and you don't need it then. I didn't bring any cigarettes with me on the trips." Yet, even when she acknowledges that the trips were "helping me out a lot and Donna and Holly helped me out a lot, too," she explains that "when it came to the pressures of school, they weren't always there."

Although Naomi didn't finish high school, she completed her GED, moved to Boston to join City Year, and had her baby. According to Naomi, the baby "helped me get out of all that, too." With great love, the AMTP staff advised Naomi through her pregnancy and included Giullia as the youngest member of the AMTP family. Naomi now has the courage and strength to build a life on her own: she is working, taking care of her baby, and attending college.

Alice's narrative begins with an intense desire to go camping. As a matter of fact, she agreed to the counseling sessions only so that she could go on the AMTP trips. Her plan was to bluff her way through the sessions. But Alice's problems at school were serious. According to her, "The major social goal of my class was to pick on me.... My boyfriend dumped me in front of our peers three times just to save face. I had no self-worth, no self-esteem" (Peterson, *The Granite State News Carroll County Independent,* February 3, 1999, 1B). She even considered suicide. The counseling sessions turned out to be critical in helping her regain control of her life. Today, Alice admits, "In my heart and in my mind, I know I probably would not be alive were it not for AMTP" (Peterson, 1B).

As a result of her involvement with the AMTP, Alice became involved in countless clubs at school, participated in winter and spring track, and managed the basketball team. Today she is an outstanding leader within the AMTP and a respected woman among the younger generation. Alice has moved to another phase in her life, in which she can give back to the organization what she feels it has given to her.

Some students are not able to manage the cycle of feeling safe and supported in the AMTP and then alone and "out there," a cycle Naomi articulates so well. San Antonio tells the story of a participant who they felt did an excellent job in an eight-day trip canoeing and rock climbing but then, a few weeks later, stole his stepfather's car. At 14, he drove to New Jersey with three of his friends, ran a toll booth, and when police started chasing him, drove faster. The teenager ended up being driven home under arrest. Cases such as this, although rare, illustrate the fragility and vulnerability of these teens, who sometimes get caught on the wrong side of their journey between safety and danger.

For AMTP teens, the path to recovery is strewn with obstacles. These teens are strong, but they rely on the support of AMTP to get them past the hard places. Trusting that they will always have the support of the organization, they have a strong foundation from which to take risks, explore life, and make healthy choices. AMTP teens know that the conditions that got them there in the first place don't change easily. In a discussion about education, it's clear that they have many insights to offer concerning the ineffectiveness of their schools and how schools put them at risk. Unfortunately, few people are listening.

Narratives of Distrust and Disrespect

Participants in the AMTP view their schools as being "too old." In other words, the ideas that guide the school are "old" ideas. This observation has nothing to do with the age of the teachers, since as Dan observes, "There are some younger ones but their ideas are older." One of these "old" ideas, Dan says, is that "kids should be seen, not heard." Expanding on this idea, he states that students "don't have authority" in the schools. Even in the few schools where students are represented on school boards, they can't vote, so their participation is useless. Repeatedly, the AMTP teens express the need to be heard. Feeling they can contribute, they eagerly wait for an opportunity to express their opinions.

Alice, who at the time of the discussion is a junior in high school, tells the story of how she is looking forward to an opportunity to talk with her school principal. The principal meets with all the seniors at the end of the school year to see what they are doing after graduation and to get their feedback on how the school can be improved. Understanding that this is the one and only chance she will have to express her opinion, she tells us:

> I was psyched when I heard about that, I'm thinking, yes, I am going to be able to at least say something.... I can't wait until next year. It's one of the things I am looking forward to in my senior year, is to be able to tell them I liked this, I didn't like this.

Although she has to wait four years to offer her insights about her school and the education she has received, Alice is grateful for the opportunity. But she and the other teens also recognize that they deserve better. They point out over and over again the exceptions—teachers who listen to them and recognize their power to think and express their views.

Teachers who give students the opportunity to participate in making decisions are consistently recognized as the good teachers. For example, Alice explains that "the class in which I seem to have accomplished most this year is the class where students have a say." Repeatedly, these teens compare the treatment they receive from the "good" teachers with the way they are normally treated. As they do, a pattern emerges. Speaking about this same teacher, Alice says, "She would come to us a lot and find out what we wanted to do, to the point where she wasn't the person up at the top that had the whip and we were just people doing it." Another student, referring to the AMTP pedagogy, explains that AMTP leads participants "without kind of leading you like a cow." Comparing San Antonio and Manoogian's pedagogy to that of other adults, Dan summarizes how these teens feel about teachers and other adults in their lives:

> A lot of adults...make you feel small. But Donna and Holly, they make you feel like you are important. They listen to you, they want your input, and I think that is the magic. They make you feel like a person.

Students don't have high expectations: to be treated like a person, not a "cow," isn't asking a lot. The experience of these teens, however, indicates that those who are meant to teach and guide them are not meeting even these minimum standards.

Continuing their critique of schools, the teens point to policies that they believe put them at risk, make no sense, or are inconsistent. For example, a male and a female student were told to leave the school building after school hours but had no place to go. It was winter, and their only option was to stay in a car for long periods. They recognized that this was a "dangerous situation," but they felt they had no choice because, as they said, there was "no place for us." What they don't understand is why the school would put their own students at risk.

The most fundamental problem at schools as defined by these teenagers is the lack of trust between teachers and students. Alice identifies three teachers in her school who "trust me thoroughly." She says, "They trust me in my decisions and they trust what I say is true." Her relationship with other teachers is different: "Teachers in my school that I can plainly see don't trust me, I stay away from." Some teachers may argue that students need to gain their teachers' trust—in other words, students begin with zero trust and move up in the "trust" scale. Yet the argument Alice makes is that to have an environment of trust in a school, "it pretty much has to start with the teachers by trusting the students." According to these students, teachers must take the first steps in creating a trusting relationship; only then will students know that they can trust their teachers and each other.

These teens don't entirely blame the teachers or even the schools for the lack of trust and disrespect they feel exists. Giving an example of a teacher who "got maced and knifed by some people he knew," Dan states, "It is situations like this that keep people not trusting.... It seems to be happening more and more." Dan sees the whole society unraveling around him. But he and the others agree that students must take responsibility for changing schools. April, who has successfully finished high school and is going to college in the fall, puts this responsibility squarely on the shoulders of students: "I think it's the students because you have to want it, you have to want to try new things. To improve things, do something."

April and Alice summarize their analyses of schools from different angles. For April, who has a teacher who has been instrumental in helping her go to college, the problem is that the good teachers need to be recognized. Alice gives a more sobering analysis, concluding, "There are good teachers...but not even their great skills can be brought out totally because of school regulations and school policies."

Listening to these students, one sees that they are spectators in the unfolding drama that takes place in their schools. Without voice or power, they carefully observe, trying to make sense of their schools. They understand, better than the adults around them, that the maze of inconsistent policies and decisions often puts them at risk, because no one takes the time to ask them what they need and desire. Despite their marginalization, these teens continue to hope that things will change. Moreover, they are willing to accept that this is their challenge. Students, they argue, need to take responsibility for changing the schools.

Experiencing Independence and Freedom

Dan uses a vivid metaphor to describe the AMTP community. He says, our community has "a common thread or tie to one another. Donna and Holly are...the center of the community for us. They're what connects everything.... It's like a spider web, they're the center of it and we are around them." The educators at the center of the spider web have a clear vision of how to create this space, or the protective web, which teens describe as "magical." Within this protective web teens can reclaim their own power—their power-from-within—so as to regain their rightful place in their schools and communities.

With great care, San Antonio, Manoogian, and the AMTP staff envision this protected space. Their mission as educators is to be "sure the atmosphere is physically and emotionally safe for everyone so students can grow in their own confidence and skill" (AMTP Mission Statement and Philosophy). For them, a safe place is one where there are love and caring, respect and trust. By creating and sustaining this safe and respectful atmosphere, a participant can "explore, be self-reflective and self-critical, honest, creative, act on his or her knowledge, believe in his or her own hopes and dreams, take risks." For the AMTP, successful participants are those who, regaining their power from within, claim their independence and their right to define their own life.

Student Power. Creating a safe place where teens can take both physical and emotional risks and reflect on their actions is fundamental to AMTP's pedagogy, because they see their primary task as helping teens overcome their sense of powerlessness. Teens, San Antonio argues, are not powerless; they simply have not been given the opportunity to experience their power. The belief that students have no power, San Antonio suggests, is a myth. The example she gives is a protest action, in which many New Hampshire students walked out of school in response to the state's refusal to celebrate Martin Luther King, Jr.'s, birthday. She also tells the story of Naomi and another AMTP participant, who, tired of the sexual harassment in their school, decided to take action. As a result of their actions, "new sexual harassment codes were written, offending students were disciplined, and a male teacher who had violated Title IX laws did not have his contract renewed." Even though Naomi found the hostility from some parents, teachers, and students so unbearable that she left school in her senior year, San Antonio believes that taking action provided the young women with an invaluable life-long lesson. San Antonio declares that these students "learned forever that they have power to interpret and change their own day-to-day experience."

Teaching from the Heart. Teens describe the AMTP as a loving community in which they feel free to enter as complete human beings. By comparing San Antonio's teaching to teaching by college professors, Dan makes an important distinction: "She is loving and caring and that's where she teaches from. She doesn't teach from a book, like college professors." In these teens' description of what it means to have teachers who teach from the heart, one finds the essential elements of a pocket of hope: a space of caring that embraces who they are and who they dream of becoming.

Providing unconditional love is understood by the AMTP staff to be a profoundly political act that provides teens with the anchor they need to begin living their lives fully. By giving unconditional love the staff means that they will join hands with these teens and sustain and guide them during their hardest struggles. Their commitment is never to turn their back on them or withdraw their love and respect.

The teens carefully describe the evidence they have that teachers are teaching from the heart. They often point out that these educators know how to listen to their problems. Knowing that they can confide in the staff, who will never repeat what they hear, will not judge them, and will respond with compassion, gives these teens the space to speak. Whereas outside AMTP, adults are often hostile to these teenagers, at AMTP they find adults who are willing and able to listen to what they have to say.

For San Antonio, listening to and taking seriously what teens have to say are not only acts of love and respect but also a radicalizing action. She says, "Something we forget is how radicalizing it is just to be taken seriously…to be taken seriously, to be given an opportunity to speak your own experience and to have it be listened to." Indeed, to feel that what they have to say matters is a transformative experience for students; it allows them to regain their confidence and begin imagining themselves differently.

A caring community where teachers teach from the heart generates the conditions necessary for individual as well as collective transformation. Teens learn to listen to their peers with the same care and respect accorded to them by their teachers. As Dan states, "When someone talks, you listen. Not just because you have to, but because you want to know what they are saying, you respect them." Naomi adds that "when you sit down to have conversations at the end of the day...you want to listen to see what they thought about the day, how it felt to them in comparison to your feelings and see if you can see the day in a different light and learn something new." Dialogue, or the sharing of their experiences so as to make sense of the world, becomes a possibility when teens believe that they have something to teach and learn from each other. The AMTP pocket of hope is one where teens experience their own as well as their collective power through the radicalizing act of dialogue.

Becoming Independent, Experiencing Freedom. A caring community that places teaching and learning at the center provides AMTP teens with the tools for self-sustained physical, intellectual, and emotional growth. Though the AMTP has an open-door policy, the participants know that the ultimate goal of the program is to assist them in becoming independent adults. San Antonio and Manoogian's concern that the teens not become dependent on the organization is evident in their pedagogy. Manoogian suggests that both in the outdoors experience and in the counseling sessions, "whenever possible, teens need to work through the process themselves," because it is a much "richer" experience, which they can "turn around and repeat." San Antonio sees it as her responsibility "to not take away a student's power by protecting them from the struggle they must engage in order to become fully human." Trial and error, taking risks and making mistakes, are central to their pedagogy.

A key element in having the power to be an independent human being, according to San Antonio, is "the power to have, pass on, and withhold information." Initially, San Antonio and Manoogian hold the power because they know how to stay safe in the wilderness. When the teens learn to survive in the outdoors, they develop their own sense of power and control. Asking questions, finding answers, constructing together the knowledge they need to succeed are therefore key for the teens in their journey toward independence.

The transfer of power and knowledge begins in the dialogues that are initiated by San Antonio, Manoogian, and the AMTP staff. These dialogues usually begin with a question. These questions, which may be as simple as "How do you feel the day went today?" usually generate what the teens label "pretty decent conversations." The constant flow of questions creates the space for teens to regain their curiosity, to pose questions, and to invent theories that can be tested and revised.

At AMTP, the teens point out, the staff encourage questions but rarely provide direct answers. The teens are challenged to discover answers on their own. By engaging constantly in this process, AMTP teens regain the power to think critically. This is important to them, because they face real, sometimes urgent, problems that they need to be able to analyze and resolve. AMTP

works for them because learning to think critically and survive in the outdoors is a metaphor for surviving the complex realities of their day-to-day
lives.

The process by which teens progressively take more control in their trips
and forge their own path is one way they learn to gain control and guide their
own lives. Again, Dan explains with a metaphor how he views the AMTP pedagogy: "It's almost like giving you a road map and a compass and saying,
here's the goal, here you are, you've got to get to it, and here's stuff along the
way.... [AMTP staff] are just kind of there, every now and then, if you wan-
der off the path, they're kind of a compass, and the program's the map."
Naomi gives a concrete example to support Dan's vision.

> They gave us a map and told us to go hike this mountain and
> come out this way. Well, I'm not good with directions, I don't
> know how to read a map, I didn't then.... I had to teach
> myself...and we're all separated. It was a solo hike. I wasn't
> scared or anything, because there were a lot of people out on the
> trails.... I somehow took a wrong turn, and they were waiting
> down at the bottom for me, I guess, for about an hour.... And
> I finally did it. Donna said to me, "This is how your life is,
> Naomi, you're going to get lost, you're going to have all these
> bumps and stuff, but eventually you're going to come through
> and find your way out of it." So that gave me a lot of insight
> about how things are...or were.

The lesson that reading a map, getting lost, and eventually finding your
way resembles life is very clear to Naomi. The connection to her life is direct
and real. When she moved to Boston, finding her way in a new city didn't
seem very hard—she knew she could do it. She also attributes successfully
moving in with "five complete strangers" to the education she received in the
AMTP. She knows how to listen, learn, and communicate with others respectfully. Naomi's power-from-within and her ability to share power-with others
give her the strength necessary to face the challenges of being a young working mother in a new city.

Being in the outdoors is an essential part of the AMTP experience. It is in
connecting to nature that teens connect to their inner being and discover
their power-within. Nature provides both the comfort of solitude and an
extraordinary sense of freedom. Dan explains:

> The feeling, to me, is almost like joy and happiness [you feel]
> with something you can wrap yourself in. It's like a nice warm

blanket. When I go out there it's like, when you were a kid and you got hurt and ran home to Mom, and she'd hug you. That's what it's like. I get out there, and it's like I'm in one big hug. I'm warm, safe, happy.

Dan uses the outdoors to sustain and renew himself when facing difficult times. Here he feels safe and free to imagine a different future for himself:

I always had a sense of freedom being out there. In a room, you are confined. Outside there is nothing to stop you except your imagination. You can go anywhere, do anything, you know the air is fresh. You hear things that you don't normally hear. Everything is just different.

Experiencing their own power for the first time gives teens a "sense of free-dom" where "there is nothing to stop you but your imagination." April attributes this sense of freedom to being independent: "You're not depending on anybody else to make you do this, to survive through the day." For these teens, power-from-within means having "everything you need with you, in your person," and having the capacity to "get through the next day, being able to do everything you possibly can do to the best of your ability." Reclaiming their strength and power, these teens move to lead others who are beginning their own journey to recover their power and freedom.

THE POWER TO LEAD AND TAKE ACTION

AMTP staff strongly believe that their mission as educators is to develop demo-cratic leaders capable of working with others in projects of social change. The staff teach leadership by modeling an approach that teens find empowering. Thus, it's not surprising that AMTP teens describe strong leaders as those who respect, trust, and encourage those they are called to lead. Although they see the leader as responsible for getting others to the end of their journey, they also point out that while on a wilderness trip everyone must take responsi-bility for himself or herself as well as for the group. The leader, however, has the added responsibility of "reading" the individuals in the group. For exam-ple, the leader may decide to switch off partners if someone is not paddling hard enough or may have to defuse a situation that is putting the group in danger. By carefully observing participants, they argue, leaders are able to anticipate when and how to intervene.

Naomi points to an important lesson she learned in the AMTP, which she relates to being a good leader: "Encourage the slower ones…putting them [in position] to lead the group." She explains that Donna and Holly did this a lot, making sure that "we'd all [move] at the same pace, instead of leaving the [slow] person behind." As a camp counselor, Naomi uses this same strategy, believing that keeping the group together, even if moving slowly, is essential to good leadership. Competition, according to AMTP teens, can have negative results and is, therefore, encouraged only as a "fun" activity. At the AMTP, the teens learn that performing to your best ability isn't about "winning"; it's about taking care of yourself and experiencing the joys of individual—and collective—success.

Leadership opportunities on the AMTP wilderness trips prepare teens to become leaders in their communities. They test their newly developed skills in community service projects. AMTP staff and teens have been involved in painting buildings at fairgrounds in the Midwest, cleaning up the Crow Indian Reservation in Montana after tribal elections, doing trail work in the South, and picking up litter along the Blue Ridge Parkway. In New Hampshire, they painted the Effingham Town Hall, cleaned and painted the Shaker Village facilities, and at the AMTP Riverland Education and Adventure Center completed the building from top to bottom. In doing these projects, teens are not only involved in doing the work: they identify the projects, speak with people about doing them, and locate resources in the community to make the projects possible. By taking on this leadership role, these "losers" or "bad" kids reposition themselves in the community, which begins to see them as having the capacity to lead and contribute. Having changed their perception of themselves through their success in the wilds of New England, these once marginalized teens are able to reenter the community from a position of strength.

The community service projects give AMTP teens the knowledge and skills necessary to define their own projects of change. For example, Alice "got the courage" to start a program at her school called Youth Works, an organization for teens to "do the things they want to do." Her objective was to "get people off the street." She wanted to provide an alternative to drugs and alcohol—"their own place, [where they could] have a coffee." Alice, who had had the experience of having nowhere to go after school, decided to organize this coffeehouse to provide others with a safe place to relax in a healthy and positive way. By taking on projects such as Youth Works, AMTP teens demonstrate that they are capable of understanding the needs of other students, addressing them in effective ways, and taking on the challenge of contributing to transforming their schools. The AMTP gives them the self-confidence as well as the practical tools they need to return to their schools and re-invent their roles as active participants as opposed to passive spectators.

An example of AMTP teens' taking on a significant issue within their communities was the spring 1998 Teen Work Conference. AMTP staff, together with long-time allies Arnie Alpert at the American Friends Service Committee and Judy Elliot of the AFL-CIO, managed to bring together an impressive group of speakers to address issues facing teenagers in the work force.

Teens raised the need for a conference such as this one in their AMTP gatherings. Increasingly their conversations revolved around their workplaces. The staff listened and began to see a pattern. More teens were working longer and longer hours. They also noticed that as a result of teens' work schedules, the typical AMTP summer trips lasting several weeks or a month had become increasingly difficult to organize. Some basic research revealed that the New Hampshire labor force, in fact, included a rising number of teenagers. Seeking to address the teens' concerns, the organizers decided to invite speakers from the New Hampshire Department of Education, the Department of Labor, the American Friends Service Committee, and the AFL-CIO to address teens, parents, educators, and business leaders in a one-day conference.

The highlight of the conference was the presentation of the findings of the research project designed by San Antonio and Jason, a teen who was doing an internship at the AMTP office. Together with a group of teens from Manchester Central, Winnisquam, Kingswood, Nute, Laconia, and Belmont High Schools, they conducted surveys and interviewed teens. They sought information on how many teens were working, what positions they held in their workplaces, how many hours they worked, and what kinds of working conditions they encountered. They also hoped to learn the effect work was having on the school, family and social life of teens. The research results, which included both quantitative and qualitative data, were impressive. Participants from the Department of Education who had conducted a similar research project commented that they reached similar conclusions and requested that the teens collaborate with them in doing further work.

As the day progressed, teens focused on discussing issues of safety, which seemed to be a shared concern. The research conducted by the teens showed that injury in the workplace was often ignored or dismissed by managers. Participants in the conference confirmed that this was also true in their experience. For example, a teen related a story about cutting herself with broken glass and being told to "stop crying, it's only a little scratch," when she felt she needed stitches. As teens shared similar experiences, they realized that there was a systemic problem.

When Mark Mackenzie, president of the AFL-CIO in New Hampshire, explained that workers have a right to workers compensation, the teens became aware that they did not know their rights. This realization generated intense discussion, in which teens asked themselves how come they didn't know. A participant pointed out that he didn't remember "ever seeing where, if I was curious about my rights, I could go look at it, and if I saw my rights were being violated, I could find the number." He continued: "If I really felt my rights were being violated, I could find it out, but it shouldn't be a chore, you shouldn't have to go do research to find out if your rights are being violated." The conclusion he reached was that this "is helping out the employers that are violating us." By listening to each other's stories, these teens began to see a pattern: those who have power over them are not likely to inform them of their rights, even if it is the law.

If the employers do not inform teens of their rights, the audience wondered who should take on this responsibility. Teens argued that employers should be forced to post their rights where they could see them, but they were told by representatives from the Department of Labor that the department does not have the capacity to enforce this rule and they are only able to visit those sites that have the worst safety records. After giving this some thought and reflecting on the possibilities, Jason suggested that the best place to teach students their rights would be in government classes in high schools. "After all," he argued, "it's our government that comes up with these regulations.... We learn about laws and amendments...teach us even more of our rights."

The conference demonstrated much about AMTP pedagogy. Teens led the conference with their research. The dialogue was intense and focused. Adults viewed their role during the day as educating teens to embrace their own power. Moving from the teens' experience, the dialogue converged around the issue of safety, which teens identified as their main concern. Through the process of having this public dialogue, the teens came to understand that they shared similar experiences. As a result, individual experience was reconceptualized as a social problem.

The feeling of collective power at the end of the day was palpable. Before leaving, the teens asked the adults "to keep in touch." This group of adults agreed with the teens that this was an issue that deserved greater attention. The teens, thus, were reassured that someone had heard their concerns and that these adults would work with them to ensure that their needs would be addressed.

CONCLUSION

Coming from poor towns, experiencing failure at their schools, and caught up in the court system, the teens in the AMTP are seldom viewed as the future leaders of their communities. Instead, from an early age, they are tracked into a future of poverty and marginalization. Worse yet, after innumerable encounters with institutions that fail them, these teens come to agree that they and their futures are worthless. Either they become resigned to their powerlessness—becoming depressed and isolated—or they rebel in ways that inevitably land them in serious trouble.

By choosing to travel with these youth in their journey toward health and hope, AMTP challenges the institutions that have discarded them and their families. The AMTP understands its mission to be helping these youth become whole and preparing them to become engaged in social change.

AMTP's classroom is the New England wilderness. The outdoors demands that participants face challenges and take risks, within a "safe environment" constructed by their "wise" AMTP educators. In the outdoors the teens experience success paddling a canoe through rapids, hiking farther than they believed possible, camping in the snows of New Hampshire, and, as a result, come to know their power-from-within. They realize that these challenges are not so very different from those that they face in daily life.

As the teens become more familiar and comfortable with the outdoors, they wrap themselves in the "nice warm blanket" of nature. Away from their daily lives, they find the peace and the silence they need to think and dream. Listening and responding to their peers who recount stories similar to their own, they begin the process of co-constructing knowledge and questioning the power institutions and adults hold over their lives. With their collective power-with they prepare to challenge these authorities constructively and change the world around them. They find new strength to withstand the relentless negative messages that tell them they are worthless and powerless.

Slowly but surely, and with the continuous help of the AMTP staff, these teens regain their rightful place in their schools, communities, and homes and prepare to work with other teens caught in the same cycle of despair. Through service projects and political action, they relocate themselves as leaders, transforming the community's perception of them as "bad kids" or "losers." As loving, respectful, and visionary leaders who believe in sharing power with others so as to transform society, they present us with a powerful alternative to leadership models that preserve the power of some over the lives of others.

By creating an environment in which all teens, regardless of their differences, are accepted, respected, and provided with the tools to empower themselves, AMTP helps teens overcome the isolation and alienation typical of countless high schools. Teens in AMTP prove that in a safe space, where they are offered love and respect, they can learn to think critically, take responsibility for themselves and others, and become passionately engaged in their communities.

When Dan describes AMTP as a "magical" space, he immediately identifies AMTP as a pocket of hope. Here, educators who treat teens as human beings, who trust the teens' decision-making process and are willing to protect them when they take risks, receive the utmost respect from their students. Dan is deeply appreciative of this "protective spider web" that provided him with a rare and precious opportunity to chart a path in life that could easily have been denied him.

The ongoing commitment of AMTP teens to the project—returning as board members, inviting new members to participate, teaching others in the way they were taught at the AMTP, and creating organizations grounded in the same principles as this organization—is a testament to the AMTP pedagogy. As they go out into the world and create other pockets of hope, AMTP graduates join in challenging the power of those who routinely throw away poor kids. This powerful and visionary generation of leaders such as Dan, Alice, Naomi, and April who have learned to trust themselves and one another, have the potential to humanize their communities and give adults, who may have forgotten, the opportunity to reclaim their own power to dream of a better future.

CHAPTER 7

No Ordinary Teacher:
Helen Lewis of Highlander

Patricia A. Gozemba

> We've got the closest thing to a dictatorship in McDowell
> County that I ever saw.
>
> I was raised in a family that focused on unions and justice. I was
> taught to measure people by what's in their heart. I am really
> concerned about democracy here and in this country. If you are
> different, your voice is not heard in the discussion. I've always
> been enriched by different people.
>
> My true love has become justice. I had a wonderful experience
> in learning how to work towards it at Highlander, especially in
> the discussions of the Democracy Schools project. The young
> people took my breath away.
>
> There is a need here for political democracy, economic democ-
> racy, family democracy, organizational democracy. People need
> to find out what power they have.
> —Meeting of the Big Creek People in Action, Caretta, West
> Virginia, June 17, 1997

This passion for justice and democracy came from four citizens of McDowell
County, West Virginia, once a booming center of the coal and timber industries, but now one of the poorest counties in the United States. As seventeen
members of Big Creek People in Action (BCPIA) met in their community center on June 17, 1997, and one by one went around the circle deliberating

about whether they would collaborate in a Democracy Schools project with Highlander Research and Education Center of New Market, Tennessee, democracy was born again. Blacks and whites, women and men, teenagers and retirees, employed and unemployed, political activists and newcomers to community politics decided to change their world. A pocket of poverty emerged as a pocket of hope.

Though proud to be Americans—with the implied traditions of democracy, equality, and freedom—the people of Appalachia, and particularly McDowell County, have been impoverished and disenfranchised by a capitalist system that exploited and abandoned them. They far more resemble their counterparts in Third World countries than those in affluent suburban neighborhoods who are riding the current wave of economic prosperity into the new millennium. Nonetheless, the willingness of the Big Creek People in Action to struggle for themselves makes it possible to believe that they will reclaim democracy—and economic justice—in their county. Their principled commitment to rebuilding their community through grass-roots democracy provides a glimmer of hope for others disempowered by the forces of capitalism and economic globalization.

Helen Lewis and two other Highlander staff members had traveled to this meeting almost five hours over mountain roads to Caretta, West Virginia, bringing with them visitors: an educator from Australia and Eileen de los Reyes and I who were searching for an understanding of how Highlander's pedagogy works in such transformationally positive ways.

As people socialized, enjoying snacks they had all brought to share, the meeting began with Carl Rutherford of BCPIA playing guitar and Guy Carawan, longtime affiliate of Highlander and nationally known musician, playing on his banjo. The music got feet tapping and heads nodding. Community favorites got everyone singing. The ease and informality immediately brought an amazing level of comfort to all who had gathered in the BCPIA Community Center. After about 20 minutes, Franki Patton Rutherford, a member of the Board of Directors of the BCPIA, asked everyone to introduce himself or herself and to offer views about whether they should endorse entering the Democracy Schools project with Highlander.

Franki began, expressing her faith in Highlander and especially in her great mentor and ally, Helen Lewis. She spoke of the positive effect that the $2.9-million Enterprise Community Grant had on McDowell County and noted that the recently completed participatory evaluation documented people's belief that the local county government was the biggest obstacle to democracy in the county.

Other people expressed their dreams of change and their willingness to work for it. Some had run for office. Others were willing to run or work on campaigns. Many people identified problems with the educational system and suggested such ideas as action clubs and political groups for youth to build democratic expectations. They heard each other out, listening carefully and building on what previous speakers had said.

Lewis, who as a Highlander staffer had maintained connections for over 20 years in McDowell County, followed people's reflections and analysis carefully. When it was her turn to speak, Lewis wondered aloud about the ways that everyone in the room saw democracy functioning in their community. Were they seeing any of the political democracy, economic democracy, family democracy, and organizational democracy that one of them mentioned earlier?

Her question prompted Franki to suggest that they reflect on the pockets of democracy that did exist in McDowell. Someone jumped up to get out the newsprint and markers—evidently a common practice. People ticked off the BCPIA, Head Start, the Family Resource Centers, the HIV Education Project, mapping the strengths of the community infrastructure. They went on to critique their disappointments: the school system, the county commissioners, and the three private land companies that owned over 80 percent of the land in the county, most of it rich in coal and timber and all of it vastly under-assessed. With the collusion of the county political structure, the absentee landlords paid minimal taxes, impoverishing the county.

The people's assessment of democratic structures, however, affirmed their hope and stirred their desire for change. They had gathered not to complain, but to act. They had a track record. Getting the building they met in, once an abandoned public school, marked the first of several BCPIA victories. Now they were on to much larger and more fundamental issues: democracy and power. They voted unanimously to collaborate with Highlander in a Democracy Schools project for McDowell County.

THE HIGHLANDER EXPERIENCE

> The power of the Highlander experience is the strength that grows within the souls of people, working together, as they analyze and confirm their own experiences and draw upon their understanding to contribute to fundamental change.
> —Statement of Highlander's Mission (1989)

As the Big Creek People in Action, an alliance of people from 23 communities, met for two and a half hours, they became the embodiment of the theory and practice of Highlander. In resisting those forces in the county with power-over them, they tapped into their power-from-within and their power-with members of their community and Highlander, the nearly 70-year-old progressive adult community education school that continues to be a beacon of hope for Appalachia and the South. Ordinary citizens sat with their peers, discussing, reflecting on, and analyzing their common concerns and planning the action they would take to develop economic justice and democracy in their community.

Highlander's pedagogical strategies—sitting in a circle with everyone able to see everyone else, laughing, sharing life histories, analyzing, eating good food, reflecting, building community, encouraging leadership, making music, respecting peers, building skills, and taking action to transform one's life and community—were much in evidence that night. Were they at Highlander, the discussion would have taken place in a group of no more than 30 or so people sitting in a circle of rocking chairs with a breathtaking view of the Smoky Mountains—dreaming another world for their community. No matter the place—the Highlander process gives people hope, just as it did in the basement of the BCPIA Community Center. Highlander, which John Glen (1988) called "no ordinary school," and Lewis, no ordinary teacher, were in McDowell County fostering democracy. In gathering with people who, through their own powers of sharing, analysis, and reflection, were developing "the resources for collective action…working to change unjust structures and to build a genuine political and economic democracy," Lewis was making real the Statement of Highlander's Mission (1989).

Although men outnumbered women in the room, the leader, Franki Patton Rutherford, ran the meeting as if she were in a feminist or critical classroom. The people had a long view, thinking of the generations that would come after them. They listened carefully to each other. Their sense of their own power invigorated them. Sharing music of their region, food, laughter, and friendship strengthened the alliances that held the community together and created an empowerment zone in which each of them could find a meaningful place. The "teacher" in this setting, the community ally, Helen Lewis, participated in this "classroom," asking only one strategic question that prompted the community to assess what it had and what it wanted. Lewis knows how important it is to ask the question that pushes people to a more complicated level of thinking.

The Big Creek People in Action were educating themselves about possibilities and they were dreaming of better lives. About one third of the group had been to Highlander for a workshop, joining the ranks of union members, civil rights activists, environmentalists, and people committed to justice who had made the same journey—people like Pete Seeger, Eleanor Roosevelt, Septima Clark, Rosa Parks, Julian Bond, Martin Luther King, Jr., and Dorothy Cotton. The BCPIA tapped into the mutual power of people with a yearning for justice and a commitment to action making common cause. The energy created in the room sustained them through the meeting and would charge their optimism and commitment as they left to return to living some of the most difficult political and economic lives in all of the United States.

We Make the Road by Walking

The people of BCPIA are part of generations of community activists who have been touched by the adult education work of Highlander Research and Education Center. Founded in 1932 by Myles Horton, Highlander, for much of the last century, has provided a unique empowerment zone for communities and leaders longing for all forms of justice and democracy. I went to Highlander in 1997 to find the spirit of Myles Horton, whose inspirational work with labor and civil rights activists I had long admired.

I found more than I had hoped for—a new guiding spirit, Helen Lewis. Lewis, who had joined the Highlander staff in 1976 and served as interim director for a short time in 1978–1979, had worked closely with Horton, who though "retired" remained active in the life of the center until his death in 1990. Not only was she carrying forward the pedagogical practices that Horton had used so effectively to inspire ordinary people to challenge the powers arrayed against them, but as a feminist, she had expanded Horton's vision. In her 21-year affiliation with Highlander, some of Lewis's most revolutionary work took place in desperately poor communities where women led the way to revitalizing social and political life as well as local economies.

A radical activist, educator, and scholar, who, as she said, had been "fired from some of the best colleges and universities for nurturing radical students," Lewis found in Highlander a home from which she could create a rich life of activist pedagogy. When she joined Highlander, Lewis was well known for her cutting-edge rebuttal of the "deficiency" and "culture of poverty" models of Appalachia and her advancement of the theory of colonialist exploitation of the region. With the birth of the second wave of feminism, however, Lewis shifted her focus; she began to nourish the leadership skills of women, whose role she realized had been undervalued, ironically enough, in both the theoretical model of colonial exploitation and Highlander's community development work.

Lewis recognized that in many coal-mining communities in Appalachia, men were defeated and sullen, so filled with resentment and shame about what had happened to them in losing their jobs that they often were not effective leaders. Women, by contrast, realized that there was no time for that kind of indulgence. Always the sustainers of community life, they wanted to forge a future for their families, especially their children, in the mountains of Appalachia. Candie Carawan, whose affiliation with Highlander over almost

40 years made her a colleague of both Horton and Lewis, notes that "Myles felt that women, especially those with children, would have a limited role in organizing and social justice work. Helen felt that women were at the heart of many community struggles and had the stamina and skill to make a huge contribution to social change" (Carawan, personal communication, 1999). Lewis created the space for women in what she jokes about as the "blue jeans macho days" of Highlander.

Lewis, who retired in 1997, is as unassuming as she is accomplished. Not only has she left a lasting impression on communities throughout Appalachia, where she has helped develop coal-field health clinics, community education programs, and grass-roots political organizations, she is known as a prime mover and shaker in the field of Appalachian studies. Throughout her years at Highlander she continued to teach at the graduate and undergraduate levels and to publish widely. She is as comfortable collaborating with university scholars in academia as she is with Gramscian organic intellectuals like Franki Patton Rutherford, meeting in church basements and community centers "on the rough side of the mountain."

When Lewis received the Cratis D. Williams Service Award of the Appalachian Studies Association in 1996, Pat Beaver, director of the Appalachian Studies Program at Appalachia State University, who nominated her, spoke about Lewis's daring and accomplishments.

> Many of us have been engaged in scholarly research and teaching in Appalachia, but few of us have the courage to step outside the safety of tenured academic positions with regular salary increments and retirement plans. Helen has had that courage.... Because she saw the importance of adult education as a tool for community empowerment and social change, she began working...with new models of empowerment. Because she saw the possibility of community renewal and self-determination through alternative economic strategies, she conceptualized new ways of thinking about economic processes within communities and began teaching and successfully organizing in communities suffering from economic decline.... Helen's life— lived gracefully, compassionately, and with abiding good humor—sets a rigorous pace for those of us who try to keep up.... [H]er vision is on the next horizon, which few of us see clearly until Helen points the way. (Beaver, personal communication, 1996)

Lewis's vision and her work are equally appreciated in the community. A few months after she received the Appalachian Studies Award, the Mountain Association for Community Economic Development in Berea, Kentucky, presented the first Helen Lewis Community Leadership Award to her. In keeping with the creative vision of Lewis, whose name it bears, the award each year is an original piece of art work representing the spirit and accomplishment of the recipient. Sculptor Debra L. Hille designed the piece honoring Lewis as an illustration of the expression, "We make the road by walking." Hille (1996) spoke about the mixed media sculpture that she created: "My interpretation is one of an individual making her way through tall reeds. She looks back over her shoulder waving others to come on. The mirror face represents reflection, as true leaders reflect to us our own potential. The crystal and silver heart represents the faith it takes to act on our beliefs." Indeed this piece of art captures in many ways the courageous, principled, deeply philosophical, and radically committed life of this inspiring teacher, scholar, and community activist.

Demystifying and Analyzing Education and the Economy

In the late 1960s, upon first hearing Horton's "two-eyed theory of education," keeping one eye on where the person is and the other eye on where you think that person could be, Lewis liked it. It resonated with her own theory and practice and with that of Paulo Freire, whose *Pedagogy of the Oppressed* she read in 1970. "I really like Myles's theory and I think that I have always worked according to something similar—starting with where people are but seeing where you think they have the potential to be and pushing, encouraging, nagging, agitating and helping them grow in their understanding and critical consciousness."

Like Horton and Freire, she developed a firm belief in the importance of understanding the symbiotic connection between education and the economy. Drawing out this connection became the major operational principle shaping her pedagogy as she worked in alliance with rural communities. But Lewis expanded on the theory and practice of Freire and Horton by incorporating cutting-edge theories of feminist pedagogy and philosophy. Her feminism and fierce commitment to democratic pedagogy as well as her long-standing alliance with and presence in rural communities distinguished her work. She constantly put her theory to the test. As Candie Carawan remarked, "Helen, perhaps more than anyone, was willing to spend time living and working in communities. She participated in community life and gave support to community members—particularly women just emerging to speak out and take on issues—in a deep and ongoing way" (Carawan, personal communication, 1999).

In describing her educational practice, Lewis wrote perhaps the most concise guide to feminist and critical pedagogy in the 13-page introduction to *The Jellico Handbook: A Teacher's Guide to Community-Based Economics* (1988), which she co-authored with John Gaventa. *The Jellico Handbook* provides a model of democratic theory and participatory pedagogy and practice, complete with the exercises that Lewis and Gaventa used in their community development work. That work involved creating "educational programs which focused on the needs of rural, Appalachian students, predominantly women who had been unable to complete their education earlier and wanted to gain certain skills and knowledge to change their own lives and improve their rural communities" (2). To facilitate this process, Lewis first created the conditions in the classrooms where students felt comfortable "questioning the equity and relevance of the education system and confronting the inequity of the economic system" (2). Next, she offered opportunities for students to deconstruct and begin reconstructing power in their communities through purposeful confrontations with the people with power-over them. Lewis describes the movement to discovering power-from-within and building power-with this way. "By demystifying and analyzing the economy and by developing skills in planning, people begin to understand the economy, devise strategies to participate in it, to change it and/or develop their own alternatives" (1988, 3).

Throughout her career, as she has worked with students in varied educational settings from universities to rural communities, Lewis has focused on deconstructing the power that operates in the educational system and democratic capitalism. When classrooms shut out the realities of injustice and democratic practice is studied but not experienced, students become initiated into a world in which inequality is naturalized and the rights and responsibilities of democratic citizens are regarded as theoretical. But when a teacher like Helen Lewis educates her students in academia and in the community to, in the words of Freire and Donaldo Macedo, "read the word and the world," something quite different happens. Students learn what it means to be part of a democracy.

One can get a feel for Lewis's philosophy and her pedagogy by looking in particular at three of her many projects during her last 10 years at Highlander, 1987–1997. At a time whern most teachers pause to consider what they will do in retirement and many of them dream of a more relaxed pace, Helen Lewis, between the ages of 63 and 73, embarked on an exemplary decade of teaching in and working with communities relegated to the margins of society.

In her work with three community leaders and their local organizations—Maxine Waller and the Ivanhoe Civic League, from 1987 to 1989; Addie Davis and the McDowell County Economic Development Authority (EDA), from 1989 to 1992; and Franki Patton Rutherford and the McDowell County Action Network (MCCAN) and Big Creek People in Action, from 1996 to 1997—Lewis demonstrates how an eminently skilled democratic teacher forges increasingly more creative and effective strategies for developing community education programs, encouraging shared leadership, creating empowerment zones, forming alliances, and creating the conditions in which people can bring about social and political change for their community.

The projects that Lewis undertook in collaboration with these three women and their communities offer models of education that can inspire teachers and students in all educational settings: in the community, in organizations, in kindergarten, in graduate school. The story of these four women, a teacher and three "students," all of whom in turn become teachers and students, offers a model of collaboration, creativity, and persistence. The example of committed lives that Lewis, Waller, Davis, and Rutherford offer can inspire all who care about changing the world to make it a more socially just place for all people—for the long haul.

MAXINE WALLER AND THE IVANHOE CIVIC LEAGUE

> Helen is more than an academic. She is a soul educator. She always gives you stuff to feed your soul with. It's more than, "Here is the proper way to do this and we need to do it this way and this way." It was always wonderful: "How are we going to go about doing it?" And we'd go from there.... When Helen teaches you something, it's something you need to know. It's not something that is supposed to be learned....
> —Maxine Waller

Ivanhoe, Virginia, community leader Maxine Waller, feminist theologian and Catholic sister Mary Ann Hinsdale, and Lewis collaborated in participatory education, research, and community development projects with the Ivanhoe Civic League (ICL) between 1987 and 1989. They then spent periods over the next three years reflecting on their work with the people of Ivanhoe and with other communities and presenting at various academic conferences. The three women documented their work in *It Comes from the People: Community Development and Local Theology* (1995), a book offering a progressive view of adult community education and development that embodies the Highlander philosophy. As Lewis (1997) describes it, Highlander is about "education for empowerment...[it] works on the philosophy that change will occur from the bottom up as small communities begin to understand, take charge, and work together to make economic changes" (2). That philosophy comes through in Waller's explanation of what "it" refers to in the title of their book: "The magic. It's magic! It's development, it's justice, it's social justice, it's education, it's power, it's the word, it is love.... What it ain't is charity. What it ain't is apathy. What it ain't is oppression. What it ain't is sexism, racism, classism. All the ism's it ain't, But it is, it is people in control of their lives" (Hinsdale, Lewis, & Waller, 1995, 336).

In the mid-1960s, Ivanhoe residents numbered 4,500; by 1987, the population had dwindled to 600. The closing of National Carbide in 1966 and New Jersey Zinc in 1981 devastated the economic infrastructure that had sustained the community. From the mid-1960s on, people had watched schools and businesses close, church membership decline, the last train depart from town, and recreation diminish. People sought work and recreation outside Ivanhoe. The few jobs that could still be found at truck stops on the interstate became increasingly desirable.

When the county supervisors of Wythe and Carroll, the two counties Ivanhoe straddled, voted in September 1986 to sell Ivanhoe Industrial Park land, which National Carbide had left to the community, people reached their breaking point. Incensed that the county supervisors felt they had the authority to sell their land, the Ivanhoe community began to organize. Waller's energy, daring, and commitment catapulted her into local media fame as she became the spokesperson for the disenfranchised people of Ivanhoe, agitating for equality and democratic practice before local and state political bodies. The people formed the Ivanhoe Civic League (ICL) and Waller became the president, with the base of operations her dining room table. The first victory for the ICL was getting the Wythe and Carroll supervisors to rescind their vote and give Ivanhoe two years to recruit an industry for the park. As in most abandoned towns, ICL began the futile process of "chasing smokestacks," trying to find any industry that would move into their town.

In early 1987, Maxine became a fellow in the Southern and Appalachian Leadership Training (SALT) program affiliated with Highlander and began a relationship with Highlander that would last to this day. The program for community activists focused on building capacity for shared leadership within communities, so that communities could face the difficult challenges of rebuilding their social infrastructure after having been abandoned by corporations.

Around the same time that Waller became affiliated with Highlander, the Glenmary Research Center of Atlanta, Georgia, funded Highlander, and ultimately Lewis, "to make an in-depth case study of a rural community which had lost its industrial base" (Lewis, 1997, 2). The Glenmary Center also wanted a theologian to reflect on the community response and suggested Hinsdale. Lewis and Hinsdale approached Waller and the Ivanhoe Civic League, who agreed to participate in the project.

In working with the people of Ivanhoe on a daily basis for two years, Lewis came to know the community in a deep and abiding way. Whereas most of her projects were relatively short term, the Glenmary funding for the Ivanhoe project gave her opportunities for pursuing questions more deeply. Lewis (1997) recalled how she "wanted to understand more about the development of local leaders, especially women, and to try to understand how people are 'empowered,' how critical consciousness can be encouraged...how local grassroots organizations evolve, how women's organizations differ from other groups, and how conflict is dealt with" (3). In acknowledging and supporting "faith and religious convictions," Lewis added important dimensions to the Highlander focus on adult community education and community development. Candie Carawan credits Lewis with pushing Highlander to acknowledge the "identification of issues important to women as central to working for systemic change" (Carawan, personal communication, 1999).

Power in Ivanhoe

The people of Ivanhoe, like millions of Americans, had always imagined themselves practicing democracy through the simple act of voting. The comforts of a respectable salary base, guaranteed by decent-paying unionized jobs, masked their consciousness of how power and powerlessness functioned in their community. Not until they tried to bring about change in their community did the people fully understand that they had long ago ceded their power to others.

As in many towns across the country, Ivanhoe had naively succumbed to corporate paternalism, not realizing this was the way companies disguised their power-over the community and protected their own interests. But in 1986, the people of this small Virginia town realized that the survival of their community depended on their ability to take back their power. As the community began to mobilize, Waller described the transformation: "We have been on a train for the last hundred years and we've rode as passengers. And now we're not passengers; we're engineers" (Hinsdale, Lewis, & Waller, 1995, 48).

The citizens of Ivanhoe, like millions of others educated in U.S. schools, were, in all likelihood, introduced to democracy through what Lewis calls in *The Jellico Handbook* "traditional educational programs" in which "there is often a contradiction between content and method" (4). In most schools, she goes on, "What is being taught: equality, democracy, active participation is contradicted by how it is taught: authoritarian ways which encourage inequality and passivity" (4). The events in Ivanhoe prior to the community's mobilization give eloquent testimony to the ways in which authoritarian education serves the interests of capitalism to the detriment of democracy.

Yet, faced with disaster, the people of Ivanhoe took action. Sharing a nebulous belief in the guarantees of the Constitution, the promise of justice in the Bible, and some vague conceptions about equality and justice in a democracy, they felt betrayed. They formed the Ivanhoe Civic League and confronted their elected officials. Two significant lessons emerged: they could become active in the democratic process but they needed to get educated to face the challenges and achieve their rights. The ICL saw Lewis's presence in their community as an opportunity to develop a community education program that would support their efforts to take power and revitalize their community.

A Democratic Community Education Program

As a democratic teacher, Lewis did not come to Ivanhoe with an "educational package." She listened to the community's needs and with them and other educators collaborated in the development of a community education program that included economics discussion groups, Bible reflections, a participatory community research project, a general equivalency diploma (GED) program, and a college-level local history course. The community also negotiated with the regional community college to offer courses in public speaking, accounting, and community health.

The Civic League successfully created a functional community infrastructure. When a building became available in town, they raised money and rented it, naming it Ivanhoe Tech. They quickly set up offices for the ICL and created spaces for classes in literacy training, tutoring, and GED programs, as well as spaces for community meetings and gatherings.

Economics Discussions. Waller invited the Reverend Carroll Wessinger of Wytheville, community volunteer Sister Clare McBrien, and Lewis to develop economics classes, which were later renamed "economics discussions," making an important pedagogical point from the outset. In these economics discussions, the community "began to change its major focus from recruiting outside industry— 'chasing smokestacks'— to looking to smaller, local development based on the community's needs and resources" (Hinsdale, Lewis, & Waller, 1995, 73).

By using democratic practice such as sitting in a circle, sharing, listening, problem posing, participatory curriculum development, research, and assessment, Lewis reports that the "economics sessions resulted in people making 'discoveries,' becoming more critical, and changing their analysis of the situation" (Hinsdale, Lewis, & Waller, 1995, 84). As always, Lewis's pedagogy involved shifting the role of learners from passive to active mode. Knowing well that "people remember best what they have said, not what they are told" (Lewis & Gaventa, 1988, 5), Lewis engaged the class in discussion of their own lives.

The group began bonding and building a learning community. They shared Ivanhoe history and the ways in which National Carbide and New Jersey Zinc had developed Ivanhoe. Miners recalled the safety concerns they had in working in the mines and the companies' callousness regarding safety, pollution, and the future of the community. Workers began theorizing about recruiting the kinds of "clean, safe industries that would not pollute air and streams and harm people" (Hinsdale, Lewis, & Waller, 1995, 84). This process confirmed Lewis's theory that effective education "does not take place in isolation from the community...is not separated from experience. It is related to real life and uses and legitimizes the person's knowledge to solve problems in the community" (Lewis & Gaventa, 1988, 3). Students, Lewis argues, bring enormous amounts of knowledge and experience with them into the classroom—and this is the starting point for any course. In community economics discussions, adult students have knowledge based on "their work experiences, migration experiences, their family economic history" (6). All of these experiences animated discussions in Ivanhoe, providing the foundation for a collaborative learning experience that would propel the community into action.

In discussions such as those in Ivanhoe, the teacher's role, Lewis says, is that of an animator. The animator enlivens discussions, acting as a "facilitator who poses problems and gives students the confidence to analyze their problems and plan ways of overcoming them" (Lewis & Gaventa, 1988, 4). Taking on the role of animator does not make the teacher's role easier. She is critical to the learning process, continually moving the discussion to deeper levels, steering participants away from "gossiping" or "sharing their ignorance" (Lewis & Gaventa, 1988, 5). In Ivanhoe, Lewis played a strategic role, moving the community toward a deeper understanding of their place in the global economy and their choices for the future.

Bible Reflections. Five Bible reflection sessions provided an alternative way for some women in the community to become involved in revitalizing Ivanhoe. These sessions attracted women who did not feel that they could participate in economics discussions. The participatory reflection sessions, which drew on Hinsdale's training in liberation theology, became a groundbreaking exploration of local theology, resulting in a new level of what Freire (1993) calls conscientization, critical awareness with a political purpose. Lewis notes that the community in making manifest its "local theology" engaged sectors of the community often disengaged from development work. "Ivanhoe's faith and religious convictions—concepts which are often suspect in community organizing circles, since they are seen as dulling and prohibitive to the development process—helped to foster an emergence, from apathy and silence, to a community of outspoken and knowledgeable citizens who are demanding participation in the planning and direction of their community" (Lewis, 1997, 3). Notably, the Bible reflection sessions gave many local women a culturally appropriate way to reflect on the leadership role women could play in the community.

Community History. One of the community revitalization activities proposed early on by the ICL was documenting Ivanhoe's history. This project became the focus of a college-level history course that Lewis developed with the community.

Kay Early, one of the students in Lewis's local history course, comments on how that class met the needs of the people.

> When I heard that there would be a history class about Ivanhoe, at Ivanhoe Tech, I said to myself, "Now that sounds like fun. I'll just go down there and learn about Ivanhoe." Boy, was I in for a big surprise! I thought that this would be a regular class, with textbooks and a teacher who lectured and gave tests. There were no books and a teacher who said, "You, the class, will do research for the history of Ivanhoe."
>
> Researching was fun and tiresome. Some members of the class read old newspapers. Others interviewed several people for their remembrances. My topics included churches and graveyards, also farms. I spent many hours, usually on Sunday afternoons, touring every graveyard in and around Ivanhoe. Church records were vague and hard to come by. I took a week's vacation to go through my husband's grandaddy's trunk which contains old letters, ledgers, bills, tax tickets and pictures dating back to the mid 1800s.
>
> Once every week the class would meet and compare notes....
>
> During my time helping research the book I learned that most people were eager to share their experiences and remembrances with me. I learned that I did have something to contribute to our community and that I might have a talent for writing (something I had thought about doing for a long time, since grade school). (Hinsdale, Lewis, & Waller, 1995, 97-98)

Lewis and Suzanna O'Donnell compiled and edited the students' research on Ivanhoe's history in *Remembering Our Past, Building Our Future* (1990), which won the prestigious W. D. Weatherford Award for the best book on Appalachia, and a second volume, *Telling Stories, Sharing Our Lives* (1990). For students such as Early, being a part of this project was a transformative experience. Not only did participants develop their research and writing skills, they developed a sense of pride in themselves and their community.

The economics discussions, Bible reflections, and community history course provided students with democratic experiences in the classroom that stood in stark contrast to their previous education. In these classrooms, residents who had found school so alienating that many had never completed high school, found their power-from-within and built power-with each other.

Culture's Role in Education and Development

During the period when many Ivanhoe residents became involved in the community education program, ICL sponsored numerous cultural activities to help rebuild Ivanhoe's sense of community. In Ivanhoe, as in many other communities with which Lewis had worked, "cultural expression like poetry, crafts, music and religion" pulled people together (Lewis, 1997, 8). Events such as festivals, parades, potluck dinners, dances, and theater performances, always accompanied by prayer and song, helped the community build their power-from-within. In Ivanhoe these events attracted many people whose alienation and hopelessness had prevented them from participating in ICL's more overtly political activities (Lewis, 1997, 8).

Lewis points out that when people share their stories in the creation of "art, theater and music" these media become strategies that can be "used to challenge, interpret and envision the future" (Lewis, 1997, 8). A stunning example of this emerged when Ivanhoe decided to use a renewed Fourth of July celebration as a community education event. Lewis recruited a puppeteer with expertise in building large puppets. The puppeteer worked with youth and adult community volunteers to develop a puppet theater production, a morality play of sorts "with scenes based on the closing of the area's industry and the recent struggle of the community to regenerate itself" (Hinsdale, Lewis, & Waller, 1995, 115). The play became the focus of annual July 4 festivities.

In the first production, a mother and her son, a miner, "represented typical Ivanhoe residents. Other puppets represented one of the villains in Ivanhoe's history, Mr. Stinky, who closed the mines.... The politicians who impeded the community development efforts" were "represented as a gaggle of feathered creatures, including a turkey hawk and a peacock" (Hinsdale, Lewis, & Waller, 1995, 115). In examining power-over by reifying both their problems and the people responsible, community members engaged in "communal conscientization" (Freire, 1993). A takeoff on the song "Proud Mary" provided a new refrain, "Selling Us Down the River," clearly locating their recognition of the way they had been victimized (Hinsdale, Lewis, & Waller, 1995, p. 115). But the play was far from a defeatist project; the "children of Ivanhoe, dressed as little chickens, rose up, survived, and pranced about" (Hinsdale, Lewis, & Waller, 1995, 115).

Action for Political and Social Change

The importance of education and civic pride in developing a community's ability to challenge power-over was made evident six months after Lewis began working with ICL. In February 1988, about "170 people from Ivanhoe attended a public hearing seeking Community Development Block Grant money" (Hinsdale, Lewis, & Waller, 1995, 74). The Ivanhoe community had worked with a professor from Virginia Polytechnic Institute in pulling together a well-thought-out proposal that would draw about 100 jobs to Ivanhoe. After the public meeting, at which all seemed to be going well for Ivanhoe, the proposal was mistakenly disqualified by the elected officials. At the next meeting, the Ivanhoe forces, empowered by their recent educational and cultural activities, publicly confronted the officials, questioning their intentions. Verbal rancor followed, with Waller steadfastly voicing the dismay of the community. In this democratic moment, when with protest the people won the right to compete for the grant, the dis-ease of the public officials became eminently clear. The Ivanhoe Civic League learned "how scared and upset elected officials can become when grassroots groups attempt to practice democracy by trying to participate in decision making and planning for their own communities" (Hinsdale, Lewis, & Waller, 1995, 75). As county officials used their power to limit the ICL's political and economic impact, Ivanhoe learned an important lesson in power-over—one that they would not soon forget.

Not well loved by the county government, members of the Civic League used the skills they developed through the community education program to apply for numerous foundation grants. They received funding for their newsletter, for general operation, and for housing rehabilitation in the community. The Civic League also set up Self Help and Resource Exchange (SHARE), which offered people food at discounted rates in exchange for several hours of volunteer work (Hinsdale, Lewis, & Waller, 1995, 77). Grants and program opportunities secured by the Civic League soon made them the "biggest employer in town" (Hinsdale, Lewis, & Waller, 1995, 77). The passengers had most definitely become engineers.

The community education and cultural revitalization programs in Ivanhoe helped people realize their power-from-within and augured well for building a coalition of people involved in the Civic League who could ensure its continuity. According to Lewis, however, the structural needs that did not get met were the democratization of the Civic League and the building of shared leadership. Waller's charismatic leadership brought many improvements to Ivanhoe, but her inability to share power weakened the organization and its overall impact. In addition, Ivanhoe, divided as it was into two counties, never found a strategy that would allow it to challenge the traditional power vested in the two boards of county supervisors successfully. Because Ivanhoe lacked alliances with other communities, the Ivanhoe Civic League could be too easily dismissed as a group of "troublemakers."

As Lewis shifted the focus of her work from Ivanhoe to other projects, she had an expanded vision of what, ideally, could happen in communities. The month after she left Ivanhoe in 1989, she taught in a summer program in Berea, Kentucky, sponsored by the Appalachian Ministries Education Research Center (AMERC) and funded by the Benedum Foundation. There she explored and reflected on the lessons of Ivanhoe. In future development projects, she concluded, she would insist on shared leadership and build it in more carefully from the outset. Also, she would assure that any communities that she worked with build alliances with other communities so they could not be isolated and ignored by the political structure, as happened in Ivanhoe. In 1989, Lewis began putting this new vision into practice in McDowell County.

ADDIE DAVIS AND THE MCDOWELL COUNTY ECONOMIC
DEVELOPMENT AUTHORITY

> Helen makes you think. I don't know, with Helen, you were more willing to try things. Helen would sit back, and she always had this little twinkle in her eye, and she'd say, "Yeah, that might work." Or she'd say, "Yeah, well, you may want to do this." Helen never told you what to do. When you decided what you wanted to do, then she'd give you all the help she could, but it would be your idea first.
> —Addie Davis

In the international slugfest of business and industrial courtship, grandmother Addie Davis selects her punches carefully.

The retired teacher, who once ran one-room schools in coal country, now is trying to wake McDowell County from a deep economic slumber.

Davis, as director of the McDowell County Economic Development Authority, says her first task is to convince people they can, and must, be in charge of their own destiny. Marching to the slogan, "McDowell Can Do," she is trying to inspire confidence in an unemployment-weary work force.

"It's not that we're trying to build false images. We're trying to get our people to dream again," she said.

—Frank Hutchins, *Charleston* [WV] *Daily Mail* (January 8, 1991)

Pedagogy of Transformation

That Helen Lewis gravitated toward working with Addie Davis seems almost predictable. As a teacher, Davis had long used democratic pedagogy in the classroom in a way that built power-from-within and allowed "students" to position themselves to develop power-with allies. She also had a track record of building shared leadership and alliances among communities in McDowell.

Theater—A Catalyst for Change. In 1985, when all of the coal mines in McDowell County were closing, devastating the county's economy, Davis worked with students in a governor's-sponsored Summer Youth Program in Bradshaw. Instead of having them do the expected tasks of picking up trash and cutting down weeds, she had young people gather oral histories of the community and develop socially and politically conscious theater—a theater of the oppressed. The first year of her program met with such success that she expanded it the next year to include three towns—Bradshaw, Iaeger, and the predominantly black town of Keystone. Lewis recalls, "At the end of the summer, the kids would do this play around the issues that they'd heard and all the families would come. Addie would open it up for discussion, asking, 'What can we do about this?'"

To Lewis, the potential for galvanizing community action through theater seemed limitless, and Davis's strategy of involving young people, who still remained hopeful and were not so defeated by the failing economic system in McDowell, seemed brilliant. This process, dramatizing community issues and problems and getting the people involved in a cross-generational dialogue about solutions, empowered participants and encouraged them to act.

The empowerment zone that Davis created came at a critical time in

McDowell's history and in the lives of its young people. McDowell's population plummeted from 90,000 in the late 1950s to 25,000 in the early 1990s. The economy was devastated; in the Big Creek District, for example, 92 percent of the families with children in school lived below the poverty level. Virtually ignored by state government, the county threatened to secede from the state in the 1980s. "The rest of the state urged it to do so," notes Caroline Carpenter of the Benedum Foundation, "but whether it was spite or lack of a place to accept it, the county remained in West Virginia" (Carpenter, personal communication, 1993).

In order to bring change to their communities, people had to begin believing in themselves. Davis taught Lewis that theater offered one opportunity for rebuilding that belief. Davis reflected on the strategy this way: "There's something about combining theater and oral history that frees people. It's almost as if you've lived in a box and you get up and do a scene and it's as if somebody cut a window and you saw light and you never have to live in darkness again." That window on the world empowered individuals to become agents of change and Davis realized that this was the first step toward making democracy come alive in McDowell County. "Addie once said, and I think it is true," Lewis remarks, "that this theater work was the beginning of the real community development program in McDowell County."

In 1988 when Lewis and Waller and other people from Ivanhoe attended a workshop run by Davis, their imaginations were sparked and they went back to Ivanhoe to create the Fourth of July play with large puppets. In Davis, Lewis saw a leader who had charisma but who held firmly to the principle of shared leadership that expanded the circle of leaders and united people.

A Democratic Teacher. From her first teaching assignment in a one-room schoolhouse with 60 students from grades one through eight, Davis mastered the art of collaboration and so did her students. She laughs, thinking about it: "I'm amazed how much the third grade learned from the fourth grade. I would say, 'Are you through with your geography? Well how about helping Johnny over here who's having a real bad time with multiplication tables?' They learned sharing. They helped each other out."

She left the school system in 1988, because she became disenchanted with its bureaucratization, lack of creativity, and unresponsiveness to the problems of children. The change that she wanted to bring about in society—to make the promise of democracy more real for the community—seemed impossible to achieve in the schools. In her fifties and eligible to collect her teacher's pension, she began a career in journalism, writing for the *Welch Daily News* and the *Industrial News*, where she was able to raise the consciousness of greater numbers of people about what was happening to their economy.

In addition to writing about the problems faced by her community, Davis, along with other citizens in Bradshaw, formed the Sandy River District Action Committee (SRDAC), the first community group in McDowell to organize around community economic development. Her interest in a countywide approach, drawing McDowell's geographically isolated towns into alliance, led her to get appointed to the board of the McDowell County Economic Development Authority (EDA) and eventually to assume the executive director position.

Davis recognized all too well the kinds of divisions that thwarted alliances among the 78 communities in McDowell County's mountainous 425 square miles. Communities throughout McDowell, separated by rough mountain roads, had built intense rivalries based on occupation, race, ethnicity, and class that frequently manifested in battles between high school sports teams and the like. Undoubtedly, the isolation of the communities served the interests of the virtual owners of the towns, the absentee corporate landlords. Davis was raised in a timbering family that, like farmers, considered itself culturally distinct from the people involved in the coal industry. But she understood that although in times of prosperity those in timbering, farming, and mining could afford to see themselves as distinct cultures, during the economic demise of the county, precipitated by the closing of the mines, social and political divisions became a luxury.

Davis as EDA Director. By fall 1989, when Davis became the McDowell County EDA director, Lewis had concluded the major part of her work in Ivanhoe. While teaching in the AMERC program in Berea, Kentucky, Lewis met with Benedum Foundation Program Officer Caroline Carpenter, who was interested in funding an AMERC project in West Virginia to pull together leaders from the community and the clergy to talk about community-based development. With the demise of community leadership from corporations, the United Mine Workers, and other community groups that had fallen apart, churches remained the only viable forces for renewal in hard-hit communities. Lewis suggested to Carpenter that they look at McDowell County, since it was one of the hardest hit areas of economic depression in the coal fields. The alliance between Lewis and Davis would become critical to the AMERC project. Between 1990 and 1994, Benedum funded a five-year program of community development workshops in McDowell through Davis's office at the EDA.

The AMERC workshops engaged clergy and community folks in identifying community development projects and developing skills necessary to carry out their dreams. Lewis and Highlander, "always a beacon of light," according to Davis, gave her the institutional support she needed over the long haul in her revolutionary effort to get the people of McDowell to dream again.

The workshops resulted in the emergence of community development groups in 15 communities and created pockets of hope all over McDowell County, demonstrating the ways in which democratic pedagogy leads to an enlivened civic sense and a longing for democracy. Once people understood the way power operated and the rights and responsibilities of citizens in a democracy, there was no stopping them.

The Workshops of 1990: Building Power-from-Within

Davis, Lewis, and Carpenter gathered a committee of ministers and community leaders, among them Franki Patton Rutherford of Caretta, to plan four workshops for the winter of 1990 and decide which communities would host them. In making the selection of communities, the Church/Community Coalition looked for interested citizens and clergy and invited people from every community where even minimal community efforts were under way. Despite rough winter weather in the mountains, about 50 people attended each all-day Saturday workshop.

The pedagogy of the four workshops followed the Highlander method of discussions in a circle with leaders to facilitate discussion, provide information, and pose questions, creating an empowerment zone where people could solve their problems. They also hosted inspirational speakers and community organizers, including Maxine Waller, who came to talk about Ivanhoe. Topics of discussion included, Starting Your Own Business, Tourism, How Communities Can Make Changes, Fund Raising, Studying Your Community, and Church and Community Development. By attending various sessions, individuals began building a diverse knowledge base, which they could share with other people in their communities.

Having learned from the Ivanhoe experience that large-scale change required involvement of multiple communities, Davis and Lewis assured that each of the workshops involved participants from at least 10 communities. As each community explained its current community organizations and potential for development, other citizens of McDowell had the opportunity to imagine what might be possible for them and how they could build on the work already accomplished. They began to dream. Davis remembers, "We had Episcopalian and Methodist ministers and Catholic priests. Normally the black community and the white community just didn't meet together and, boy, we made a difference there." The meetings were historic in that they were the first time the geographically isolated communities of McDowell County met together to consider their futures.

As in all Highlander educational efforts, culture played a preeminent role, and here, Davis's expertise with oral histories and theater gave many communities an opportunity to recover their pride and imagine new possibilities. "Cultural activities were always a focal point while I was EDA director," Davis recalls. An important function, Davis believes, was "to sell the people to themselves—give them evidence of their worth. When people have low self-esteem, it seems they are too defeated to try anything. I tried to use their history to make them see how much they had contributed to humanity." People got to learn about each others' communities and their neighbors in these thoroughly pleasurable ways.

It was in these workshops that the people from Caretta determined to get the abandoned Caretta School building for their community center; they subsequently formed Big Creek People in Action to do just that. The planning and encouragement they received from workshops made it possible for them to achieve their dream. Other community organizations also emerged, all of which went on to become focal points of their community's overall education and development plan.

By the end of 1990, Lewis recalls, there were 10 communities with very viable community organizations, and they wanted more workshops with more opportunities to learn, form alliances, and develop leadership. A critical mass of people had built their own power-from-within and were poised to do more.

The Workshops of 1991: Building Power-With

For 1991, the Benedum Foundation came through with another grant of $25,000 to be used to award 10 "community mini-grants" of $2,000 to civic organizations in McDowell that were "voluntarily trying to improve their own communities." To help communities learn how to prepare grants and expand their dreams for their communities, Davis, Lewis, and the Church/Community Coalition developed a plan for five more structured workshops. The collaborative effort to develop 10 excellent grant proposals would be a powerful pedagogical strategy, from which would emerge community organizations that would spearhead social, political, and economic change in McDowell County to this day. The 10 community organizations had increased to 15 by the end of 1991.

While the members of the organizations who would attend the 1991 workshops would develop the rules for the mini-grants, Benedum made one stipulation, according to Lewis: there had to be three of the same members of each community in attendance at three workshops in order to be eligible for a mini-grant. This rule assured the continued development of shared leadership.

The 1991 workshops taught people the skills to assess their community's social capacity, develop a project, and write a proposal for $2,000. These skills would have a "multiplier effect," providing the emerging community organizations with the analytic and technical skills to assess the strengths and weaknesses of their communities and develop future projects. Lewis, whose skills in community mapping, social capacity assessment, and grant writing made her a natural to teach many of the workshop sessions, constantly called upon other resource people in the area to build networks of allies for the communities. Davis had much earlier followed the same practice; she and some of her friends led workshops focused on collecting oral histories and developing a play, and she continually brought in allies involved in cultural revitalization.

Lewis remembers that two months after she taught the workshop on community mapping and social capacity assessment, another workshop was held. Much to everyone's amazement, the BCPIA had "mapped their whole community and interviewed every house in their community and put all their findings on a computer. They had kids running around taking pictures of stuff in their community. It was very exciting."

As the workshops progressed, the 15 organizations solidified, and 10 of them collaboratively put together mini-grant proposals. Communities and organizations read each others' proposals and worked to strengthen them. They learned from what the others had written and how they had done their research. They sharpened their writing and presentation skills and began looking at the positive social capacity of their communities rather than the deficits brought on by their abandonment by the coal industry. During this cycle of workshops, it became clear that social capacity had been built or discovered in communities. Lewis notes that "broader groups formed, which the churches and ministers were either a part of and continued to be a part of, just as members, but they were not playing any leadership roles by then."

Over 150 people showed up at the awards event to honor the grant recipients. Each group getting a $2,000 check had baked a cake, Lewis remembers, and "decorated it to show what they had done in their community." The award-winning projects ranged from creating a recreation center, to running a tutoring program for students, to creating a statue in honor of coal miners.

At the end of the 1991 cycle of workshops, Lewis turned to other writing, teaching, and organizing projects, but she had helped sow the seeds for future development activities in the county. Between 1992 and 1994, Davis, while remaining in touch with Lewis, continued building the community infrastructure of McDowell County.

The Workshops of 1992 and 1993: Challenging Power-Over
Lewis speaks with pride about Davis's work in the 1992 and 1993 series of

workshops, which took a decidedly more political bent because the citizens were becoming more aware of the lack of democratic process in their lives. "The workshops were sort of democracy schools. They were about what was going on in the government and what government was supposed to be doing. People started voter registration campaigns and registered hundreds of new voters." Lewis chuckles that "Addie began to get flak because [the county officials began to] think that she's building herself into a powerful political figure."

Among the so-called radical activities that Davis engaged in was working with a group called Youth of McDowell County to put together a handbook, *Democracy and Local Government* (1994), which could be used in schools and by organizations and citizens to figure out how to make their government more democratic and responsive. Davis and the youth crusaded to make the promise of democracy and the Constitution a real part of people's lives. In the preface to the book they said, "Our Constitution insures that we have government of the people, by the people, and for the people. The only way this can happen is if PEOPLE get involved" (Davis, i). As the people of McDowell County slowly began to understand their rights, they began to look at both government and themselves with higher expectations.

Creating Bigger Dreams, 1994

In late 1993 the McDowell County Family Resource Network, which had been part of the workshops, learned about the request for proposals for the newly initiated federal Empowerment Zones and Enterprise Communities (EZ/EC) programs. About 15 representatives of the community organizations involved in the workshops went up to Charleston, West Virginia, in February 1994, to an informational meeting sponsored by the United States Department of Agriculture. Lewis notes that the growing sophistication of the group made it possible for them to branch out and compete. For the purposes of the EZ/EC grant and to distinguish themselves from the EDA, which the county commissioners continued to harass, the group constituted themselves as the McDowell County Action Network (MCCAN) and received funds from the community action program, Council of the Southern Mountains, to help develop their grant application. Lewis proudly points out that "these community groups were so strong that they could compete on an equal basis with people like the welfare department, mental health programs, and other such agencies."

The organizing that had gone into the workshops beginning in 1989 had created a strong grass-roots network. In Ivanhoe, Lewis had learned that working "with one community...was not empowering enough. They [couldn't] get enough power to deal with the local government, [and] instead [were] marginalized and pushed aside as troublemakers." In McDowell, the project "organized enough groups so that they had some power and support amongst themselves and they could learn from each other and not be in competition."

Before McDowell was awarded its EZ/EC grant, Davis, whose desire to return to writing persisted and whose husband wanted to take a job in Virginia, decided that she would leave the EDA job and move to Virginia. With her "McDowell Can Do" spirit she had nurtured many empowerment zones where people could begin to dream again. Her legacy to McDowell County was the kind of intense community action that persists there to this day. By initially building on the social capacity of churches and drawing them into a ministry of development, Davis and Lewis tapped into a very important source of energy that drew in a critical mass of people. Davis's work throughout the county modeled the importance of sharing power-with, and people who never knew their neighbors one mountain over (which sometimes was three miles down the road) began to realize what valuable potential allies they had to help create change in their communities and their county.

In 1993, when Caroline Carpenter from the Benedum Foundation accepted the Scrivner Award for designing the pilot project of mini-grants in McDowell, she affirmed the model of community development that Davis and Lewis had fostered. Paying tribute to the power of the people, Carpenter told this story:

> The pilot project helped unify this county, imbued a new spirit in it that even the old guard county politicians are noticing. Many communities are still going on and adding new layers. One of the local results was a coal miners' statue to commemorate the county residents. The mini-grant only covered the landscaping but the workshops triggered three of the participants to use their own resources. After a couple of workshops, the three put their heads together and figured out that they could ask $100 per name to be engraved at the base of the statue. They came up with criteria, such as worked in the mines ten years or died in a mining disaster. Each of the three women got five names to start. The statue now stands in its own park by the side of the road. At the base of the statue there are 475 names engraved. They had to get an extra slab of marble to accommodate the overflow. In June, this group will host the First Coal Miner's Festival. Ruth Cooper, who was one of the women, commented to others, "We didn't know what we was getting into, but we now know that no project is too large for

us." (Carpenter, personal communication, 1993)

Communities all over McDowell County were proud of what they accomplished between 1989 and 1994. In December 1994, their hard work was rewarded with a $2.9 million Enterprise Community (EC) grant. In Caretta, the Big Creek People in Action decided that what they had learned from the people of the county could help them achieve even more.

FRANKI PATTON RUTHERFORD: THE MCDOWELL COUNTY ACTION NETWORK AND THE BIG CREEK PEOPLE IN ACTION

> At my very first meeting at Highlander in 1977 with the Appalachian Health Care Providers group, I met Helen. She was making a presentation to the group and I was just a young person, about 27, working in my community trying to do good. I listened to her and I can remember thinking, "Oh God, I want to be like her when I grow up."... My first impression of Helen was of a hell-raising activist woman.... I wasn't used to seeing too many people like that, women or men.
> —Franki Patton Rutherford

Hell-Raising Activist Women

The opening vignette of this chapter presented a snapshot of Franki Patton Rutherford of Big Creek People in Action facilitating a meeting where people decided they would collaborate with Highlander on the Democracy Schools Project. Since Rutherford had first met Lewis at Highlander and set her sights on becoming a "hell-raising activist woman" just like her, 20 years had passed. On June 17, 1997, it was clear that Rutherford had achieved her goal and in a sense so had Lewis. As a quintessential democratic teacher, Lewis had mentored Rutherford and been there for her—always ready to listen, always ready to reflect with her, always ready to raise some hell.

At their first meeting at Highlander in 1977, Rutherford came across *Colonialism in Modern America: The Appalachian Case* (1978), a collection of essays edited by Lewis and others. The essay that made the biggest impression on Rutherford was written by Lewis and Ed Knipe, "The Colonialism Model: The Appalachian Case." Rutherford reflects, "I agreed with what it said. It was a life changing experience." Later she picked up Harry Caudill's *Night Comes to the Cumberlands* (1974). Rutherford recalls the "Aha experience" she had reading each of the books: "I was no longer a second rate, no good #**!, one of those people the Vista volunteer missionaries had to come down to save from themselves. I just put every bit of that behind me.... But

I was so angry.... I had to take some action to make it better." Rutherford, who had finished one year of college, went through her own crash course in colonialism and power, gaining the insights that she needed to reconcile her conflicting feelings about being from Appalachia.

From 1977 on Rutherford, who worked in community health, collaborated with Lewis on a variety of small projects and maintained a connection through programs at Highlander. By 1989, when she allied herself with Davis and Lewis in the development workshops in McDowell, she had already become a community leader, working with allies to develop the Public Service District for Coalwood and Caretta which brought clean water back to their communities. The community organizing work inspired by Davis and Lewis between 1989 and 1994 came at an important juncture in Rutherford's life, teaching her new skills, helping her understand more about shared leadership, and aiding her in building strong alliances and networks.

Democratic Teacher/Researcher and a Participatory Project

In February 1996, the USDA, which administers the EZ/EC program, selected McDowell County as one of 10 rural EZ/EC sites for a pilot participatory evaluation project of their $2.9-million grant. The Community Partnership Center of the University of Tennessee chose Lewis as the regional researcher and MCCAN chose Rutherford as the local coordinator. Lewis and Rutherford then trained together to lead evaluation teams. From April 1996 through December 1996, the MCCAN Citizens Learning Team engaged in a democratic teaching and learning experience as they evaluated the funded programs in their Enterprise Community to prepare to submit a final report to the people of the county and to the federal government in March 1997. The following passage from their final report indicates the democratic way that a teacher/researcher like Lewis, working in alliance with a community, approaches such a process:

> All members of the group [Citizens Learning Team] had con-
> siderable skills and experience in staff and committee work
> although none had worked with a participatory evaluation pro-
> ject before.... At session four there was considerable frustration
> and confusion. The workbook seemed to add to the confusion
> and the notebook assignments seemed academic and not help-
> ful. We decided to draft our own tools and develop our own
> research methodology.... In later evaluations all members men-
> tioned that this was a turning point but that it should have
> come earlier so we could have been further along with the
> process by this point. (Rutherford & Lewis, 1997, 17)

Here one can get a sense of the participatory and collaborative process Lewis uses in all of her teaching. Clearly, Lewis created an empowerment zone in which the "students" felt free to critique the packaged federal materials that were passed on to them for learning the participatory evaluation processes. The students took up the challenge of creating materials that would be more useful to them. In rejecting what university professionals had determined would be the best materials for the participatory evaluation process, the students took hold of their own learning process and developed their own power-from-within. They gained confidence in their decision-making process and, significantly, took action.

Lewis's flexibility in educational settings allows students to summon their creative energies and often to create more work for themselves. The kind of enthusiasm that she exudes about the process of learning opens wide the space for the students to become independent learners. In the report, it becomes clear that the students' very active role in the classroom came as a result of Lewis serving, as she says in *The Jellico Handbook* (1988), as a "facilitator who poses problems and gives students the confidence to analyze their problems and plan ways of overcoming them" (4). What flows from this practice, she adds, is that the "students learn to speak out, take the lead, and make changes in their lives and in their communities" (4). Democratic educational projects intentionally build a longing for more democratic lives.

Not surprisingly one of the major findings of the evaluation was a call for "reforming the political system" of McDowell County. The team contended, "There needs to be developed an education program targeting civic leadership, democracy and community organizing so that the political system can become democratic and a tool for County revitalization rather than a barrier and hindrance to the process" (Rutherford & Lewis, 1997, 14-15). Inspired by Lewis, Rutherford and others in BCPIA committed themselves more passionately to challenging the political system and building democracy in their county.

Democracy Schools

During 1996, 10 members of BCPIA, diverse in race, ethnicity, age, creed, and sexual orientation, went to Highlander to participate in workshops refining the concept of the Democracy Schools, a new project that Highlander hoped would revitalize communities without power. It was not long after, on June 17, 1997, at the meeting described in the opening vignette of this chapter, that the BCPIA voted to begin their Democracy Schools project. Having played an instrumental role at Highlander in conceptualizing the Democracy Schools and defining the project's goals, the BCPIA was determined:

- to counter myths of democracy, understand our history and current realities of power and the alienation of people so that we work to build a culture of democracy;
- to develop workshops with community groups at Highlander and in the region focusing on greater democratic participation and access to decision-making by using a workshop agenda that will allow participants to learn and share tools, strategies, and models in order to practice democracy in their communities and homes;
- to facilitate a dialogue within communities about the barriers to effective participation in democracy;
- to network community groups who are working on issues of democracy in their organizations, local government, workplaces or national and global situations;
- to provide material for communities wanting to begin a process of democratic renewal; AND
- to develop a way to network groups following the workshops in order to support sustainable democratic practices at home, school, in the community, in the workplace, and in the electoral process. (*Highlander Working Paper on Democracy Schools,* 1997)

BCPIA's passion for democracy grew out of every aspect of its members' lives. After having successfully built their community center, participated in the Enterprise Community development projects, and then analyzed their successes and failures through participatory evaluation, they were ready to turn to their larger goal: bringing the revolutionary concept of democracy to Big Creek District and eventually to all of McDowell County.

Lewis had played a major role in helping Rutherford and her community articulate, through the EC evaluation, the vision that would become the foundation for the Democracy Schools project. Although not officially linked with McDowell County after 1997, Lewis stayed connected. Rutherford spoke in 1999 about the role that Lewis continued to play in her life. "She has just taken me under her wing and helped me to do the things that I've done in my life. She's always only been a telephone call away to talk with about things. And in times of need, she's jumped in her car and come to the county. She is like a rock."

By early 1999, nearly 40 members of BCPIA had participated in Democracy Schools workshops at Highlander. As Rutherford explains, "Highlander is a safe place where we can talk about some really significant problems in the county without a whole lot of fear and intimidation."

In a conversation in April 1999 reflecting on the growth of the Democracy Schools project, Rutherford shared with Lewis her excitement about the direction that the project was taking. She commented that there was universal agreement about becoming more inclusive: "We talked a lot about how we could involve people who are not involved very much—women, African-Americans, poor folks, less educated folks, young people—and give them more powerful voices." She added that foremost in everyone's mind was a need for better public education that was oriented around "liberal arts education, preparing critical thinkers for the future instead of employees." Lewis praised these ideas and asked what their strategies were.

Rutherford explained that in the summer of 1999, BCPIA would hire Linda Vance, a mother from Bradshaw, who had been receiving public assistance, to begin organizing throughout the district. Vance, she went on, had gone to Highlander a few times with BCPIA for training, and Rutherford described her transformation with pride:

> She's been turned on to democracy. She used to vote but that was the only thing that she saw as democracy....In the last election, she was going from precinct to precinct to check on who had voted. She called me and said, "We're going to the next precinct. They threatened to arrest us at the last precinct. If I go down to the precinct and they arrest me, are you going to bring my bail so you can get me out of jail?" And she went from voting, to just thinking that it was the best thing to get thrown in jail for standing up for democracy.

In addition, Rutherford noted, youth were now connected with the Democracy Schools project. On the first weekend of April 1999, Rutherford had escorted three youth from BCPIA, one of them her daughter, Jess, to a youth Democracy School workshop at Highlander. At nearly 50, Rutherford was one of four elders whom the youth allowed to listen in and become "allies for youth." She commented that "all the young people at Highlander really touched my heart because they convinced me that I absolutely did not have to worry about the work that I consider important, my life work, being carried on by very caring committed people who know the issues in a deep way." One of the groups at the workshop who made an impact on the McDowell group was "a really strong contingent of young gay teenagers who spoke about their oppression." Rutherford felt elated that the whole group saw "racism, sexism, classism, and homophobia as barriers that the establishment has put between the different groups to keep them from organizing together."

After their Highlander experience, the three youth from BCPIA applied to the Appalachian Community Fund for start-up money for the Young Leaders Action Council and got it. Supported by Highlander and their elders, they have begun to "make the path by walking."

In 1999, the county commissioners and many of the other entrenched politicians who had wanted to fire Addie Davis from the EDA position when she worked with youth on a voter registration campaign and the *Democracy and Local Government Handbook* (1994) were beginning to see their nightmares come true.

Taking Risks

Dynamic individuals like Lewis and Rutherford change over 24 years, but what has endured for both of them, since their meeting at Highlander, is a passion for democracy and social and economic justice. The spirit of Lewis manifests itself in Rutherford who through the AMERC workshops, the participatory evaluation project of the MCCAN Enterprise Community Grant, and the start of the Democracy Schools in McDowell, demonstrated the skills, politics, and passion needed to transform individuals and communities. As Lewis approached 75 she embarked on a new teaching assignment for the fall semester of 1999 at Appalachian State University and in 2001 she is finishing work on a new book. As Rutherford, approached 50 in 2000, she took the risk of quitting her job of 20 years at Tug River Health Clinic and accepting the executive director position at BCPIA. This meant raising money for her own salary as well as for the support of the many projects of BCPIA. There is some irony in the worry that Lewis expressed to Rutherford about the risk that she was taking. After all, Lewis has been the ultimate risk taker herself and Rutherford knows it.

CONCLUSION

Between 1987 and 1997, Lewis's intense community work with Maxine Waller, Addie Davis, and Franki Patton Rutherford allowed her to develop an especially insightful analysis of the connection among education, the economy, and democracy in communities that were struggling to come back. Moreover, her two decades of recognizing and nurturing women leaders turned out to be critical in broadening the mission of Highlander Research and Education Center and in extending its cultural strategy. Lewis sums it up: "What I admired so much of the whole women's movement was the reliance on stories. That's what I've done a lot of writing and talking about is moving from people's stories to analysis. That whole feminist methodology has been extremely influential in anthropology and sociology—a more qualitative methodology." She credits many of the women leaders and the communities that she has worked with over the years as her teachers and inspiration in developing "suggestions and guidelines for rebuilding communities, strategies for building social capital and developing socially responsible, democratic, sustainable communities" (Lewis, forthcoming).

Pedagogy for Democracy: A 12-Step Program
Still inspired by the lessons she learned from the women of Appalachia, Lewis wrote "Rebuilding Communities: A 12-Step Recovery Program" (forthcoming). Her incisive wit and deeply nurtured wisdom from years of working in academia and in hard-hit communities shine through as she wryly confronts the co-dependent model of industrial recruitment and advances a recovery program built on democratic education, sustainability, people development, culture, inclusivity, use of local resources, and sound ecology (Lewis, forthcoming). She charts the course: "The 12 steps are not a straight forward stairway to community revitalization. It is more like dance steps. Sometimes you go two steps forward and one step back to repeat number 1" (Lewis, forthcoming).

Lewis's 12 steps offer sound advice for development in communities and a guide for developing learning communities at all educational levels using democratic pedagogy that will prepare students to become citizens capable of taking up their democratic responsibilities:

1. Understand your history, share memories
2. Mobilize/organize/revive community
3. Profile and assess your local community
4. Analyze and envision alternatives
5. Educate the community
6. Build confidence and pride
7. Develop local projects
8. Strengthen your organization—develop shared leadership
9. Collaborate and build coalitions
10. Take political power
11. Initiate economic activity
12. Enter the local/regional/national/international planning process.

The democratic teacher who considers the principles at work in these steps can imagine the ways in which many of the strategies for building democratic capacity in the community will work in the classroom. With the exception of the economic focus of steps 11 and 12, all of the other steps speak to ways of creating community in a classroom that will encourage learning and build citizenship. The steps provoke a teacher to think about banishing alienation and isolation and valuing individuals and the unique talents that each of them has. Aware of the need to subvert the usual power-over mode of operation in most classrooms, the democratic teacher can break that grip simply by allowing students to know each other through what they want to share of their lives and by encouraging collaborative rather than competitive work. Lewis describes the exhilaration for the teacher in seeing her power-over shift in the classroom:

> It's the most exciting experience in the world to sit in the back row and see other people do what you pushed them to do. Instead of being up front yourself, you see students take over a class and run it. It's wonderful. But you've got to have a bit of humility. It's an ego thing…all of those old ideas of being respected as a teacher of being listened to and being the one who has the word and the knowledge and the expertise to talk. It's giving up the idea that you're the only one who knows.

Once the classroom has been transformed into an empowerment zone, the teacher's challenge is to foster a learning community like the AMERC Workshops, the Citizens Learning Team in McDowell, or the local history class in Ivanhoe. The focus on projects that allow students to understand in more depth their own communities, both inside and outside schools, builds "confidence and pride," intellectual capacity, and community spirit. In the arts and humanities, science, or social sciences, potential projects abound— from studying the literature or music of the region or local cultures to producing plays, recording oral histories, statistically surveying community needs and capacities, or analyzing the ecology of local natural resources. Through these projects, students can connect to their larger school, college, or university community or to the community outside, opening up a web of potential alliances and becoming active participants in the world around them. That is, after all, a primary goal of an education—initiation into the rights and responsibilities of democratic citizenship.

Risk Taking and Democratic Pedagogy
Maxine Waller's striking metaphor for the transformation of Ivanhoe citizens from "passengers" to "engineers" parallels the hopes of all democratic teachers for their students. Surely, if more students leave schools prepared to be "engineers" rather than "passengers," our democracy will remain more vital and the power-over that seems so natural in our society will be chal-

lenged more routinely by people committed to a just and equitable society. Democratic teachers play a critical role in this vision of democracy. Ironically, a commitment to democracy in the classroom involves taking serious risks. Some teachers, like Helen Lewis, have been fired for this kind of "radical" activity. But "radical" teachers and students, like "radical" citizens, are usually just people who believe in democracy and want to participate in it.

Democracy, however, unsettles entrenched politicians and corporations. They understand quite well what Lewis calls "the symbiotic connection" between educational and economic systems, and they recognize they have a vested interest in maintaining the current educational system, which uses power-over to train submissive citizens more interested in consumerism than critical thinking. That's why a program that Lewis started was defunded when college students began analyzing and reflecting on black lung disease and strip mining in their communities. Lewis recalls that "the coal companies offered $7 million for the college to get rid of a whole social work program that I had developed." Although those affluent donors allied with local politicians had their way with Lewis's program, that did not stop her. She went on to teach and do research at other prestigious universities as well as at Highlander Research and Education Center. Unlike other academics, she never allowed herself to be confined to formal classrooms. Her work in alliance with poor communities throughout Appalachia spanned her entire career. Lewis, no ordinary teacher, has left behind an extraordinary legacy of empowered citizens, both young and old, who in the face of seemingly insurmountable opposition have rekindled democracy and the fight for social and economic justice in their communities.

Works Cited

Alvarado, S. (2000, Spring). *MassParents News.* Boston.

Bowles, S., & Gintis, H. (1976). *Schooling in capitalist America: Educational reform and the contradictions of economic life.* New York: Basic Books.

C., Joy. (1996). The phone call. *Harvard Educational Review, 66,* (2) 175–177.

Caudill, H. (1974). *Night comes to the Cumberlands.* Boston: Little, Brown and Co.

The Center for Education Reform. (1998). *A nation still at risk: An education manifesto.* http://www.edreform.com/pubs/manifest.htm

Crowley, M. (2000, May 9). Finneran maneuvers to force vouchers. *Boston Globe,* pp. 1, A24.

Davis, A. (1994). *Democracy and local government.* Welch, WV: McDowell County Economic Development Authority.

Dolci, D. (1984). *The world is one creature.* New York: Amity House.

Dunphy, P. (2000, April). Charter schools fail promises. *MTA Today.* p. 4.

Freire, P. (1993). *Pedagogy of the oppressed.* Twentieth Anniversary Edition. New York: Continuum Press. Originally published in 1970.

———. (1994). *Pedagogy of hope.* New York: The Continuum Publishing Company.

Freire, P., & Macedo, D. (1987). *Literacy: Reading the word and the world.* South Hadley, MA: Bergin & Garvey.

Giroux, H. (1988). *Teachers as intellectuals: Toward a critical pedagogy of learning.* Westport, CT : Bergin & Garvey.

Glen, J. (1988). *Highlander, no ordinary school.* Lexington, KY: University of Kentucky Press.

Gozemba, P. A., & de los Reyes, E. (1996, Fall). A dialogue of hope: Faculty in the 1990s. *Thought and Action, The NEA Higher Education Journal 12* (2), 117–132.

Hall, B. (2000, April 30). Opinion remains divided on charter schools. *Boston Globe,* p. J9.

Handy, E.S.C., & Handy, E.G. (1972). *Native planters of old Hawaii.* Honolulu: Bishop Museum Press.

Handy, E.S.C., & Pukui, Mary K. (1972). *The Polynesian family system in Ka'u, Hawai'i.* Tokyo: Charles E. Tuttle.

Hart, E. (1997, Summer). At Salem State: A mentoring community success. *Thought and Action, The NEA Higher Education Journal, 12* (2), 51–59.

Highlander Research and Education Center. (1989). Statement of Highlander's mission. *Highlander Research and Education Center: An approach to education presented through a collection of writings.* New Market, TN: Highlander Research and Education Center.

Highlander Research and Education Center. (1997). *Highlander working paper on democracy schools.* Unpublished paper.

Hille, D. (1996). *Dedication of the Helen Lewis Community Leadership Award.* Speech presented to the Mountain Association for Community Economic Development, Berea, KY.

Hinsdale, M., Lewis, H. M., & Waller, S. M. (1995). *It comes from the people: Community development and local theology.* Philadelphia: Temple University Press.

hooks, b. (1994). *Teaching to transgress: Education as the practice of freedom.* New York: Routledge.

Horton, M. (1990). *The long haul: An autobiography.* New York: Doubleday.

Horton, M., & Freire, P. (1991). *We make the road by walking: Conversations on education and social change.* Philadelphia: Temple University Press.

Hutchins, Frank. (1991, January 8) "McDowell Can Do." *Charleston* [WV] *Daily Mail,* p. 1.

Kozol, J. (1967). *Death at an early age: The destruction of the hearts and minds of Negro children in the Boston public schools.* Boston: Houghton Mifflin.

———. (1991). *Savage inequalities: Children in America's schools.* New York: Crown Publishers.

Lather, P. (1991). *Getting smart: Feminist research and pedagogy with/in the postmodern.* New York: Routledge.

Lewis, H. M. (1997, June). *Participatory research in community development and local theology: Ivanhoe, Virginia, United States of America.* Paper presented at The World Congress on Participatory Action Research, Cartagena, Colombia.

Lewis, H. M. (forthcoming). Rebuilding communities: A 12-step recovery program. In S. Keefe (Ed.), *Culturally-relevant practice in Appalachia: A sourcebook for practitioners in health, education, community planning and related fields.*

Lewis, H. M., Johnson, L., & Askins, Donald. (Eds.) (1978). *Colonialism in modern America: The Appalachian case.* Boone, NC: Appalachian Consortium Press.

Lewis, H. M., & Gaventa, J. (1988). *The Jellico handbook: A teacher's guide to community-based economics.* New Market, TN: Highlander Research and Education Center.

Lewis, H. M., & O'Donnell, S. (Eds.) (1990). *Remembering our past, building our future.* (Vol. I). Ivanhoe, VA: Ivanhoe Civic League.

————. (1990). *Telling our stories, sharing our lives.* (Vol. II). Ivanhoe,VA: Ivanhoe Civic League.

Mansbridge, J. (1996). Using power/fighting power: The polity. In Seyla Benhabib (Ed.), *Democracy and difference: Contesting the boundaries of the political.* Princeton, NJ: Princeton University Press.

Massachusetts Department of Education. Massachusetts youth risk behavior survey results. (1995). Boston, MA.
http://www.doe.mass.edu/lss/yrb95/yrb95111.html#c6

McLaren, P., & da Silva, T. T. (1993). Decentering pedagogy: Critical literacy, resistance and the politics of memory. In Peter McLaren and Peter Leonard (Eds.), *Paulo Freire: A critical encounter.* New York: Routledge.

Meier, D. (1995). *The power of their ideas: Lessons for America from a small school in Harlem.* Boston: Beacon Press.

Meyer, M. A. (1998). *Native Hawaiian epistemology: Contemporary narratives.* Unpublished doctoral dissertation, Harvard University.

National Center for Fair and Open Testing. (1998, November 23). Educators criticize new Massachusetts Comprehensive Assessment System (MCAS) exams.
http://www.fairtest.org/pr/mcaspr.htm

National Commission on Excellence in Education. (1983). *A nation at risk: An education manifesto.* http://www.ed.gov/pubs/NatAtRisk/risk.html

Office of Instructional Services. (1995). *Secondary training manual for school mediation.* Honolulu: Hawai'i Department of Education.

Palmer, P. (1998). *The courage to teach: Exploring the inner landscape of a teacher's life.* San Francisco: Jossey-Bass Publishers.

Park, P., Brydon-Miller, M. Hall, B., & Jackson, T. (Eds.) (1993). *What is participatory research? Voices of change: Participatory research in the United States and Canada.* Toronto: OISE Press.

Peterson, N. (1999, February 3). Appalachian Mountain Teen Project helping teens in troubled times. *The Granite State News Carroll County Independent,* pp. 1B, 3B.

Putnam, R. (2000). *Bowling alone: The collapse and revival of American community.* New York: Simon & Schuster.

Rutherford, F. P., & Lewis, H. M. (1997). *McDowell county enterprise community report.* New Market, TN: Highlander Research and Education Center.

San Antonio, D. (1995). *A critique of the Appalachian Mountain Teen Project: Suggested adaptations using ecological theory.* Unpublished paper.

————. (1997). *The drive behind the dream.* Unpublished paper.

Stake, R. E. (1994). Case studies. In N.K. Denzin & Y.S. Lincoln (Eds.), *Handbook of qualitative research.* London: Sage Publications.

Starhawk. (1987). *Truth or dare: Encounters with power, authority, and mystery.* San Francisco: Harper & Row.

Steinberg, J. (2000, April 13). Blue books closed, students boycott standardized tests. *New York Times.* pp. 1, A22.

Weiler, K. (1991). Freire and a feminist pedagogy of difference. *Harvard Educational Review,* 61 (4), 449–474.

Wolin, S. S. (1996). Fugitive democracy. In Seyla Benhabib (Ed.), *Democracy and difference: Contesting the boundaries of the political.* Princeton, NJ: Princeton University Press.

Wolk, S. (1998). *A democratic classroom.* Portsmouth, NH: Heinemann.

ERRATUM

The following text was inadvertently omitted from page 60:

Much has happened in the United States since we began the LIIP. In the 1990s, federal, state, and local actions against immigrants and students for whom English is a second language have been relentless. California's propositions 187 (seeking to prevent illegal aliens from receiving public benefits), 209 (dismantling affirmative action) and 227 (dismantling bilingual education); English-only bills introduced in Congress; the raising of TOEFL, SAT scores for admittance into public colleges; and the national testing and standards movement are some of the manifestations of the actions against immigrants, especially those who don't speak English. Access to higher education continues to become more and more difficult for students for whom English is a second language.

For teachers who see these trends as acts of injustice, the challenge is to ensure that all students—regardless of their country of origin, race, class, or ability to speak English—are able to access higher education. Within that context, it is essential for students who are non-native speakers of English to understand that language is both a tool of oppression and liberation. It is not enough to teach grammar, syntax, and punctuation. The standards must be higher, with students learning to use language to name, read, and act in the world. For those courageous teachers who choose to work with these students, the journey begins where the students are at—wherever that may be. From there, protected by a pocket of hope and encouraged through democratic teaching, all students can learn to access their power-from-within and develop their power-with others so as to reach the destination they envision for themselves.

Students from the LIIP have the power to read their world. Some have become teachers and educate their own students in the tradition of the LIIP. Others who have graduated plan to become lawyers, psychologists, park rangers and doctors. We are confident that the LIIP students who graduated from the program between 1993 and 1997 have the self-confidence, the leadership skills, and the critical-thinking and language skills necessary for inventing their own pockets of hope and struggling for democracy. We anticipate that they will break the cycle of oppression, raise the question, and rise to action.

About the Authors

EILEEN DE LOS REYES is Assistant Professor of Learning and Teaching, Harvard Graduate School of Education, Harvard University.

PATRICIA A. GOZEMBA is Professor of English and Women's Studies, Salem State College.

Please remember that this is a library book,
and that it belongs only temporarily to each
person who uses it. Be considerate. Do
not write in this, or any, library book.

DATE DUE

ILL 7576670 9/7/04			

DEMCO 38-297